Existence and Utopia

The Social and Political Thought of MARTIN BUBER

Bernard Susser

Rutherford • Madison • Teaneck
Fairleigh Dickinson University Press
London and Toronto: Associated University Presses

Associated University Presses, Inc.
4 Cornwall Drive
East Brunswick, New Jersey 08816

Associated University Presses
69 Fleet Street
London EC4Y 1EU, England

Associated University Presses
Toronto ME5 1A7, Canada

Library of Congress Cataloging in Publication Data
Susser, Bernard, 1942-
Existence and utopia.
Bibliography: p.
Includes index.
1. Buber, Martin, 1848-1965. 2. Community—
Philosophy. 3. Utopias. 4. Zionism and Judaism. I. Title.
B3213.B84S86   301   78-75188
ISBN 0-8386-2292-5

Printed in the United States of America

To my mother and father

Contents

Acknowledgments

This book is a record of a dialogue in more than one sense. I have shared my thoughts with many and received timely and helpful comments and criticisms. My gratitude goes especially to Julian Franklin, Herbert Deane, Daniel Elazar, and Paul Flohr. Margot Cohn, Martin Buber's personal secretary and since his death in charge of the Martin Buber Archive at the Hebrew University Library in Jerusalem, was of invaluable assistance in organizing material, locating documents, and pointing out manuscripts that I would have otherwise missed. In the course of preparing this work I have been generously aided by the National Foundation for Jewish Culture, the Memorial Foundation, the Israel Academy for Science, and Bar Ilan University.

I would also like to thank the following publishers for permission to quote from copyrighted material:

Schocken Books Inc. Reprinted by permission of Schocken Books Inc. from *On Judaism* by Martin Buber. Copyright ©1967 by Schocken Books Inc.

Macmillan Publishing Co., Inc. and Routledge Kegan Paul Ltd. *Between Man and Man* by Martin Buber. Copyright ©1965. Macmillan Publishing Co., Inc., Routledge and Kegan Paul Ltd., England.

And Susan, thanks.

Introduction

Perhaps more than any other contemporary philosopher, Martin Buber has become popular. Although he established no school and left few professing disciples, Buber's influence is deep and pervasive. The vogue he enjoyed in the fifties and sixties continues to flourish, the Buber-related literature—both academic and popular—expands yearly, and his terminology (*I-Thou*, dialogue, encounter) has so become the common coin of Western speech that its source has been obscured. Buber has taken his place in the Pantheon of contemporary cultural heroes.*Inevitably, the distance between Buber as persona and as person has widened. The sharply etched lines of his intellectual profile have blurred into a cannonized and out-of-focus public image that is as blandly benign as it is inaccurate.

While Buber is, of course, not guilty for the sentimentalization that has overtaken his thought, his passionate eloquence and disarming powers as a stylist are at least partially responsible for it. Whatever one's ideological predilections, Buber possesses the uncanny ability of bridging the psychic distance between the written word and the reader's heart. It is enough to pick up some small essay and to read a page or two for the power of his personal address to make itself felt. His words have a way of benumbing doubt and hypnotizing the critical sense. Even the most self-consciously detached

* At Grace Cathedral in San Francisco, Bishop Pike placed Martin Buber alongside Albert Einstein, John Glenn, and Thurgood Marshall in a stained-glass display of "secular saints."

readers will often find themselves seduced by the lyrical humanity that animates Buber's writing. Unfortunately this threatens to leave his readers with two equally unattractive choices: either to accept uncritically or, being uncomfortable with the compelling experience, to reject uncritically. As strange as it may sound, the philosopher of dialogue succeeds only rarely in drawing his readers into dialogue.

Professional readers, that is, the academic community concerned with Buber, have too often fared no better than the general reading public. Either the attempt to recreate the 'Buber experience' has led to a fruitless attempt at outdoing Buber at his own art, with the scholar cast as *artiste manqué*, or so aloof and impersonal (indeed, often hostile) a posture is struck that nothing is left of Buber but a skeleton of terms and definitions. Those who would try to avoid Scylla and Charybdis by presenting "fair and accurate exposition," face the problems of both. Either detachment misses the 'experience' or the 'experience' overwhelms the detachment.

The problem is complicated further still because Buber was an intense and engaged public advocate who took some very unpopular stands, particularly in public matters. Here again, either the jagged edges of his position are dulled to make him some kind of general, inoffensive humanist, or the ideological thrust of his thought is polemically joined or parried.

To avoid these pitfalls—and I am certain that I have not avoided them entirely—Buber's teaching on dialogue is, ironically, the best guide. Dialogue does not entail intellectual naiveté or suspension of the critical faculties. But neither does it mean debate in which pre-conceived positions are argued and justified. Rather it is, above all, an attempt to uncover and relate to the human source of what is being said with the totality of human powers at one's disposal. To take part in dialogue is to pass beyond the intransitive posture of onlooker and to enter into a relationship in which the reality of the 'other' becomes present and immediate. The philosophy of dialogue says nothing about the ultimate acceptance or rejection of my partner's position.

An essay on Buber along these lines demands a variety of perspectives. While nothing can take the place of systematic analysis, it must, if we are to be true to Buber's teaching, turn on an encounter with the man himself. The work needs to mirror its *subject* (in both senses of the term) by reflecting the man, his mind, and method in its own alternation of engagement, rigor, sensibility and judgment, by being both a careful study of his ideas and the record of a dialogue.

In order to let the voice of the man be heard as authentically as possible, I have cited Buber's words with a frequency that, perhaps, is excessive by conventional standards. But Buber is difficult to paraphrase, and even in translation his philosophical personality insinuates its way between the lines into the reader's attention.

The specific focus of this writer's concern is with politics and social thought. But Buber's intellectual retina saw the world as a seamless unity, and as such an introduction to Buber as a social thinker is ipso facto an introduction to his thought as a whole. Any conceptual apparatus comprehensive enough to contain his political ideas will necessarily be large enough to lend perspective to the many other fields to which he turned his energies.

As I have said, dialogue involves engagement. But engagement inevitably draws the scholar's personal perspective out of the hidden interstices where it normally lies, into the reader's field of vision. As such it is important to make my own views clear. My sympathy for Buber's ideas has waned from the initial enthusiasm I felt for them. They appear to me less in themselves, that is, when made to stand without the stylistic support of Buber's eloquence, than a first reading would indicate. I believe that this is not an uncommon reaction. But this does not mean I have become hostile. Simply put: I remain unconverted but not unmoved.

Existence and Utopia

1

The Origins of a Philosophical Temperament

If hopeful Fancy once, in daring flight,
Her longings to the infinite expanded,
Yet now a narrow space contents her quite,
Since Time's wild wave so many a fortune stranded.

Goethe

Two rival *Weltanschauungen* contended for mastery in the mind of Martin Buber. Neither was ever able to establish itself exclusively; each shared in a tense synthesis with its rival-partner. The two—existentialism and utopianism— grew tentatively into a synthesis during the first two decades of the century and to the end of Buber's life never came to peace. The unresolved, and in the nature of Buber's thought unresolvable, tension between these two modes of philosophic perception was the driving energy for his lifetime's work.

Existentialism, the rubric most often applied to Buber, connotes a certain appreciation of contingency, of the world's impenetrability and intractability, of the fragility of human achievements and successes. If the Existentialists launch their fiercest assaults against the undermining power of despair and nihilism, it is only because these feelings are so naturally attendant upon the existentialist enterprise. To be sure, existentialism is not an ideologically determinate philosophy—that is, it is compatible with virtually all political positions—nevertheless, there is an unmistakably brooding and anxious quality that suffuses all its myriad varieties. Visionaries have only a cramped berth in this type of world; they are replaced either by the profound pessimist who resigns himself to oblivion, the stubborn person who refuses to bow under but instead seeks coherence in chaos, or the God-tortured person who leaps into the only 'certainty' he or she knows—the arms of heaven.

At the other pole stands the Utopian who views the world not as a set of imperatives but as an array of potentialities. Utopians are concerned less with the reality they confront than with the ideal they envision, less with the present than with the future. The only imperative they recognize is the idea of perfection, the only demands they know as valid are the absolute demands of justice and happiness. They are set against compromise, for the millennium cannot be achieved through bargaining. They represent the relentless spirit of the unconditional.

That these two *Weltanschauungen* might settle simultaneously into the mind of a single man, to say nothing of a thinker of distinction, seems at first sight highly improbable. The two perspectives appear irreconcilable both philosophically and temperamentally. That Martin Buber was able to combine them into a unified and coherent outlook is some measure of the "atypical" nature of his thought.

A search for the roots of this synthesis—and they are essential for its understanding—leads inevitably to the manifold intellectual exposures of Buber's formative years. While no attempt at a full intellectual biography is intended, it is nevertheless imperative, before turning to the more well-known mature thought, to consider those elements in Buber's early years that account for the development of his unique philosophical personality.

It was in the highly charged atmosphere of the *fin de siècle* that the young Buber left his grandfather's home in the Polish Pale to study in the universities of Germany, Austria, and Switzerland. His education to that point had been in Polish grammar and intermediate schools, and the sudden move into the swirling intellectual and aesthetic life of the German and Austrian universities had an intoxicating effect on the young student's mind.[1]

His past education, in particular the teachings of his grandfather, seemed to him at this moment very foreign to the world of poets and artists in which he traveled. His grandfather, Solomon Buber, a Jewish scholar of significance,[2] had taught him Hebrew and Bible, and exposed him to the Hasidic communities that flourished in the Pale. In a few years' time, the memories of the Hasidic rabbis and the unreserved dancing and singing of their Hasidim would be the spark that would light his way back to Judaism, but now the "young esthete,"[3] from his vantage point on the fashionable promenades and cafes of Vienna, remembered their uncouth appearance and their unseemly frenzy, if he remembered them at all.[4]

His major areas of study were philosophy and art history. Although his early personality displayed considerably greater affinities to the latter, the ardent aestheticism of these early years corresponded closely with the philosophical mysticism he espoused.[5] He experienced in his mystical flights the same untrammeled union with the 'pure', the 'unconditioned' that so moved him in the realm of aesthetics. The real concerns of daily life seemed defiled and unworthy by comparison.

Buber was by no means exceptional in these sensibilities. The general revolt against Comtean positivism was at its height at century's end and nowhere so dramatically as in Germany where the Enlightenment had made only weak inroads. Whatever may divide the various *fin de siècle* manifestations of intellectual ferment—from anthroposophy to *Lebensphilosophie*—they concurred in rejecting rationalism and turning to the evocative powers of the imagination, to *mythos*, to great moments of poetic discovery, and to the mystery of the *Erlebnis*.[6] They rebelled against structure, regularity, and convention, recognizing as valid only the dictates of the creative mind, the flash of artistic revelation. These aesthetic tastes became, in Buber's thought, a proclivity for mysticism when translated into the language of philosophy and for utopian socialism in the formulation of politics.

The utopian urge that projects its ideal past the confusing difficulties of the moment onto the screen of the future shares an affinity of spirit and thought structure with mysticism, which abstracts itself from the here and now for union with the thoroughly independent and absolute. They both posit a vision of perfection that lies beyond the everyday—the one in temporal, the other in ontological terms. What is demanded in both cases is a freeing of oneself from the limitations imposed by reality.

It is not surprising, therefore, that mysticism and utopianism had parallel histories (one might even say a single history) in the unfolding of Buber's thought. So long as the mystical mood persisted, so did the commitment to an undiluted form of utopianism. A number of years later, when Buber gradually renounced his mystical orientation in favor of an existential philosophy of dialogue, his utopianism too began to incorporate elements of political realism. This was neither a sudden nor a complete conversion in either area; it was rather the product of a growing realization that required nearly two decades to crystallize fully. But at the turn of the century, there were very few influences that mitigated his youthful, unqualified voluntarism.

Nowhere is the mystical-aesthetic utopianism of these early years more explicitly enunciated than in the recently published "Alte und neue Gemeinschaft,"[7] a speech delivered to the *Neue Gemeinschaft* circle[8] of Berlin in 1900. In this, his first major essay, the twenty-two-year-old Buber distinguishes between the old *Gemeinschaft* rooted in utility and calculation and the revolutionary *Gemeinschaft* of the future—adumbrated by the *Neue Gemeinschaft* circle—that renounces instrumentality in favor of the 'co-essentiality' [*Wesensverwandtschaft*], that is part of the "blissful, blessed fusion with all things in time and space." In the florid and breathless language of his early mysticism, Buber writes that the *Neue Gemeinschaft* will be subject to no end but "life itself," "life that is liberated from all boundaries and concepts." "We would prefer," he proclaims

> to crash into the valley like a wild, wondrously beautiful mountain stream and exhaust our strength rather than to permit ourselves to be harnessed and our strength exploited.[9]

The spiritualized community that Buber envisages is a kind of *Civitas Dei* for those initiated in *Erlebnis* mysticism. For the great *Erlebnis* teaches the essential unity of all the world and the initiate recognizes that there exists an identity between the deepest strata of his subjective consciousness and the universal community of being. In these sacral moments of "festive communion," the brotherhood of mankind, indeed the unity of all being, is glimpsed by the inward eye.

But there will be those, Buber explains, who wish to extend this experience from these "blessed" but infrequent moments of epiphany to the everyday, to endow all of life (*das Leben*) with a new meaning and direction derived from the experience of the endless unity of becoming.

> A few of us want to live the ideal—to extend the inner commonality [*Gemeinsamkeit*] [of the cosmos experienced in those sacred moments] to [existential] particularity [*Eigenheit*]. I believe they will be able to live it. According to the ideal they will live ... the meaning of the universe, the endless unity of becoming.[10]

Far from the ignoble life of the cities, Buber concludes, there are many fallow and uninhabited lands that await us. There is no need to destroy in order to build. A thoroughly new "order of things" in which free creativity takes the place of purposefulness will grow out of the hearts of people revolutionized by the *Erlebnis* of being's unity. "Our *Gemeinschaft* does not will revolution," he proclaims, "it is revolution."[11]

With reality a willing partner and the age-old problem of revolution set to rest, "the instinctive unity of existence of primordial man" can become fact. The *Neue Gemeinschaft* is, indeed, the herald of such a "post-social" community. While the form of social organization to prevail may be described as anarchism, it is not anarchism as a political ideology—as such it would be subject to the entangling dilemmas that beset all ideologies—but anarchism as the mystical concomitant of the *Erlebnis* that reveals the world's inner unity.[12]

The utopian community Buber envisages is not to be understood in sociological terms, that is, as the harmony of coordinated interests or even as the solidarity between those committed to a political ideal; it is, rather, the mystical vision that superimposes community from realms beyond the reach of sociological categories. "Co-essentiality," [*Wesensverwandtschaft*] is not dialogue; there is no meeting, only participation in a greater unity.

As with so many of his contemporaries, the heroic figure of Friedrich Nietzsche looms large in Buber's early work. To be sure, it is not the tragic and tortured Nietzsche who inspires him, but Nietzsche the enemy of convention and prophet of unconditional living.[13] Already as a high-school student in Lvov, the youthful Buber was so profoundly moved by Nietzsche that he completed a Polish translation of the first part of *Also Sprach Zarathustra*.[14]

There were many points of contact between Nietzsche and the *fin de siècle* romantics that permitted this type of perfunctory synthesis without forcing a radical choice between them. They were unanimous in denigrating scientific rationalism and in glorifying the powers of intuition, "life-force," and creativity. They joined in condemning the small-minded philistinism of German society and in disdaining the unimaginative routine of the Burger's daily life. But this was a synthesis of merely apparent affinities in the face of crucial differences in *Weltanschauung* that would tolerate no long-term reconciliation. The *Schwärmerei* of hedonist aesthetics and mystical utopianism could come to no more than a temporary truce with Nietzsche's uncompromisingly this-worldly temperament, just as the unsuspecting innocence of Buber's voluntarism could not coexist with the cynical and 'unmasking' tendencies in Nietzsche's thought. Besides, Buber's early writings indicate little appreciation of the problematic nature of human and social life—the very hallmark of Nietzsche's ruthless intellect. Nietzsche saw the world of politics as faithfully reflecting the human material it served, so that any fundamental rehabilitation of public life required nothing less than a reorientation in the human perspective. The young Buber, for his part, accepted Nietzsche's Promethean strivings but took little heed of the existential ballast that lent weight and stability to this thought.

Nevertheless, the seed of doubt had been planted. It would require time and disappointments to develop, but Nietzsche's admonitions regarding the powers of corruption in Western culture and his exhortations for the spiritual renewal of man would become the core of Buber's later social and political philosophy.

Nietzsche may seem a strange catalyst, but it was in great measure due to his influence that Buber became involved in the Zionist movement.[15] From the vantage point afforded by Nietzsche's critique of barren intellectuality and call for "the heroic man who creates and transcends himself,"[16] Buber came to look at the abject state of European Jewry. So viewed, they appeared to him "poverty-stricken, distorted and sickly."[17] Their lives participated virtually not at all in the self-reliant, virile creativity that Nietzsche commended. Instead, they were homeless, subordinated to others, and unable to fashion their own future. Culturally they suffered either from a self-perpetuating provincialism to which art, literature, and all the liberating ideas of the Jewish Enlightenment were foreign or from a parasitic aping of Western styles that rejected the Jewish tradition out of hand. What was necessary was a national revival that would bring the real Jewish life of the masses[18] into contact with the productive forces of contemporary Europe and liberate Jewish civilization from the obscurantism that held it fast. The one indispensable precondition for this revival was a national homeland and cultural autonomy. This brought him to Zionism.[19]

Predictably, the Jewish 'renaissance' that Buber and his circle championed was not conceived as a specifically political resurgence. The term 'renaissance' was not of accidental usage; it was meant to evoke the associations that Burckhardt had given it in his historical studies. Renaissance connoted the spiritual reawakening of an entire civilization.[20] The political Zionists—Herzl and his followers—considered popular enlightenment secondary to the main goal of gaining international political recognition for the necessity of a Jewish state. Buber and his friends—the "Democratic Opposition"[21]—felt that national renaissance could never result from a declaration of goodwill on the part of others. Any meaningful transformation must come from within, and to this end, national education was vital. The people had to be prepared for the land and not simply the land for the people.[22]

For Buber, the young Nietzschean-esthete, the spark of revitalization would come from the engaged national artist, "Die Schaffenden." These Jewish Zarathustras are the "secret kings of the people"[23] who are able to elicit the "genuine" and "true" from the national genius[24] and thereby further the struggle for their people's redemption. They represent pure and uncompromising artistic dispositions that are to revolutionize the stubborn and gloomy reality of the

Jewish masses. Characteristically, the young Buber expresses neither fear that their purity be tarnished in the confrontation, nor concern that artistic ardor is unequal to the struggle. This striking lack of 'suspicion' is a sure indication of his lasting enthrallment with Nietzschean heroics and, perhaps, of his tender years and secure student existence.

The strivings for national renewal attendant upon the Zionist movement became, among the young intellectuals, a determined search for spiritual roots in Jewish history and literature. The *Haskalah* (Jewish Enlightenment) with its strident rationalistic orientation no more filled the needs of these young students than did the traditional rabbinic Judaism of the Talmudic academies. Interestingly, many young intellectuals found what they were searching for in Hasidism.

The regenerative potentialities of Hasidism had found an early expression in the writings of Moses Hess[26] but four decades were to pass before being taken up again by Jewish writers. Roughtly at the turn of the century, Ahad Haam, Berdishewski, and others discovered the 'originality' and 'depth' of the Hasidic tradition, and Buber, falling under their influence, began to acquaint himself with Hasidic sources.[27] The appeal that Hasidism had for the young Buber is not difficult to understand. Besides lending substance to his Zionist position, the kabbalistic leanings of Hasidism as well as its focus on the heroic figure of the *Zaddik* were at one with his own mystical Nietzschean disposition.

But Hasidism injected a new and critical ingredient into Buber's thought that marks a turning point in his intellectual development. It *began* the process of redirecting his mystical energies from the singular aesthetic-philosophical *Erlebnis* that meets the Absolute by transcending the *hic et nunc*, to a "world affirming" mysticism that approaches the Absolute through the realities of daily life. As Buber saw it, Hasidism had immanentized the mystical urge; in his words, it was mysticism "become ethos."[28] Rather than retaining his Olympian purity, the Hasidic *Zaddik* is convinced that the road to God leads through the sanctification of this world. "Infinity," the Baal Shem-Tov had said, "shall be contained in every deed of man, in his speaking and seeing, listening and walking, standing still and lying down."[29]

The *Neue Gemeinschaft* and "Die Schaffenden," by contrast, circumvented real predicaments either by translating them into metaphysics and resolving them philosophically or by proclaiming that the undefiled aesthetic revelation would effect concrete social change. From the Hasidic perspective both were illegitimate because the ideal and real remained separate and unconfronted. "Whoever says that the words of the Torah are one thing and the words of the world another must be regarded as a man who denies God."[30] To redeem the world meant, first of all, to descend to where unholiness abounds. "If you want to raise a man from the mud and filth," the *Zaddik* warned,

> do not think it is enough to keep standing on top and reaching down to him a helping hand. You must go all the way down yourself, down into the mud and filth. Then take hold of him with strong hands and pull him and yourself out into the light.[36]

Buber's account of his "conversion" to Hasidism highlights this 'worldly mysticism'. He relates how, chancing upon a saying of the Baal Shem-Tov (the founder of Hasidism), he was overwhelmed and "experienced the Hasidic soul."[32] The Baal Shem-Tov's words were: "He takes unto himself the quality of fervor. He arises from sleep with fervor, for he is hallowed and become another man and is worthy to create, and is become like the Holy One, blessed be He, when He created the world."[33] Sleeping and waking, the most routine of human actions, could be hallowed with divine fervor. "Each morning is a new summons," to prove that "the life of man is open to the absolute in every situation and in each activity."[34] Hasidism taught him that the Absolute could become 'real' through human agency. "Man's being created in the image of God," Buber recollects, "I grasped as deed, as becoming, as task."[35]

But despite his exuberance in praise of Hasidic 'worldly mysticism', the Buber of 1904 is still far from renouncing his own proclivities to the unconditioned *Erlebnis*. In fact, his early interpretations of Hasidism itself betray clear signs of this tendency. What seems to have initially stood out for him in the Hasidic tradition was precisely the element of spiritual ecstasy that leads to "the shaking off of the last chains, the liberation which is lifted above everything earthly."[36] The "core" of Hasidism, he wrote, was "a highly realistic guide to ecstasy as the way to the summit of existence." Only in joyful rapture does the soul "awaken and fulfill itself until, free from all lack it matures to the divine."[37]

Nevertheless, there was a considerable development from the earliest days of the *Neue Gemeinschaft* to the early works on Hasidism. While in "Alte und neue Gemeinschaft" reality is altogether spiritualized, some two years later, "Die Schaffenden," as national educators, face a factually unredeemed world with which they must grapple. To be sure, their 'struggle' is exclusively aesthetic, but it is already an art in the service of social needs. Hasidism's reality-centered activism represents, as has been shown, a further step in the direction of social responsibility. The *Zaddik*'s concern with communal matters is, for example, one of Buber's most basic premises. But whatever intellectual development is manifest, there is nothing to indicate that Buber advanced beyond the unmitigated utopian voluntarism of his earliest essays. Indeed, more than a decade passed before Buber, in his late thirties, began to incorporate the 'sense of the tragic' into his writings.

Much the same marriage of social engagement and philosophical voluntarism characterizes Buber's response to his more formal academic education. The sociological works of Tönnies, the socio-philosophical writings of Dilthey and

Simmel, the philosophical critique of language he learned from Fritz Mauthner, are all refracted through the utopian-mystical activism of his early years. And if Hasidism was instrumental in channeling his mystical energies to the real social world, it was his academic mentors who taught him the uniqueness of this interpersonal sphere as well as the modalities of human interrelation and who permitted him to define his communal yearnings in more than mythopoeic terms.

Tönnies's celebrated dichotomy between *Gemeinschaft* and *Gesellschaft* was one of a number of such distinctions that struggled to articulate the transformation that had overtaken European civilization since the French Enlightenment. Nietzsche's Apollo and Dionysis, Weber's traditional vs. legal-rational authority, Spengler's occidental and oriental, as well as the popular distinctions between civilization and *Kultur* and between old and new nations, all, in one form or another, arrayed the forces of creativity, naturalness, spontaneity, and youth against those of artificiality, overregimentation, conventionality, and effete sophistication. There is also an element of backward-looking nostalgia and unease with the modern that marks these dichotomies as the formulations of an age in transition. Buber's *I-Thou* and *I-It* relationships, as will be seen, need to be appreciated in this context.

Already in "Alte und neue Gemeinschaft," his very first essay, the distinction between the comunity rooted in purposefulness (*Zweck*) and the 'post-social' community that transcends all sociological categories resounds with the echoes of Tönnies' typology. To be sure, Buber is hortatory and mystical rather than analytic, but the source of his inspiration is clear. Very interestingly, Buber takes Tönnies to task for his unimaginative empiricism, more precisely, for failing to recognize that *Zweck* may be dispensed with in social life, but again it is the criticism of one deeply in debt.[38]

Whatever may be the full historical and sociological import of the *Gemeinschaft-Gesellschaft* typology, Buber's focus was, no doubt, on the kind of human association involved in each. *Gesellschaft*, which represents Hobbes's "civil society" and Marx's bourgeois capitalism[39] distilled into a sociological 'ideal type,' is "a fusion of interests over a specific positively defined area. Within the area it involves a 'compromise' of interests and parties but it only mitigates the deeper-lying separateness which in essential respects remains untouched."[40] It is a "mere coexistence of people independent from each other."[41] The dominant human motive in *Gesellschaft* is *Kurwillen* or 'rational' will, that is, viewing men and material in marketplace terms of management, allocation, and control.

At the other pole *Gemeinschaft*, modelled on a romanticized version of the medieval community, is a state of natural rather than superimposed social harmony. It does not signify an artificial truce, or management of conflict, but rather a fundamental unity in which people are joined intrinsically to one another. *Naturwillen*, its characteristic perspective, is associated with friendship, spontaneity, and directness.

Buber seems to have read Tönnies as the activist reads the academic—for inspiration rather than explanation. Tönnies' historical 'ideal types' become, in the young Buber's hands, critical normative tools to stimulate action in the present.[42] His ardent commitment to social renewal transforms a quasi-scientific dichotomy into moral categories and finally, some two decades later in *I and Thou*, into a sweeping phenomenology and ethic of human relations. The implicit critique and grudging acceptance of industrialized society contained in the term *Gesellschaft*, as well as the tacit approbation of organic solidarity in *Gemeinschaft*[43] are the embryonic models for the *I-It* and *I-Thou* relationships.

Furthermore, the influence of Tönnies is evident insofar as Buber begins to appreciate society—indeed, all human groupings whether economic, political, or national—in terms of the quality of human intercourse that underlies it. "Das Zwischenmenschliche,"[44] a term he coins at this time, expresses the yet imprecise feeling that what exists between man and man is not reducible to what takes place in each partner or even to the sum of what takes place in both. The social dimension is sui generis and constitutes the heart of all formal human organization. Not surprisingly, Buber's objectives are not purely academic; the need to gear human life to "das Zwischenmenschliche" is couched in the imperative.

In similar fashion, the activist in Buber, translates the scholarly speculations of *Lebensphilosophie* from the intransitive vocabulary of academia to the dynamic and personal terms of the passionate advocate. Buber attended the lectures of both Dilthey and Simmel at the turn of the century and later acknowledged that *Lebensphilosophie* was an important influence on his early thought.[45] Already in "Alte und Neue Gemeinschaft," the young Buber had glorified *das Leben*— that mysterious and incommunicable essence—as the axis of "neue Gemeinschaft."

Certain aspects of the *Lebensphilosophie* school of philosophy and historiography have particular interest in regard to the unfolding of Buber's philosophical temperament.[46] By 'life', *Lebensphilosophie* meant that totality of human experience of which the changing forms of art, literature, philosophy, religion, politics, and so on, are only partial expressions. This myriad faceted kaleidoscope could never be comprehended in even the vastest philosophical system because it is by its very nature in the state of 'becoming' and the philosopher, as part of the moving stream, speaks, perforce, with the consciousness of a given vantage point. One can no more lift oneself above the arena of Heraclitean change than one can become 'part of' an era that is not one's own. All that one may know are the various manifestations through which this evolving consciousness articulates itself. All absolutes, be they in the nature of the thing in itself, Platonic ideas, or the dialectic of history, are futile, one-sided attempts to compress the incompressible. They represent the urge to find a final resting place.

The embodiment of a particular consciousness into a concrete social or political form is similarly only a transitory phase of 'becoming', never a *terminus ad quem*. 'Becoming' repeatedly crystallizes into various institutions and orderings only to find them outdated, frequently even partners to obscurantism. The clearest symptom of an idea's obsolescence is its attempt to barricade itself against the onrush of that which it no longer knows how to manage.

But given the irreducible singularity of each era, how is historical knowledge, indeed, knowledge of realities other than one's own possible? To enter the living consciousness of this evolving human spirit the investigator must forsake the prejudices of his or her own particularity and cross the boundary between the self and the phenomenon in question, in Dilthey's words, between the "self and the non-self." Culture, the large tableau in which consciousness is most richly represented, is the window through which one may peer into the *Innerlichkeit* of another age. The ability to do this, *Verstehen* in Dilthey's terminology, consists of fathoming the inner state of another mind through the medium of its outward movements. It is a "transposition of myself," a *Nacherleben* that pierces the barriers between closed-off individuals and permits them to sense, with something approaching personal immediacy, the moods and qualities of the other. *Verstehen*, as opposed to the purely intellectual process of *Erklaren*, requires the totality of the searcher's efforts, "the cooperation of all the powers of the mind."[47] It is this ability that sets the *Geisteswissenschaften* off from the natural sciences and which was *Lebensphilosophie*'s rejoinder to the Kantian dilemma of the epistemological inaccessibility of the thing in itself.

Notably, for our purposes, the same involvement that is required to grasp the essence of another historical period is also indispensable when another human being stands before us. "We strive keenly," Dilthey writes, "to press through every facial expression and every word to the inner mind of the speaker."[48] But it is not simply the other individual that one comes to understand by this method. "It is only in comparing myself with others that I come to experience what is individual in myself; only then do I become conscious of that in my own existence which differs from others."[49] *Verstehen* is the means for "rediscovering myself in the Thou."[50]

Despite its avowedly academic character, it should not be surprising that for Buber, *Lebensphilosophie* represented a vindication of the 'engaged' individual. Passive detachment, besides being morally indefensible, was now shown to be an epistemological blunder. The *ens realissimum* could be approached only through active, exhaustively human relation and would yield its truth to no partial, sedentary method. To avoid reducing historical figures or, for that matter, those one daily encounters, to stereotyped abstractions, to see the "whole man, in the full diversity of his powers; the willing, feeling, thinking being,"[51] a leap of empathetic transposition was imperative. The pursuit of human truth was no spectator sport.[52]

Buber's differences with *Lebensphilosophie*, which found their expression in later years, center precisely on the alluring but illusory promise of 'engagement' that the latter proffered. The concept of "life," Buber wrote retrospectively, was a "questionable abstraction, all the more questionable since it pretended to remain especially close to the concrete."[53] As Kierkegaard had taken his lecturer Hegel to task for not responding to the question, "How do I live a life?", Buber complains that for all of Dilthey's concern with the "whole man" and with real "lived experience" he failed to grapple with the most fundamental of problems—what is to be done?

True, *Lebensphilosophie*'s historicism had effectively shaken the presumption and smugness of the system makers,

but this selfsame relativism also attacked the roots of belief—
leading beyond humility to skepticism, even paralysis. Characteristically, Buber navigates a careful course between the
poles of skepticism and security. He draws upon the 'engaged' and 'open-ended' aspects of *Lebensphilosophie* to
justify commitment and creativity, while transforming its
relativist historico-epistemological method into a tool for the
pursuit of situational moral knowledge. If, on the one hand,
this knowledge is not systematically or definitively acquira-
ble, neither, on the other hand, is it the relative chameleon-
like knowledge of historicism. Reality may be unique at each
meeting, yet this diversity rests upon a discoverable ontological constant that provides those who seek with the imperatives for action.

Interestingly, Buber's utopian mystical voluntarism found
philosophical corroboration in *Lebensphilosophie*'s aversion
to structure and fixity. If, as Dilthey had contended, the
dynamic flux of history could never be contained in static
forms and a congealed form is symptomatic of an idea that
has lost its vitality, Buber inferred that the codification of
religion, the institutionalization of public order, the regula-
tion of human relations, pointed to the moribund state of
these phenomena. And as much as the mature Buber may
have revised these views in favor of the necessity of organization and authority, he never abandoned the conviction—
one could almost say it was a personality trait—that established order represented a kind of failure of nerve, a ready
substitute for the directness and spontaneity he preferred.[54]

While *Lebensphilosophie* attacked the proposition that
truth could be definitively systematized, Fritz Mauthner, an
early associate of Buber, questioned the very ability of
language to faithfully convey thought or describe reality.[55]
Words, he maintained, cannot express reality "as it really is."
Reality is a world apart, and language, although it may
maneuver to encircle it, can never entirely capture it. To
ascend the "ladder" of knowledge, Mauthner writes, "I must

destroy language behind me and in me step by step. I must destroy every rung of the ladder while climbing upon it."[56] More programmatically stated, his thesis is that "knowledge of the world through language is impossible, that there is no science of the world and that language is an insufficient instrument for knowledge."[57] Indeed, Mauthner adds elsewhere, "through language men have made it impossible for themselves to ever act to know each other."[58]

Clearly, this kind of skepticism could easily lead to an immobilizing nihilism. Mauthner himself went far in this direction rejecting, among other things, the validity of abstractions, of science, of moral knowledge, even the possibility of self-knowledge.[59] Paradoxically, Buber turned the thrust of Mauthner's skepticism in the direction of his own mystical activism. The formal tool of language is, in fact, unsuited for the expression of true moral knowledge. Only in relation, in encountering others beyond the reach of words, does the extrinsic give way to the essential. Moreover, if Mauthner was right about the limits of language, it only vindicated the privileged status that Buber accorded to mystical knowledge.

Buber absorbed this perspective on Mauthner's *Sprachkritik* from the man who was in many ways his model and intellectual alter ego—Gustav Landauer.[60] The dramatic relations and fascinating cross-fertilization between these two men are in themselves subjects for a full-scale essay, but it may safely be said that the impress of Landauer, both as thinker and personality, is pervasively evident in Buber's thought and philosophical temperament.

They met at one of the *Neue Gemeinschaft* circle meetings, and against the background of shared interests in mysticism[61] became fast friends. Buber followed Landauer (who was nine years his senior) when he rejected the naive utopianism and *Vereinsspielerei* of the *Neue Gemeinschaft*.[62] He again concurred with Landauer in his critical reevaluation of Mauthner's *Sprachkritik*.[63] But far the most basic and enduring of Landauer's influences on his young friend was the romantic, secularly spiritual, libertarian socialism he professed.[64]

From Landauer's quasi-religious perspective, Marx and his followers were not 'radical' enough—in the sense of cutting to the roots of the socio-political difficulties they faced. The Marxists had identified the problem, *tout court*, with a particular economic system, consequently their solution was appropriately simple: its destruction. With capitalism gone, they believed that a 'new communist man' unaffected by the vices of the past would arise to build a truly human world. Landauer rejected these 'Marxist'[65] views as mechanical, naive, and dangerous.

Whatever may have stood between Landauer and his conservative and religious opponents, they were at one in appreciating human transformation as the fundamental problem of all revolutionary activity. True revolution, Landauer argued, was not to be understood as a primarily political upheaval in which power changed hands or ownership was passed from class to class; to be 'radical', that is, to prevent the new order from simply replacing old injustice with some fresh variant, the revolution needed to transform the human material out of which all social orders were composed. For the political conservative, the identification of real social change with subjective metamorphosis vindicated a position of philosophical resignation as well as an Olympian disdain for the shortsighted impetuosity of the revolutionary; the intractable and unsavory were, after all, a fixed part of human nature. Laundauer, however, was convinced that by a great act of dedication and will—resembling nothing so much as a religious conversion—people could recreate themselves as well as their environment. If the axis of revolution ran through each individual so that without personal regeneration no real social improvement were possible, revolutionary activity necessarily consisted in the concerted effort to penetrate the "thick crust" that had formed over one's soul. Notably, Landauer's magnum opus is not a socialist 'manifesto' but an *Aufruf zum Sozialismus*,[66] a call, an appeal to the slumbering powers of vitality and love to make themselves felt in the world. "Socialism," he declared, "is the desire to create a new reality with the power of a certain ideal."[67]

Not surprisingly, the Marxist 'leap' into the era of freedom by, what seemed to Landauer, a mere 'technical' reshuffling of power and ownership was a shallow and escapist alternative to the too formidable challenge of human renewal. Having conceived of change in facile 'objective' terms, the Marxists were not averse to highly questionble methods so long as they achieved these limited goals. Their conceptual narrowness blinded them to the broader human drama of revolution and its deep moral underpinnings so they could, with zeal and good conscience, destroy the revolution's inner integrity for the sake of its 'objective' success.

Much the same 'technical' perspective was evident in their mechanical beliefs that class war was inevitable, that the dictatorship of the proletariat would of itself give way to anarchist harmony and that the classless society was the result of the dialectical unfolding of history. "There is nothing ahead of us," Landauer exhorted, "it is only within us."[68] Moreover, Marxism's manipulative and authoritarian cast was but another symptom of its lack of contact with those vital spiritual powers that make people free to create without external coercion.

The parliamentary Social Democrats and Bernsteinian evolutionary socialists were not much better in Landauer's view. They had, in effect, sold the socialist dream for a mess of porridge. They too, in their own way, were unable to transcend the technical perspective; hence they had forfeited the high-minded spiritual motives of real socialism in favor of pragmatic efforts to raise the standards of living. Revolution or evolution was, in fact, not the proper question: this consisted in the polar choice between commitment to a radical human transformation and a program of technical, extrinsic *bouleversement*.

Even this very summary presentation of Landauer's views, highlights their "elective affinity" to the Promethean voluntarism of the young Buber. There is a similar moral earnestness, a very comparable stress on human self-transformation, and a common belief in the vital—indeed, the mystical—capacities upon which the utopian community rested. Landauer's ideas cannot but have added substance and depth to Buber's emerging philosophy. Indeed, it was through Buber that Landauer's views reached their widest audience after he was murdered during the abortive Bavarian revolution of 1919. So much of Landauer's spiritual passion was absorbed, reworked, and perpetuated by Buber that it involves little exaggeration to call him the 'executor' of Landauer's political testament.

Buber's encounter with Hasidism in 1904 marks a caesura in his public career. He turned his energies to study and reflection, producing his first Hasidic works as well as editing *Die Gesellschaft*,[69] an important periodical devoted to social issues. When, after five years of relative withdrawal, Buber returned to the public arena, he emerged as a highly sought-after writer and speaker. He was after all something of an anomaly: a young intellectual, conversant with Western culture, who rejected the orthodox, scorned the reformers, but yet spoke of Judaism and spoke with authority. During the next decade Buber expounded his ideas to a large audience of avid Jewish youth, alienated intellectuals and the generally curious in a series of remarkable addresses, essays, and public forums. They established his reputation as spokesman and teacher for a new generation of committed Jews who had found their way back to Judaism without sacrificing their 'critical spirit' or Western culture. The uniqueness of Buber's public image and something of the wonder it caused were captured by Ludwig Lewisohn when he declared that Buber was "either a shocking anachronism or almost a miracle."[70]

The early addresses on Judaism (1909-1911)[71] manifest conspicuously those characteristics that have been identified with the young Buber in the foregoing pages. Even a cursory reading leaves the impression of uncompromising ardor and contempt for "small-minded" political 'realism'. The surging, often turgid style is ideally suited to the utopian-mystical activism Buber champions; and even if he now confronts social problems somewhat more analytically than in the earliest writings, the essays' defining quality remains an epic state of mind that will brook no compromise in the realization of its loftiest aims.

Whether it was due to the mellowness that grows with age, the disappointment and shock brought on by world war,[72] the failure of the Bavarian Soviet, the brutal murder of Landauer[73] or his growing isolation and powerlessness in the Zionist movement[74] (likely all of the above taken together), Buber's utopianism underwent a fundamental revision in the years following the early addresses. To study the development of his writings in the prewar and war period is, therefore, to be witness to the emergence of that philosophical personality outlined at the opening of this chapter—the marriage of utopian yearnings and existential anxiety.

Perhaps most representative of Buber's rapturous voluntarism in the earliest essays are his exhortations for the 'renewal' of Judaism. Renewal, he insists, must be total and all consuming or not at all. "For by renewal I do not in any way mean something gradual, a sum total of minor changes. I mean something sudden and immense—by no means a continuation or an improvement but a return and transformation."[75] He bemoans the absence, in his uninspired age, of those impassioned ones who march under the banner of the "sudden and immense."

All activities of the typical man of today are governed by the concept of evolution, that is the concept of gradual change— or, as it is also called, progress—emerging from the collective effect of many small causes. This concept['s] ... effect upon the realm of the mind and the will has been highly deleterious ... The extinction of heroic, unconditional living in our time must to a great extent be ascribed to this sense. Once the great doer expected to alter the face of the world with his deed, and to inform all becoming with his own will. He did not feel that he was subject to the conditions of the world, for he was grounded in the unconditionality of God, Whose word he sensed in the decisions he made as clearly as he felt the blood in his veins. This confidence in the suprahuman has been undermined; man's consciousness of God and deed had already been stifled in the cradle; all one could hope for was to become the exponent of some small "progress." And whoever can no longer desire the impossible will be able to achieve nothing more than the all-too possible. Thus the power of the spirit was replaced by busyness, and the might of sacrifice by bargaining skill.[76]

Notably, both mystic and utopian activist are united in the "great doer" who overcomes mundane contingencies by being "grounded in the unconditionality of God."

The difficulties of social and national renewal, Buber told his audiences, do not reflect vexing objective hinderances but rather are symptomatic of deficiency at the subjective level— in this case the absence of heroic and unconditional dedication. Consequently, he argued that the 'Jewish problem' was a fundamentally subjective one representing the unhealthy state of the Jewish "soul." The Jews, he explained, are the most dualistic of peoples, spiritual yet materialistic, cohesive yet homeless, creative yet sterile. In no other people has this "primary dualism" been so profound and hence in no other has the vision of unity been so desperately sought after. Both problem and solution derive from a state of mind. "Nowhere," he writes, has dualism been

as strong, as dominant or as central as it has been, and is, in the Jew. Nowhere has it been realized in such purity and so fully; nowhere has it had so determining an effect upon character and destiny; nowhere has it created anything as momentous, as paradoxical, as heroic, as wonderous as this marvel: the Jews striving for unity. It is this striving for unity that makes Judaism a phenomenon of mankind, that transforms the Jewish question into a human question.[77]

In an argument reminiscent of Marx's dialectical self-transcendence of the proletariat, Buber contends that "Judaism's fundamental significance for mankind" has to do with its desire to resolve inner dualism.

Conscious as is no other community of the primary dualism, knowing and typifying division more than any other community, it proclaims a world in which dualism will be abolished, a world of God which needs to be realized in both the life of the individual man and the life of the community: the world of unity.[78]

More specifically,

striving to evolve unity out of the division of his I, he [the Jew] conceived the unitary God. Striving to evolve unity out of the division of the human community, he conceived the idea of universal justice. Striving to evolve unity out of the division of all living matter, he conceived universal love. Striving to evolve unity out of the division of the world he created the messianic which later, again under the guiding participation of Jews, was reduced in scope, made finite and called Socialism.[79]

Already in 1912 the momentum of the "all or nothing" person who dashed impetuously through the early essays is moderated by an incipient realism, a growing recognition of limits. Not that Buber's ardor has cooled—this is the unshakable constant of his career—but it has been redirected from the unconditional, fate-transforming act to the resolute decision—whatever its actual 'success' in the world may be. There are, Buber explains, two rival tendencies in each "human soul," the "forming" and the "formless" (*Gestaltende* and *Gestaltlose*) that, following his 'psychologizing' orientation, determine the course of history. The "formless" individual shrinks from decision, content to follow the well-worn path of least resistance. The "forming" individual decides to accept responsibility for his or her world even while recognizing the limits of human power. It is, in fact, "necessary and urgent" that the "forming" individual

> come to know the experience of the limit, of the unformable, of the insuperable obstacles of the soul. Yet it is in his potentiality and in the sweep of his vision to experience the power of formation and from there to conquer new land daily, to plant the borderstake further on. Those in and to whom this creative power reveals itself to such a degree are the truly formed, the formers of mankind. But those over whom inert matter triumphs are the eternal army of the realistic opposition.[80]

But even when such slow hard-fought progress (of the kind Buber had formerly disdained) finally achieves some measure of success

> the formless ever again break into their domain and break up the form . . . therefore the formed is transformed, and the struggle for form is a process that begins ever anew. . . it is then self-evident and yet an ever new occurrence that, in the empirical process of life the formers are defeated. It cannot be otherwise but that the formless . . . triumph empirically over the spirit.[81]

The prophets, archetypes of heroic unconditionality in the early essays,[82] now begin to exhibit signs of suffering, ineffectuality, and defeat. Instead of informing "all becoming with his will," the prophet is typically outcast and unheard, fighting the scorn of an apathetic people, at times defending himself against their wrathful designs.[83]

Even the term 'unconditionality' undergoes serious modification. No longer is the unconditional person confident of achieving the "impossible," the "superhuman." Individuals "who are compelled toward unconditionality" are now seen as those "who choose, who make decisions," who are "dedicated to their goal."[84] It is not partial success they reject but indecision and spiritual sluggishness.

Moreover, replacing the exclusive emphasis on subjectivity, there also appears at this time a counter tendency which stresses action directed toward the objective world. "Jewish religiosity," Buber asserts, means "the absolute value of man's deed." This entails being aware

> that the fullness of the world's destiny, namelessly interwoven, passes through our hands. It is said in the *Mishnah*, "every man shall say: 'it is for me that the world was created'." And again, "every man shall say: 'the world rests on me'," which is corroborated by the Hasidic text: "yes, he is the only one in the world and its continued existence depends on his deed."[85]

"Genuine religiosity," he adds in clear reference to his own past, "has nothing in common with the fancies of romantic hearts or the self-pleasure of aestheticizing souls ... genuine religiosity is doing." It wants to "sculpt the unconditional out of the matter of this world. The countenance of God reposes, invisible, in an earthen block; it must be wrought, carved out of it. To engage in this work means to be religious—nothing else."[86] Late in the autumn of 1914[87] these incipient biases were confirmed and dramatized by an "everyday event" that Buber recounted some years later. With Olympian solemnity he writes:

> What happened was nothing more than one forenoon, after a morning of 'religious' enthusiasm, I had a visit from an unknown young man, without being there in spirit. I certainly did not fail to let the meeting be friendly, I did not treat him any more remissly than all his contemporaries who were in the habit of seeking me out about this time of day as an oracle that is ready to listen to reason. I conversed attentively and openly with him—only I omitted to guess the questions which he did not put. Later, not long after, I learned from one of his friends—he himself was no longer alive—the essential content of these questions; I learned that he had come to me not casually but borne by destiny, not for a chat but for a decision. He had come to me in this hour. What do we expect

when we are in despair and yet go to a man? Surely a presence by means of which we are told that nevertheless there is meaning. Since then I have given up the 'religious' which is nothing but the exception, extraction, exaltation, ecstasy, or it has given me up. I possess nothing but the everyday out of which I am never taken. The mystery is never disclosed, it has escaped or it has made its dwelling here where everything happens as it happens. I know no fullness but each mortal hour's fullness of claim and responsibility. . . .[88]

Much the same repudiation of spiritualizing reality is contained in a short philosophical dialogue written at this time, in which a narrator dissents from the mysticism championed by his interlocutor. "Beyond this," the narrator continues his argument,

I lack the mystic's negation. I can negate conviction but never the slightest actual thing. The mystic manages, truly or apparently, to annihilate the entire world . . . in order to press forward to God. But I am enormously concerned with just this world, this painful and precious fullness of all that I see, hear, taste. I cannot wish away any part of its reality. I can only wish that I might heighten this reality.[89]

"It took . . . five years," Buber reminisced many years later, "for this recognition to ripen to expression."[90] It is worth noting, if only parenthetically, that this transformation from a *Wirklichkeitsfremd* subjectivism to an engaged 'ethic of responsibility' was part of a larger transformation that many German intellectuals underwent during and after the war. Karl Jaspers, for example, speaks for his generation when he describes the impact of the war:

Up until then my life had been a spiritual striving . . . untroubled by general happenings and without political consciousness, though with momentary forebodings of possible distant dangers. All intentness centered on my own private life, on the high moments of commission with those closest to me. Contemplation of the works of the spirit, research, continual intercourse with things timeless, were the purpose and meaning of life's activities. Then in 1914 the World War

caused the great breach in our European existence. The
paradisiacal life before the World War, naive despite all its
sublime spirituality could never return.[91]

Far the surest symptom of Buber's transformation during
these years was his growing suspicion of the millenial enthusiasm that so many intellectuals—of both right and left—
expressed first in regard to the war and later the Munich
Soviet. Despite his participation in a small group of intellectuals (known as the *Fortokreis*) that attempted, in the spring
and summer of 1914, to avert the war, it cannot be said that
at war's outbreak Buber was *au-dessus de la mêlée*.[92] It is not
surprising, given his deep-seated utopian-mystical predilections, that when the national *Erlebnis* associated with the
'ideas of 1914' swept over Germany, Buber was carried
away.[93] Indeed, his early wartime writings display such
fervent German nationalism that they were understandably
withheld from the public eye in later years. He became
virtually apocalyptic in his expectations. The war, specifically
a German victory, would resolve everything from the Jewish
problem to the future of European democracy.[94]Whether it
was due to Landauer's vitriolic attacks against his friend's
dangerous naivité[95] or to the general spirit of frustration and
war fatigue that set in after the initial burst of enthusiasm
gave way to the unromantic prospect of a protracted trench
war,[96] Buber soon disavowed nationalist zeal and recognized
as groundless his earlier buoyant optimism. The crushing,
indeed, embarrassing disappointment he suffered was a lesson he could not easily forget. It created an anxious inner
sentry who sounded the alarm when his hopes outran his
limitations.

The collapse of Kurt Eisner's Bavarian revolution drove
this lesson home only too well. Landauer, who was minister
of "public enlightenment" in Eisner's government, obsti-
nately refused to abandon hope in the foundering revolution.[97] In a dramatic reversal of roles, it was now Buber who

cautioned against quixotic aspirations. Some ten weeks before Landauer's death, Buber wrote movingly of a visit to
Munich and of his encounter with the revolutionaries. He
sensed a heavy apocalyptic air hanging over their night-long
discussions—the apocalypse of catastrophe. "Doom shone
out of Eisner's polished manner, he was marked." Landauer,
for his part, strained every nerve to maintain his faith in the
revolution.[98] He could not but win Buber's praise, yet it was
the heavy-hearted panegyric accorded to a doomed martyr.
On May 2, 1919, Gustav Landauer was viciously beaten to
death by a band of counter revolutionaries. Buber's reaction
to the murder of his 'Socrates' can only be imagined.[99]

Writing shortly afterward, Buber returns to the theme of
human limitations—with a vengeance. While mystical rapture is "pure and undefilable"—"not so the deed."

> No matter how free its intention, how pure its manifestation
> it is at the mercy of its own consequences; and even the most
> sublime deed, which does not waste so much as a glance at
> the lowlands of causality, is dragged into the mud as soon as
> it enters the world and becomes visible. . . . There is no
> undefilable perfection here; everywhere the impure challenges
> the pure, dragging it down, distorting it; all about him
> gloating derision apprises the heroic victim of its futility, and
> the abyss pronounces its inexorable sentence on the dying to
> whom victory is denied.[100]

"Human nature," far from being that wonderously pliant
substance transformable by will and dedication

> resists with all its active and latent energy the commanding
> will to mold it, pulling the deed down into its destructive
> vortex; . . . [it] does not merely impede all transformation,
> but—and this is much worse—pollutes, distorts, and corrodes
> whatever transformation might have already begun.[101]

The forty-one-year-old Buber stood at the threshold of his
intellectual and public career. Notwithstanding the existential gravity of the foregoing lines, the utopian urge remained

fundamental to his outlook. He had incorporated two contrary but reciprocally fructifying philosophical perspectives, and what is more, rather than striking a mutually neutralizing 'prudent' balance, he insisted on preserving the full force of each imperative intact. Herein lies both the heroic pathos of his work and the tension from which it springs.

2

The Narrow Ridge

I have occasionally described my standpoint to my friends as the "narrow ridge." I wanted by this to express that I did not rest on the broad upland of a system that includes a series of sure statements about the absolute, but on a narrow ridge between the gulfs where there is no sureness of expressible knowledge but the certainty of meeting what remains undisclosed.

Buber

THE critical moment in Buber's intellectual genesis had come relatively late in life. At thirty-five he was still what Hegel called a "beautiful soul": that type of subjective disposition "which empties the objective of all content,"[1] which "consists in yearning," and a soulful "transparent purity."[2] Only when the first four decades of his life were behind him—a time when most thinkers have long since formed an intellectual personality—does he haltingly begin speaking in that voice by which he is now recognized. Moreover, the transformation he underwent was largely due to external wartime stimuli that compelled a retreat from his utopian voluntarism rather than to an inner evolution of latent tendencies. The mature Buber who emerges from the tragedies of war and revolution is, in a sense, a compound personality, unable, on the one hand, to free himself from the long-ingrained habits of visionary enthusiasm and, on the other, unable to avoid the dark lessons of human corruption and failure.

I and Thou, which is at once the first of his mature works[3] and his magnum opus, conveys this uneasy duality dramatically. To Buber the world appears irremediably twofold: either inspired and extraordinary or pedestrian and all too ordinary, either beyond the reach of causality and contingency or inexorably at their mercy. No golden mean between the poles of *I-Thou* and *I-It* can be struck; the intrusion of one dissolves the other forthwith. Buber has, in effect, incorporated his syncretic thinking into the phenomenology of human relations presented in *I and Thou*.[4]

The *I-Thou* relation itself contains a striking structural reflection of this dualizing tendency. At the one pole, it is structureless, without specific content, beyond causality and will, unbounded, atemporal, unplanned, and unconditioned—the very definition of a mystical experience. At the other pole, Buber insists that only concrete and specific individuals can so relate, that relation must be to a similarly palpable and existent subject, that there is no loss of self on either side in such a relation and that the object to which one relates need have no lofty or exceptional character. This is the voice of worldliness and facticity.

In fact, Buber's entire thought structure betrays signs of this 'double vision'. The two major headings under which the bulk of his mature philosophy may be subsumed—the philosophy of dialogue and the philosophy of realization (*Verwirklichung*)—are, interestingly, constituted of very different materials. The philosophy of dialogue as epitomized in *I and Thou* sets the *I-Thou* relation beyond unaided human will in the unconditional realm of 'grace'. 'Activism' has no place in its attainment. To desire it, is to render it impossible. On the other hand, the philosophy of realization whose goal is true communal life, is meliorist and intensely activist as well as being avowedly subject to the limitations of circumstance. These two philosophical moods reflect the two halves of Buber's philosophical personality: at the one pole mystical, subjectivist, undefiled, at the other Promethean, worldly wise, sober. And while Buber makes every attempt to amalgamate the polar elements into a coherent whole, it is perhaps inevitable that the seams of his synthesis should, on occasion, become visible.

Yet, whatever may be their biographical causes and structural effects, it is precisely in the uneasy coexistence of these perspectives that Buber's uniqueness lies. This bipolarity lends richness and dialectical depth to his philosophical voice, encourages a mutually affecting interplay of 'is' and 'ought', and permits the realist and the visionary—the *Vita Activa* and the *Vita Contemplativa*—to jointly assume responsibility for moral political decisions. To be sure, compounding an 'unconditional' vision with a contingent world cannot but produce intellectual friction, indeed, at times more anxiety than clarity, but from this friction Buber's characteristic warmth and light are generated.

Clearly this 'synthesis' is not the outcome of logical speculation—as discursive logic it is meaningless—it is rather a dynamic lived unity that accepts paradox as the only formulation apposite to the human condition. Resolving the paradox, that is, reducing the antinomy between the existentialist's *hic et nunc* and the visionary's model of perfection to a manageable, conciliatory third position, is a seductive but escapist simplification. This antinomy is man's unshakeable burden; he is the creature who ever conceives perfection but lives in imperfection. In Buber's majestic prose:

> Whoever affirms the thesis and repudiates the antithesis violates the sense of the situation. Whoever tries to think a synthesis destroys the sense of the situation. Whoever strives to relativize the antinomies annuls the sense of the situation. Whoever would settle the conflict between antinomies by some means short of his own life transgresses against the sense of the situation. It is the sense of the situation that it is to be lived in all its antinomies—only lived—and lived ever again, ever anew, unpredictably, without possibility of anticipation or prescription.[5]

Buber's philosophy of "realization," of incorporating the absolute into the real, enjoins the pursuit of the possible with the vision of the perfect before one's eyes. It aims at infusing existence with the maximum of utopia it can contain at any given moment—at helping "the world become God-real."[6] This is no counsel of perfection, only an imperative to bring forth out of a stubborn reality what is possible at each meeting—*quantum satis*. To pass beyond what is legitimately possible for the sake of the ideal is to fall into dangerous quixotism; to hypostatize a particular reality without trying its potentialities is to transgress through aimlessness and cynicism. Sensing what might be called the 'force field' of each pole without reduction or dilution, alive to the moment's malleability as well as to its stubbornness, cognizant of his own powers and of their limits, the "realizing" person locates the furthest point of possible advance. "The important thing," Buber insists, "is to realize how tremendously difficult it is—and then to believe, believe nevertheless."[7]

There can be little doubt that Buber's worldly activism with its transcendent overtones is indebted to the spirit of Judaism. The Jewish tradition's stress on social justice and on the efficacy of human action, particularly in its world-affirming Hasidic variant, were pervasively interlaced with his ethically vitalist communitarian socialism. By way of comparison, Christianity's relationship to the 'social gospel', both in its American and continental versions, was strikingly ambiguous. The sober pessimism of classical Christianity did not easily reconcile itself to theologically prescribed social activism. By and large the translation of 'transcendent' religious ideals to 'immanent' social ones—what a recent Jesuit critic of Buber calls "religious secularism"[8]—has been vigorously resisted by Christian thinkers. Perhaps no better indication of this can be found than in the tendency of major Christian thinkers—Barth, Niebuhr, Tillich, and Maritain come to mind—to abandon an initial commitment to socialism under the impact of Christian 'realism'.

As seen by Buber, 'transcendent' and 'immanent' are not mutually exclusive categories; their unification is in fact the heart of the religious imperative. For Christian sensibilities, on the other hand, the abyss between worldly and divine is generally regarded as so profound as to discourage attempts at synthesis. So that while Buber grasps the transcendent-immanent duality as the great challenge of history, his Christian counterpart generally regards it as a humility-inducing verity.

In this spirit, one Christian critic takes Buber to task for his inability to "offer any future but the human, the social."[9] The notion that life in a true socialist community is a "sacramental existence," or that socialism is the central content of prophetic messianism for the present time is vehemently and predictably rejected. There is a "grave danger," he argues, in giving such a deeply religious meaning to a worldly, nontranscendent vision of human happiness, the danger that religion will

> be transformed into something very different, some modern form of Judaism, something man can "acquire," unrelated to God, dialectical, moralistic, and in one sense or another, progressive.[10]

Buber can promise nothing, this critic complained, "except a flat, shallow, socialistic, futuristic, perfection."[11] Even Buber's view of prophecy, normally the stronghold of transcendence, is vitiated by his social activism.

> [It] is wanting in the transcendent element implied by fulfillment; it never rises above itself, and because it remains imprisoned within the scheme of its own thought, it is finally precipitated into the paradox . . . of social utopianism.[12]

For his part, Buber appreciates social activism not as the secularization of religious ideals but as the sanctification of the world. Judaism, he repeats tirelessly, speaks to the real individual in the concrete circumstances of his or her daily routine: to "his emotions and his will, his actions and abstentions, his life at home and in the marketplace, in the temple and in the popular assembly."[13] There are no special precincts to which religiosity is confined, no special actions through which it may be manifested, no special time suited for its practice. Religiosity is simply where, through human agency, the unconditional purity of the absolute is made to touch the common and unglorified moments of real life. Buber liked to call this point of contact the "narrow ridge."

He speaks of the "narrow ridge" as the "rocky" and elusive path far from the open and accessible "broad upland" in which the "systems" prevail.[14] It is where the existentialist moment and the utopian urge confront each other and negotiate, in "holy insecurity," for the moment's best possibilities. Although the evocative associations of this philosophical metaphor are meant to be considerably broader than what has just been indicated (more on this will follow), in all its variants the "narrow ridge" never leaves the fullness of real life; it is traversed in everyday, often unheralded moments when a person seriously faces both the "demands of the spirit" and of "the historical hour."

This brings us to Buber's ambivalent but highly instructive relationship to the 'Christian realism' of Sören Kierkegaard. The quarrel between them is most clearly reflected in two ostensibly similar but substantively antithetical philosophical metaphors used to depict the religious person's moment of sanctification. For Kierkegaard, only the "single one"—the solitary individual who leaves the crowd far behind—can enter the "narrow pass" and encounter the divine. This "pass" is envisaged as the line between God and the world, accessible only to those who renounce all but their spiritual individuality and present themselves unaccompanied and unburdened. In this spirit Kierkegaard confides to his diary "I stand like a lonely pine tree egoistically shut off, pointing to the skies and casting no shadow."[15]

The "question" Buber puts to the "single one" is simply whether piety and holiness are indeed opposed to "the earth and the fullness thereof," whether purity and worldliness are mutually excluding alternatives. Buber's answer is unequivocal. The "narrow ridge" he insists, never leads out of the actual world of people and things. To hypostatize the crowd as fallen and worthy of abandonment is not only factually unwarranted, it fails, besides, to hear the Voice that often speaks in the vernacular to the social collectives of which each individual is inexorably part.

But for Kierkegaard, since the "single one" is he who "does not have to do essentially with others," it follows that he is "as sharply opposed as possible to politics."[16] For politics is the realm of the "crowd," the mire of "untruth," where his undefiled aloneness before God is overwhelmed by the depravity of the many. One must choose, Kierkegaard's 'Christian realism' declares, God or the world, "either-or."

There is no attempt on Buber's part to 'refute' Kierkegaard's somber teaching by presenting an alternative, embellished, picture of the "crowd." The world of politics involves risking one's soul, of that there is no doubt. But when one comes to realize that "creation is not a hurdle on the road to God, [but] the road itself,"[17] then no part of the God-given world may be wished away or withdrawn for purity's sake. On the "narrow ridge," Buber writes, the "relation with God . . . includes and encompasses the possibility of relation with all otherness." To be truly a "single one" means to change "the crowd into single ones." Just at "the place where he stands, whether lifted up or unnoticed, he does what he can, with the powers he possesses . . . to make the crowd no longer a crowd."[18]

If Buber can speak the words "either-or" at all, it is only in regard to assuming responsibility, that is, accepting or not accepting personal accountability for the possibilities his reality offers him. The following passage captures the somewhat stylized, passionate, almost libidinal thrust of Buber's Promethean existentialism.

He [the "single one"] must face the hour which approaches him, the biographical and historical hour, just as it is, in its whole world content and apparently senseless contradiction, without weakening the impact of otherness in it. He must hear the message, stark and untransfigured, which is deliverd to him out of this hour, presented by this situation as it arrives. Nor must he translate for himself its wild and crude profaneness into the chastely religious: he must recognize that the question put to him, with which the speech of the situation is fraught—whether it sound with angels' or devils' tongues—remains God's question to him, of course without the devils thereby being turned into angels. It is a question wondrously tuned in the wild crude sound. And he, the single one, must answer by what he does and does not do, he must accept and answer for the hour, the hour of the world, as it is given to him, entrusted to him. Reduction is forbidden; you are not at liberty to select what suits you, the whole cruel hour is at stake, the whole claims you, and you must answer—Him.[19]

A more direct confrontation with 'Christian realism', in which some of these same ideas are reiterated in less rapturous form, is evidenced in Buber's comments on two of his German contemporaries of the mid-1930s: the Roman Catholic jurist Carl Schmitt and the Lutheran theologian Friederich Gogarten. Both Schmitt and Gogarten present, in legal and theological terms respectively, extended arguments contending that the state as constituted represents the exclusive context in which political and ethical judgments may be made. They base this judgemnt, in large measure, on the "radical evil" in people which the "sovereign state by its right over the life and property of its subjects" is able to control. Because of their assessments of human nature and the consequent urgency of the state's protective role, Schmitt and Gogarten reject any desideratum that is independent of the state as it exists in the present.

Buber's response once again reflects the multi-dimensionality of his religio-political imagination.[20] "I do not see," he argues, "how [man's] being unredeemed can be broken off from its dialectical connection with redemption." What characterizes man "is his potentiality," the fact that "he remains the center of all surprise in the world." As such Schmitt and Gogarten err in speaking of the *State* in static terms; there is only an "historical state" reflecting the dynamic order achieved at any given time. To be a "single one" means, in this context, to envisage a "right order" toward which a path leads out of the established order of the present. Yet for all that, Buber adds in a characteristic note of caution, the "surprise" man brings to the world "is fettered surprise, only inwardly is it without bonds; and his fetters are strong."[21]

It would be mistaken to take these various statments as expressions of a'reformist'—even a passionately 'reformist'— position. Reformism, as Buber saw it, while admittedly working for genuine improvements was entirely present-centered because it had lost contact with the utopian vision that endowed its efforts with more than transient significance. Buber's social thought is above all characterized by a looking beyond the moment while acting through it. In religious terms it is an immanentized messianism. There are few passages in the entire corpus of Buber's writings that more forcefully get to the heart of this philosophical vision than the following: "A drop of Messianic consummation must be mingled with every hour, otherwise the hour is godless despite all piety and devotion."[22]

Accordingly, the messianic moment in Buber's thought is quite nearly omnipresent. Virtually every field of study he undertook culminates in an eschatological vision; whether in politics, Zionism, Hasidism, or even biblical criticism, his thought is crowned by a messianic dream. Moreover, above the peculiarities imposed by each field, the lines of his thought meet in a single vision.[23] But it is nevertheless a messianism sui generis: an existentially tempered messianism, a messianism "become ethos."

The view from the "narrow ridge" is, as has been observed, far more commanding and comprehensive than indicated to this point. It is the unifying vantage point that provides dispositional, if not systematic, coherence to Buber's thought. Virtually everything he wrote is illuminated from this perspective. The remainder of this chapter will follow the various aspects of the "narrow ridge" as it deals with ideology, socialism, the philosophy of history, and interhuman relations.

Philosophy on the "narrow ridge," in all its variants, has a distinctly unacademic flavor to it, being tentative, unsystematic, situational, hortatory, personalist and, for the most part, free of jargon. If we were to cast about for a common expression adequate to its spirit, the nearest we could come would be "standing face to face with life." As such, few things are so foreign to the spirit of the "narrow ridge" as formal philosophical systems and, on a more programmatic level, mass movements with their schematic ideological perspectives. Much as Buber resisted the attempts of the aforementioned Christian thinkers to neatly categorize the holy and profane, the pure "single one" and the corrupted many, insisting instead on a more inclusive contrapuntal interplay between them, so he opposes the ideologist's tendency to mediate phenomena through set categories that impoverish reality's inexhaustible complexity.

The tendency to ideological reduction is particularly acute in the present time because of the massive social transformations that have shaken the belief systems of the past. Very much in the existentialist tradition, Buber highlights the 'loss of nerve' that craves the reassuring security of the 'total' ideology.[24] But paradoxically, this very exposedness and vulnerability also undermines the credibility of the great philosophic systems—Aristotelian, Thomist, and Hegelian-Marxist in Buber's view—encouraging thereby an unmediated confrontation between man and his world as well as dramatizing the greatest of philosophical imperatives: "know thyself." Historical periods of this sort are relatively infrequent and, when they do occur, are characterized by such intense intellectual turmoil that they quickly burn themselves out in bursts of agitated luminescence. Nevertheless, both the 'authentic' philosophical questions as well as the great protective ideologies are born out of them.

Buber's "narrow ridge" also attempts to avoid the tyranny of either-or concepts. By placing 'life' (the term has a demiurgic ring for Buber) before principles, the imperious claims of ideological reduction are undermined, and the irresolvably dialectical texture of real experience rises up before one's eyes. Philosophy on the "narrow ridge" seeks to preserve the paradoxical fullness of lived life rendered superfluous by the tailored abstractions of ideological systems. Perhaps most odious of these contemporary reductions, Buber complains, is the unwarranted choice the ideologies present between individualism and collectivism.

Individualism, which is historically prior to collectivism, raises "loneliness" to the power of a system. "To save himself from the despair with which his solitary state threatens him, man resorts to the expedient of glorifying it."[25] Individualism is the bravado born of social atomism, that, by making a virtue of necessity, mitigates the massive displacements and psychological anxieties occasioned by liberal capitalism. As an ideology it presents a kind of social nominalism that denies the existence of 'society' and recognizes only concrete individuals as 'real'.

For Buber, the most representative articulation of the individualist viewpoint—with ideological conclusions given philosophical support and refinement—is the thought of Martin Heidegger.[26] Here one finds a symptomatic inability to recognize any relation as 'essential' apart from the reflexive relationship to oneself.[27]

> The man of real existence in Heidegger's sense, the man of "self-being," who in Heidegger's view is the goal of life, is not the man who really lives with man, but the man who can no longer live with man, the man who now knows real life only in communication with himself. But that is only a semblance of real life, an exalted and unblessed game of the spirit. This modern man and this modern game have found their expression in Heidegger's philosophy.[28]

Heidegger's isolation surpasses even the withdrawal of Kierkegaard's "single one." For while the latter *can* relate to 'otherness' but chooses to limit his essential dealings to God, the former is cut off by a hopeless incapacity to truly breach the barriers of selfhood. "Wherever his existence is essential," Buber paraphrases Heidegger, "he is alone."[29]

If Heidegger's *reductio* reflects the dilemma of contemporary individualism (Buber has, in effect, analyzed Heidegger in partisan Sociology of Knowledge terms), Max Stirner's solopsism is the anachronistic avant-garde of this same tendency. For Stirner retreats so far into his selfhood that all 'otherness' becomes some kind of synonym for "myself." There can be no relation or responsibility—not even to Being as with Heidegger—for everything outside myself is essentially unreal. Not that there is "no-exit" from selfhood, there is nowhere to exit to. "The loss of reality which responsibility and truth have suffered in our time has here if not its spiritual origin certainly its exact conceptual prediction."[30]

Although the individualist *reductio* manages to schematize much that is threatening and uncontrolled, it does not succeed, Buber warns, in protecting against the anxiety of solitude. For individualism is a kind of 'emperor's clothing' that cannot cover 'exposedness' but merely prevents its acknowledgment. As such it cannot provide real security and its ideological counterpart, collectivism, rises to meet the crisis.

Collectivism has the great advantage of its irrefutable tangibility. It is loud, visible, and convincingly monolithic. Like the celebrated frontispiece of Hobbes's *Leviathan*, the many become one, a large "group I," that is essentially Stirner's solipsist man *writ large*.

Here the human being tries to escape his destiny of solitude by becoming completely embedded in one of the massive modern group formations. The more massive, unbroken and powerful in its achievements this is, the more man is able to feel that he is saved from both forms of homelessness, the social and the cosmic. There is obviously no further reason for dread of life since one need only fit oneself into the "general will" and let one's own responsibility for existence which has become too complicated, be absorbed into collective responsibility, which proves itself able to meet all complications. ... The collective pledges itself to provide total security. There is nothing imaginary here [as in individualism], a dense reality rules, and the "general" itself appears to have become real.[31]

This "organized atrophy of personal existence"[32] which collectivism represents, Buber concludes with an optimism that is difficult to fathom, "is the last barrier raised by man against a meeting with himself."[33]

It requires no elaborate argument to demonstrate that individualism and collectivism, despite the affecting power of Buber's account, have more complicated and concrete sources in the economic, technical, and political history of the past three centuries. To be sure, Buber possesses the rare ability to approach and address his readers with the immediacy of a living voice, but normally this involves jettisoning all the cumbersome and distracting minutiae of the real historical process that diminish the dramatic impact of human encounter. Buber the lyricist undermines Buber the analyst. Paradoxically, the drive of philosophy on the "narrow ridge" to come "face to face with life" without shrinking from any of its features ends by cutting away large sections of socio-historical reality that do not sit well with its heroic and personalist ambiance.

This paradox originates in the "double vision" which was mentioned earlier. Buber's intellectual seams are here distinctly visible. The activist-realist, on the one hand, cannot forsake the real historical moment. He insists on working through it and castigates those who withdraw into the 'self' or the 'crowd' to avoid responsibility. His words strive mightily to make the 'here and now' palpable, almost tactile in the reader's hands. But as this 'here and now' is approached, it proves to be quite elusive, more the 'here and now' as a principle than as a hard fact. The subjectivist-visionary retreats from these hard facts by refracting them through the prism of inner life. They thereby lose their specificity and become functions of mental states. Individualism and collectivism appear, when so viewed, alternate spiritual escapes from social, even cosmic, anxiety and solitude. Thus the picture projected by Buber's 'double vision' mismatches a tangible immediacy that is all but physical with a psychologized analysis that hollows out much of its substantiality.

Entirely consonant with this approach is Buber's discussion of community. Community represents the 'third way' that transcends both individualism and collectivism because it is not a *reductio* but a comprehensive alternative born out of relation to an undiminished reality. To expose oneself to the world in this way is to be a "single one," that is, an individual whose *I* is neither impoverished by withdrawal from otherness or benumbed by capitulation to it. His is an integral *I*, alive to its personal existence and responsibility while open to and accountable for the world in which it moves.

Community can begin only with such "single ones," for "one must truly be able to say *I* in order to know the mystery of the *Thou* in its whole truth." That is to say, "only the man who has become a 'single one', a self, a real person, is able to have a complete relation to the other self."[34] When a number of such persons become a group, there arises an "essential *We*" which is the cornerstone of community. By *We* Buber means

a community of several independent persons, who have reached a self and self-responsibility, the community resting on the basis of this self and self-responsibility and being made possible by them. The special character of the *We* is shown in the essential relation existing or arising temporarily between its members; that is, in the holding sway within the *We* of an ontic directness which is the decisive presupposition of the *I-Thou* relationship. The *We* includes the *Thou* potentially. Only

men who are capable of truly saying *Thou* to one another can
truly say *We* with one another.[35]

There is then a progression from the ability to say *I* (the
point at which Kierkegaard and Heidegger stop) to the
capacity to relate to a *Thou*, to the potentiality to become a
We.

Much as with individualism and collectivism, community,
after closer examination, proves to be more indebted to a
philosophical orientation, a certain spiritual maturity, than
to concrete social organization, more an offshoot of dialogue
and the *I-Thou* relation than a category of empirical sociological analysis. Standing "face to face" with life better describes
the subject's posture than the object's attributes.

Although community and the *I-Thou* relationship are
profoundly related, they are neither identical nor even the
same phenomenon in the plural and singular cases respectively. Beyond its significance as a charmed category of
interpersonal relations and as an inspiring theological metaphor for the Divine-human encounter, the *I-Thou* relation is
intended no less as a pure distillate of the socialist ethos.
Community, by contrast, refers to actual living together—
with all the compromise-demanding difficulties inexorably
associated with it. In terms of Buber's 'double vision', *I-Thou*
captures the unalloyed ideal while community is its translation—as in most translations something is lost—into immanent, worldly terms. From one perspective, community is the
I-Thou relation as seen through the prism of the "reality
principle."

Just as Buber's "narrow ridge" strives to experience the
world without prejudice or reduction, his socialism is
founded upon the unreserved meeting between man and
man. The *I-Thou* relationship in which the other becomes
fully 'present' is, on the interhuman level, the functional
equivalent of Buber's epistemological tenet that on the
"narrow ridge" one is assured of "meeting what remains

undisclosed." So appreciated, socialism constitutes an organic part of his thinking related to the most pivotal of his philosophical principles and not merely an incidental political persuasion.

Here is not the place for a full treatment of *I and Thou*—there exist numerous adequate accounts.[36] What concerns this writer is its place in Buber's socialism, that is, how socialism, perceived as a specific quality underlying human relations, is apprehended through the categories of *I-Thou* and *I-It*. For Buber differed in this regard from virtually the entire organized socialist movement. Socialism, he insisted, is not primarily an economic movement with standard of living, labor, and ownership at its core but rather, above all, the moral urge to create human fellowship. It is, therefore, more finely attuned to the texture of the interhuman than to the distribution of social wealth.

I-It, with its purposefulness, inessentiality, and insularity is the paradigm for nonsocialist association. The other confronted as *It* is merely an agglomerate of abilities, a fragmented object that needs to be accounted for in one's calculations. Whether in capitalist or 'socialist' societies, the *I-It* perspective

> sees the other beings around as centers of productivity which need to be recognized and employed in their specific capacities, as bundles of experienceable, influenceable, manageable, usable properties. Each one is to him a *He* or *She*, constituted thus or thus, bearing in himself such and such possibilities of which those are to be furthered in their unfolding that can be made useful for the utilitarian goal.[37]

By contrast, the *I-Thou* relation is the prototypical embodiment of socialist life. The *I* of *I-Thou* approaches the other as a self-existing subject rather than seeking to control or utilize his or her specific capacities. His inalienably autonomous existence, the indefeasible otherness glimpsed in the epiphany of the dialogical moment, rules out reducing him to a serviceable quantum of energy suited for some extrinsic purpose. 'True' socialism, Buber declares, is social living with this as the formative principle—"the real living together of men, genuineness from man to man and unmediated relations."[38]

But intellectual archetypes are, by their very nature, heuristic rather than operationally concrete. Clearly, the *I-Thou* relation can have no programmatic political content because it resists organization, evades the very best-laid plans and, as the soul of spontaneity, is necessarily ephemeral, elusive, and exceptional. Similarly *I-It*, despite its pristine qualities as a model, is helplessly inadequate for describing a specific political reality because all of the real world of politics, including Buber's socialism, falls into this category. One can hardly conceive of politics, or for that matter of industry, science, education, or even charity or martyrdom without purposefulness and deliberation. Still, as the crystallized typological polarities of social existence, the *I-Thou* and *I-It* relations present, apart from their manifest philosophical and theological substance, a unique inventory of the inter-human as the infrastructure of political life.

Closely paralleling the perspective of the "narrow ridge" in which direct, personal confrontation with the world is contrasted with the extrinsic and mediated concepts of the philosophical systems, the *I-Thou* and *I-It* relations (as noted above) represent the direct and the mediated relations respectively in their interhuman form. If socialism entails knowing the 'Truth' of the other by approaching him as *Thou*, philosophical 'authenticity' involves an open, inclusive, and interior relation to Being. So that despite Buber's consciously unsystematic and situational philosophical personality, there is, nevertheless, a master thread—the "narrow ridge" in all its aspects—that runs through the fabric of his thought.[39]

When theoretical paradigms are converted into real political terms, community replaces *I-Thou* as the programmatic content of socialism. Whereas *I-Thou* is limited to two discrete individuals, community is a public entity; while *I-Thou* is beyond intentionality, community is preserved only through deliberate decision; if *I-Thou* is unaffected by causality, community lives in a phenomenal world of constraining facticity; although *I-Thou* is evanescent and incorporeal, community may be constructed out of enduring materials. Even with all these obvious differences, community is, nevertheless, a derivative of the *I-Thou* relation. Without having glimpsed the *Thou* in another the formative principle of community is wanting. "Only men who are capable of truly saying *Thou* to one another can truly say *We* with one another."[40] The ability to say *Thou* is, then, the precondition and not the condition of community.

In community one does not live in a permanent *I-Thou* relation but, as it were, at its threshold. For just as the ability to say *Thou* precedes the saying of *We*, the "essential" relations characteristic of community is the "decisive presupposition of the *I-Thou* relationship. The *We* includes the *Thou* potentially."[41] More simply stated: the relation is reciprocal, experiencing the *Thou* is the sine qua non for creating community, while community presents the most conducive environment for experiencing the *Thou*. For the "directness" and "essential relations" of community are given to transcending themselves and for a singular moment a person may reveal the *Thou* to a comrade. And while community is not built through such moments, they are among its sublimest ends—the inner logic of community raised to its quintessential power.

Community in itself, however, lies squarely in the world of *I-It* inasmuch as utilizing, experiencing, evaluating are necessarily involved. As lofty as the urge to community may be, its realization "embraces in itself hard 'calculation',"[42] and involves "the common and active management of what it has in common."[43] The many different examples Buber presents of community clearly bear out this point. He includes the solidarity of a revolutionary group dedicated to popular education,[44] the fellowship of partisan activists against a terrorist regime,[45] the Hasidic community,[46] and kibbutz socialism.[47] What distinguishes these groups is a life in common that inevitably entails intentionality and not that which momentarily transpires between single members. As Buber puts it:

> It is not a matter of intimacy at all but rather one of openness. A real community need not consist of people who are perpetually together; but it must consist of people who, precisely because they are comrades, have mutual access to one another are ready for one another. A real community is one which in every point of its being possesses potentially at least the whole character of the community.[48]

Yet, despite its intentionality, in community one does not "see others as economic objects but as partners in a common life."[49] Communality is human solidarity embodied in social organization, the materialization of a spiritual urge. As such it has little to do with physical proximity or economic partnership, with joint ownership or with living "on one street or in one village." It is rather a question of "common life." They must "help one another to live, produce together, consume together, in short really be together in a way that one has to do with his neighbor."[50]

But if community is the immanentization of an urge whose source is transcendent (rooted in the ontology of the *Thou*), it must constantly retain its ties to transcendence if it is not to lose the fructifying polarity of 'is' and 'ought', that is, if it is to keep its footing on the "narrow ridge." In this sense, Buber conceives of socialism as a religious category, as the embodiment of religious inspiration.

> Religious socialism can only mean that religion and socialism are essentially directed to each other, that each of them needs the covenant with the other for the fulfillment of its own essence. *Religio*, that is the human person's binding of himself to God, can only attain its full reality in the will for a

community of the human race, out of which alone God can prepare His kingdom. *Socialitas*, that is mankind's becoming a fellowship, man's becoming a fellow to man, cannot develop otherwise than out of a common relation to the divine center, even if this be again and still nameless. Unity with God and community among the creatures belong together. Religion without socialism is disembodied spirit, therefore not genuine spirit; socialism without religion is body emptied of spirit, hence also not genuine body. But—socialism without religion does not hear the divine address, it does not aim at a response, still it happens that it responds; religion without socialism hears the call but does not respond.[51]

Buber speaks of community's tie to transcendence as the relation to a "center." "True community," he writes, arises

in a living, reciprocal relation to a single living center, and in a living, reciprocal relationship to one another. The second event has its source in the first but is not immediately given with it. . . . A community is built upon a living, reciprocal relationship, but the builder is the living, active center.[52]

This "center," community's transcendent archetype, is the generating point of contact; the binding joint that permits the movement of individuals toward each other. Metaphorically speaking, each individual is a spoke off the radiating "center." The "center" binds individuals together in light of a commonly conceived purpose much as an audience which witnesses a great theatrical event is forged into a unity. As both archetype and communal catalyst, the "center" is irreplaceable; without it community degenerates into an uninspired aggregation.

Paradoxically, if the "center" creates community, it does so—and with this the argument is brought full circle—only out of "single ones." Community is comprised of individuals whose moral responsibility is intensely personal without thereby being private or self-sufficient. Responsibility on the "narrow ridge" surpasses concern with the purity of one's own soul and includes accountability for the social body of which one is part. So that while community arises through the will of "single ones," it is more than the sum of the units that compose it—"something essential and irreplaceable, meant by God as such and answerable to Him as such."[53]

Community is, then, the translation of an ineffable meta-political ideal into a real political program; but it is for all that, Buber admits, a utopian vision. In fact, it is the heart of the entire utopian socialist tradition. As such we shall next turn to consider Buber's attempt at rehabilitating the utopian-communal urge so badly tarnished by generations of Marxist scorn.

3

The Rehabilitation of Utopia

Only where the state ends; there begins the human being who is not superfluous.

Nietzsche

I will once be classified among the late Utopian Socialists,[1] Buber told his lifelong friend, Ernst Simon. While this may very well be true, it is not the whole truth. For the existential dimension provides Buber with an uncommon perspective which creates a utopianism sui generis. He conceives a pristine ideal that may rank, in terms of lofty inspiration, with many of the great historic utopias. Yet it is not a scheme that lives a tranquil life outside the world of real people. Vision involves responsibility and responsibility brings one down, invariably, to the imperatives of the here and now. These imperatives merge with and necessarily modify the ideal, making the Utopian a creative realizer rather than a technician or oracle.

The dialectic between ideal and real that is so characteristic of Buber, allows far more freedom of intellectual movement than is common among those generally called Utopians. For the latter, ideal and real hover on the verge of unity awaiting only the assent of some willing philanthropist or the imminent mass recognition of 'the truth'. The Utopian perceives a reality which shall soon be or at best, must inevitably be. His utopia is the single point of reference to which all else is potential, auxiliary, or peripheral. It is inconceivable for modern Utopian Socialists to offer programs which in their judgment are unattainable or involve Herculean difficulties.

Buber, by contrast, is not nearly so limited. His thought operates effectively on two levels and derives its dynamism from the shifting interplay between them. The two spheres—the real and the ideal—are independent in that they are not necessarily developing toward one another and insofar as each is a detached point of reference from which the other may be judged. The actual world that Buber confronts is not swept into the folds of his vision to become merely the "before" to his utopian "after," or the embryonic herald of an imminent world. If utopia is "a picture of society designed as though there were no other factors at work than conscious human will,"[2] the here and now—its independence, its nay-saying power, the compromises and concessions it enjoins—need to be approached with the utmost seriousness.

Buber's religious perspective sets him off from other Utopians as well by deepening and adding to his caution. He cannot agree that the problem which faces all visionaries, is, at its root, attributable to a particular organization of society or form of government. No doubt they exert powerful influences for good or evil, but utopias that end with a mechanical reshuffling of institutions or even with radical changes in the loci of power have merely cleared the ground and set the stage without taking the crucial step toward the heart of socialist life, that is, the fraternity between man and man. And this stage is not amenable to organization or manipulation; it is the inescapable human problem that seizes one when the technical obstructions of organization are overcome.

The religious thinker's introspective sight grasps humanity as a paradox of potentialities, the source of surprise in history, the battleground of good and evil. The religious perspective cannot rest content with the scheming of the Utopians which seems shallow, even childish in its attempt to treat the intransigent complexity of the human spirit as if it were a neat pile of transparently assessable qualities requiring only this or that ordering. Religious thinkers

realize as well that social life, the reflection of this complexity, is too rich and unpredictable to be compassed in schemes
and arranged in advance. Their concern is therefore not with
the details of an attractive idyll but with a truly regenerated
world. Buber consistently refrained from utopian constructions and detailed blueprints; it was the utopian idea, the
"should be" in its pure form that attracted him.

We are here in the presence of a spirit that in some respects
is closer to Plato and More than to Marx. What draws Buber
is the power of the ideal as a model; an ideal not framed into
a specific historic reality nor set to culminate from certain
definite processes.

> It [utopia] is bound up with something suprapersonal that
> communes with the soul without being governed by it. What
> is at work here is the longing for that rightness which, in
> religious or philosophical vision, is experienced as revelation
> or idea.[3]

Buber might well subscribe to Plato's admission in the
Republic that the ideal he constructs is beyond the reach of
humans to achieve, or at least to achieve *in perpetuum*. For
the ideal does not gain validity from its practicability or its
drawing power as a political platform—its validity is generated entirely by the intrinsic merit it possesses. Both Plato
and More intended to create a timeless utopia and despite
their use of the social and institutional material they found at
hand, both sought to condense an eternal ideal into a
concrete framework: justice in the case of Plato and the
elevation of altruism in place of pride and greed in More. In
some sense the same may be said of Buber and the ideal of
human fraternity. For him,

> . . . all "socialist" tendencies, programs and parties are real or
> fictitious according to whether they serve as strength, direc-
> tion and instruments of real *Socialitas*—mankind's really
> becoming a fellowship.[4]

But Buber would not feel comfortable, despite these affinities, in the company of the aforementioned 'philosophical' Utopians. For them utopia was a literary exercise that served to convey an idea in more attractive dress, or, as with Plato, a vision of perfection that existed outside of the "cave" of human practice.[5] The ideal was cut off from practice except insofar as individual readers, under the influence of the work, might be disposed to favor their proposals. As a model without a movement, it became intellectual grist for the academies and edifying reading for the scholars, without having any appreciable effect on the conduct of human affairs. Missing entirely was the "fierce interplay of doctrine and action, planning and experiment."[6]

Needless to say, for the philosopher of 'realization', these contemplative models were not the last word. Not only did belief enjoin action, it was tested verified, often first truly understood, in the moment of struggle. To make truth one's own it was necessary to attempt its implementation in the here and now. The "unity of theory and practice" was for Buber an axiomatic truth.

Buber would disassociate himself from the classical Utopians on yet another ground. For while they were wise in seeing the power of an ideal as the heart of utopianism— rather than, say, an economic or historical analysis—they had encrusted this vital ideal into an immobile structure. By offering what purported to be a picture of the realized ideal, often in dizzying detail, they had, in fact, vitiated its living image and effective power.

The disciple of *Lebensphilosophie* was not inclined to see in a static utopia the goal he was seeking. The 'authentic' visionary, Buber observes, seeks to present "perfection in the light of the absolute, but at the same time as something towards which an active path leads from the present."[7] As such, the ideal will not assume the same characteristics and qualities in all cases. To be realized, it must be dynamically understood and flexibly introduced.

The vision of "what should be"—independent though it may
sometimes appear of personal will—is yet inseparable from a
critical and fundamental relationship to the existing conditions of humanity.[8]

Buber's ahistorical approach permits him to isolate the
pure utopian ideal in a way not found among Utopians who
translate their ideas into concrete programs or who see their
plans emerging only from certain specific conditions. This
distilling of the pure ideal from the variegated annals of the
utopian socialist tradition is characteristic of Buber's approach to intellectual history and serves as the key to
understanding his work on the subject. *Paths in Utopia*
should not be approached as a history of utopian activity or
as an account of the patterns of utopian thought. It is rather
an attempt to relive the birth, growth, and maturation of the
essential utopian ideal.[9] By finding and tracing the master
thread that runs through the entire fabric of utopianism,
Buber hopes to produce a yardstick with which to judge the
various paths in utopia, their aberrations and fidelity.

That man is a 'social animal' is surely one of the great
truisms of the Western intellectual tradition. One noted
scholar ties together all the elements of Aristotle's celebrated
doctrine comprehensively: "He (man) needs this community
not only for self-preservation, security and perfection of his
physical existence but above all because only in it is a good
education and control of life by law and justice possible."[10]In
Aristotle's own phrase, humans live socially for the sake of
"noble actions and not mere companionship."[11] Community
is the indispensable background for the human *telos*—it
provides the 'paraphernalia', the order and leisure requisite
for the good life. As such, society and the state are 'natural'
phenomena, that is, they emerge from the very character of
humanity.[12]
    Although Buber agrees that community is 'natural', he
would hesitate to subordinate it to a further and presumably
loftier end, the good life. The "interhuman," Buber contends,

is not context but *telos*. Far from being a functional step in the process of human development, the "genuine community of human beings" is the "primary aspiration of all history."[13] It does, indeed, exist for the sake of man's "higher nature," but one errs to see this in terms of the "life of reason," for, Buber writes, the "fundamental fact of human existence is man with man. What is peculiarly characteristic of the human world is above all that something takes place between one being and another the like of which can be found nowhere in nature."[14] "Mere companionship," which Aristotle disdains, is for the philosopher of *I* and *Thou*, in its more vital and positive aspects, the consummate human activity.

Clearly, one may be thoroughly 'social' in the Aristotelian sense and still pass over "the life between man and man." Being 'social' in this sense means utilizing the interhuman for its functional benefits. But for Buber it is not by passing beyond community that one attains to the allegedly higher goals of justice and law, but only through meeting. Justice, for example, cannot be found in the intellect and then applied to the world of people, but can only emerge through the encounter with others: by recognizing in others that irreducible otherness that makes them worthy of the same treatment as ourselves.

It is precisely in this going beyond the 'social' as merely natural and functional, that is, in humanizing the natural, in raising "mere companionship" to communal life at the threshhold of the *I-Thou* relationship that Buber sees the heart of the utopian idea. Community, the real living and working together of people, is the *goal* of the utopian urge. Fidelity to the utopian 'idea' must be measured by the degree of commitment to the restructuring of society for the purpose of community. To make community secondary to any other goal, to utilize it for its side effects or its tactical value is to take a false path in utopia.

Contemporary society, when seen in light of community, is woefully lacking. Capitalism, with its pervasive individualist competition, Buber writes, has all but overwhelmed the islands of human association that managed to survive the breakdown of the medieval *Gemeinschaft*.[15] The top-heavy and omnipresent state crushes initiative and prevents the growth of independent associations—except insofar as they are depersonalized unions of convenience whose aim is profit or narrow self interest.[16] Allied to the state is the technical, scientific, industrial complex that weighs down heavily upon human spontaneity and undermines the ability to relate to others.[17] Rootless, atomized, and lonely

> . . . the life between man and man gets lost in the process; the autonomous relationships become meaningless, personal relationships wither, and the very spirit of man hires itself out as a functionary.[18]

Proceeding from this very 'contemporary' critique of society, the ground is prepared for utopian vision, for "all suffering under a social order that is senseless prepares the soul for vision and what the soul receives in this vision strengthens and deepens its insight into the perversity of what is perverted."[19] The core idea of this negation of perversity that arises dialectically as the utopian vision is, as has been indicated, the life of community. True socialism is "real community between men, direct life-relations between *I* and *Thou*, genuine society, genuine fellowship."[20] Building around this central idea, Buber sets up a number of supporting propositions which, when taken together, represent the utopian idea in its fullness. [21] These propositions are, for Buber, implicit corollaries of the urge to community.

Since community involves a real "life in common," "mutual access," and the triumph of the "between" over both individualism and collectivism, only circumstances that dispose people to encounter each other directly and essentially are conducive to bring it about. The formal, imposed 'harmony' of a centralized bureaucracy—even if it should call itself 'socialist'—is an obstacle that must be overcome before human fellowship can become fact. Meeting cannot take place in an over-regulated atmosphere; it presupposes an independent, spontaneous individual, who confronts others and freely binds himself to them in comradery and solidarity. Voluntarism and freely interacting individuals are then the first principles that the process of societal restructuring must adhere to if it is to end in community. Buber makes the point forcefully when he writes:

> Centralization versus decentralization is not a proper question. Centralized socialism is not socialism. Socialism in which the relations of authority were changed to the benefit of the workers, without a change in the relations between men is not socialism. Not only by the relations between workers and employers is contemporary humanity flawed but by the decay of human relations in general.[22]

Given this position, it is not surprising that Buber proclaims: "I declare in favor of the rebirth of the commune."[23]

The commune is a living, "organic" cell that performs its own essential functions and moves toward its goals with the "diversity in unity" that results from freely associating persons. Insofar as the moment's reality permits, such groups handle their own affairs, growing into maturity and responsibility in the process. To subordinate this independence is to suffocate the community's breath of life. Delegation of authority—be it even to workers' councils—is to add "passive economic representation" to the already numbing political representation. "For community . . . declares itself primarily in the common and active management of what it has in common, and without this it cannot exist."[24]

Settling accounts with his own past, Buber emphasizes that the commune has nothing in common with the self-pleasure of an intellectual experiment but

> embraces within itself hard 'calculation', adverse 'chance' and the sudden access of anxiety. It is a community of tribulation and only because of that a community of spirit; community of toil and only because of that a community of salvation.[25]

> Community lives . . . in the midst of a simple, unexalted, unselected reality, a reality not so much chosen by them as sent to them just as it is . . . A community of faith truly exists only when it is a community of work.[26]

Insofar as the "lives" and not merely "certain interests" of the members are shared, insofar as the new order "implicates" people, the cooperative[27] is a truly "living" cell, capable of forming the new unit for the restructure of society.

Only a society that is built of such 'organic' units—a community of communities—is worthy of the name "commonwealth." Each cell left to itself is doomed because standing alone it will be forced to become a unit of economic interest rather than of social cohesion. "Collective egoism, that is, egoism with a clear conscience," [28] will overtake the isolated unit and transform a social experiment into a joint capitalistic venture. Only federalism, the building of the social body out of freely associating units, can preserve the social quality of association.[29]

But what is to prevent these communities themselves from rivalry and factionalism? Even more basically, what will keep each community together in a state of mutuality and harmony? Certainly, Buber would be the first to agree, simple restructuring is not sufficient. People, even when they are "implicated" (perhaps precisely because they are "implicated"), need not care for each other deeply or desire to share anything essential. They may be pressed ever so tightly together and yet have as much to do with each other as potatoes in a sack. Is one not dealing with some kind of 'leap' when one advances from restructure to regeneration?

"Assuredly," Buber would answer. Socialism seen merely as a change in the relations of power or production will, in every case, stop dead at the point of the 'leap'. It is conceived in mechanism and can end only in mechanism. "Even the greatest effort will fail if the inner condition is missing." To create a community in which individuals are held together by a genuine inner bond there is need of persons seized by an ideal, transformed by its power and struggling for its realization. Essentially, socialism is a matter of the spirit; those who take this spirit into themselves are the regenerated and the regenerators of society.

But if socialism begins with the renewal of each individual, there is no need to await some future date to commence its implementation. It begins just as soon as socialist relationships between people become a reality. The transition from capitalism to socialism, therefore, cannot be dated sharply from the moment of revolution—although, as will be seen, this is a crucial step—but is a slowly maturing, painfully difficult process that germinates in the womb of the old order and grows to fullness in the new. In Landauer's words:

> Socialism is possible and impossible at all times; it is possible when the right people are there to will and do it; it is impossible when people either do not will it or only supposedly will it, but are not capable of doing it.[30]

The enthusiastic young Buber who cried, "We are the revolution," presents in his maturity a philosophy that has, to be sure, grown and developed but nevertheless remains true to the basic principle of his youth, to wit: revolution, if it is to introduce signal and penetrating change, must be above all a revolution in people, in spirit rather than in form. Any other change is, by contrast, superficial, indeed often dangerous. Buber cites approvingly Moses Hess's observation that socialism is "either the fruit of a free spirit or it is without foundation and changes into its opposite."[31]

Exactly what the role of the state is in this process constitutes a complicated and typically many-sided question in Buber's writings. His approach is nondoctrinaire, often to the point of vagueness. At times he writes in a fairly Marxian tone, judging the state in terms of the material conditions of society.[32] At others, he speaks the language of philosophical idealism, viewing contemporary institutions and political life as reflections of the spiritlessness and atomization of the age.[33] Most often, however, the two come together in a compounded analysis that is awake to the cross-influences between idea an fact.

The origin of the modern state is generally attributed by Buber—as was highly fashionable in German academia—to the breakdown of the medieval *Gemeinschaft*, with its close associations, guilds, and cooperative ventures.[34] Growing up in its place, capitalism engendered a system of universal competition, a "war of all against all," that required—in true Hobbesian fashion—a state that could "quell the conflict between different groups."[35] Still, in itself, this would not suffice to make the state the gigantic, all-controlling institution it has become. For this, Buber insists, the general climate of international instability as well as the constant threats to national security were necessary. Psychologically, the pervasiveness of aggression and mistrust causes the individual to fear "things in general," and to find relief in "clinging desperately to the collectivity," allowing oneself to be saturated by and imbedded in one of the massive group formations of the day.[36]

Rallying round the state, "my country right or wrong," and a great deal of the hysterical nationalism of the time, are by-products of this syndrome. It produces what Buber terms a "political surplus," that is, an excess in the power of control taken from society and invested in the state.

All forms of government have this in common: each possesses more power than is required by the given conditions; in fact this excess capacity for making dispositions is actually what we understand by political power.[37]

Although there is no way of computing this surplus, it constitutes the difference between 'administration'—understood in the sense of Saint-Simon or Engels's 'withered' state—and 'government'. With this provocative but question-begging analysis, Buber pays his debt to traditional political theory and proceeds along his own way.

What is important to recall is Buber's conviction that neither narrowly materialistic nor simple idealistic explanations suffice to tell the whole truth regarding the state. The immediate antidote to the state, that is, revolution, must then follow the same pattern. To succeed, in the full sense of the word, it must change both people and material. Buber gives this position simple and definitive expression when he writes:

> Two views concerning the way stand irrevocably opposed to each other. The one demands that one begin by changing "relations" [of production or power], for only out of their being different can a change of men and their relations to one another arise. The other explains that the new orderings and institutions in the place of the old will not change one particle of life so long as they are carried by unchanged persons. This alternative is false. One must begin at both ends at once, otherwise nothing can succeed.

This is so, Buber explains, because:

> What new relations really are, even in their operation depends on what kind of human existence is put into them; but how shall humanity persist on earth if it is not preserved and confirmed by new orderings? The world of man without the soul of it in addition is no human world; but also the soul of man without the world is no human soul.[38]

'Genuine' revolution is then a double-pronged attack that converges on the state from two directions. Insofar as the state represents vested economic interests and the institutionalization of unnecessary force, counterforce *may* very well be the answer. Of its own volition, Buber concedes to Marx, the state apparatus will never decree its own dissolution. Even a "vital peace," which succeeds in reducing the attraction of the "excessive state," would not by itself effectively destroy the overbearing state apparatus, for established power is self-perpetuating and will not be easily dislodged. The revolution that comes to dismantle the state apparatus aims then not merely at a change in the "apportionment of power"—this is perfectly compatible with a new giant state and "political surplus"—but a change in the "nature" of power, that is, at reducing the "political principle" as far as it may be reduced in the existing conditions.[39] Predictably, this concrete phase of revolution, its 'what is to be done' aspect, is only very minimally discussed by Buber. The actual tactics of revolution, the organization necessary for it, the methods by which mass society and industry are to be structurally reorganized, were not very much to his taste. His is the language of the 'ought' and not of the detailed 'how'. He is above all the philosopher of social renewal; revolution, particularly in its organizational aspects, was distinctly of secondary interest.

Buber is at his strongest, by contrast, when he considers the other aspect of the struggle, the regeneration of humanity. The state reflects, as has been noted, a pervasive mentality; it is a framework that frames people as they are. The 'state' is, in fact, a state, a condition.[40] A generation of spiritless people, lacking spontaneity, relating to each other formally and inessentially, become the generation of the overarching state that steps into the vacuum left in the wake of their retreat. Where there is no initiative the state initiates; where there is no spontaneity the state imposes order; where relationships have withered the state juxtaposes individuals to one another in marching armies or in producing conglomerates.

To alter this condition is to undermine the *raison d'être* of the state.

> Men stand to one another today in a 'statual' [*staatlichen*] relationship, that is one which makes the coercive order of the state necessary and is represented by it and in it. Hence this order can be overcome to the extent that the relationship between men is replaced by another.[41]

This is possible by piercing the

> ... hard crust that has formed on mankind, if their own inner "statehood" is broken open and the slumbering, immemorial

reality aroused beneath . . . Men who are renewed in this way can renew society . . . [42]

The new "subversive" reality appears "alongside" the state—outside its benumbing reach but from within the powers latent in society.[43] Growing up inside the old forms, "in love, in work and in stillness," with the slowness and thoroughness characteristic of genuine renewal, the new order poses itself as a vital alternative to the state. Political revolution comes now to sweep away the old, to negate. The affirmation, the positive revolution, has been maturing all the while so the old system's overthrow does not signal the virgin birth of a new order but rather the institutional confirmation of an ascending reality that has gradually been displacing the old.

To this point Buber has the unmistakable appearance of a "late Utopian Socialist." He glorifies the power of will and commitment while giving only scant notice to the *I-It* world of contingency. Although we are spared the trifling minutiae of a Fourier, there is no question but that the entire system rests squarely on an a priori deductive foundation. This is the Utopian Buber, the only partially mellowed mystic who speaks the language of 'unconditionality', of all or nothing. But it is a sharply one-sided portrait that has been drawn here. In effect, it identified the pure ideal with the actual program and by so doing omitted the crucial interplay between reality and vision. To balance these soaring aspirations one needs to consider the other aspect: the existential sobriety of Buber's thought.

"It is a difficult, a tremendously difficult undertaking," Buber acknowledges,

> . . . to drive the plowshare of the normative principle through the hard sod of political fact; but the right to lift the historical moment into the light of super-history can be bought no cheaper.[44]

The utopian imperative demands, therefore, not the realization of the absolute but the creative exercise of human

decision. What is demanded is not objective achievement or
ideological purism but the attempt "to wring from each hour
its best possibilities."[45] Buber's "narrow ridge"—the ethic of
spiritual tact and authenticity—is the ethos of utopian struggle.[46]

Since the new order is not a sudden, once and for all
occurrence but an unfolding many-sided process that is
largely due to decision and will, socialist strategy must be
elastic and situational. If the "task" of Socialists is "to drive
the factual base-line of the state back to the 'principial'
[*prinzipiellen*] baseline of socialism,"[47] they must not advance
beyond the point dictated by sober political realism. "The
line which at any time limits this capacity [for local autonomy, decentralization, etc.] forms the basis of the state at
that time; in other words the degree of incapacity for a
voluntary right order determines the degree of legitimate
compulsion."[48] Only "that portion of the state which is
superfluous and without foundation at the time"[49] is legitimately dispensed with. This involves the rejection of "all
rigid delineation of ways and methods" (only ends may be
absolute) and the courage "to know that in the life of man
and human communities the straight line between two points
is often the longest."[50] "The fatal question," Buber declares,

> . . . does not take the form of a fundamental Either-Or: it is
> only a question of the right line of demarcation that has to be
> drawn ever anew—the thousandfold system of demarcation
> between the spheres which must of necessity be centralized
> and those which can operate in freedom; between the degree
> of government and the degree of autonomy; between the law
> of unity and the claims of community.[51]

The Socialist is the "custodian" of the true boundaries
between the desirable and the possible.[52]

Even community itself should not "be made into a principle," for as a fixed principle it is an abstraction rather than a
living goal. It must always "satisfy a situation" and thus it

"cannot occur once and for all time: it must always be the moment's answer to the moment's question, and nothing more."[53] The struggle for community

> . . . is a problem which . . . cannot be approached in principle, but like everything else to do with the relationship between the idea and reality, only with great spiritual tact, with the constant and tireless weighing and measuring of the right proportion between them.[54]

Politics is truly "the art of the possible."[55]

Buber is neither the avowed enemy of the state nor sympathetic to any simplistic anarchist doctrine.[56] One of his foremost students summarizes his position well:

> He feared the domination of the political principle over the spontaneity of society—yet he saw in this principle a necessary and legitimate principle of all human and social experience. Buber knew very well that weak and unstable government or leadership will not necessarily insure social freedom—on the contrary, they are even liable to strengthen the tendency of the political principle to dominate and create a "political surplus." Therefore, Buber never demanded the reduction of state power for its own sake, rather he saw its proper boundary according to the context, avoiding the trap of facile formulations.[57]

The proclivity to dismiss Buber as a hopelessly quixotic Utopian[58] stems, therefore, from an incomplete grasp of the dialectical polarity in his thought: he appears the anarchist only when viewed through the prism of unclouded ideals. The true spirit of Buber is tautly strained between "the demands of the spirit and the historical hour." As he puts it elsewhere: "In every moment utopia must make contact—the contact of life—with topia."[59] Neither the unworldly, principled moralist, who sees only what should be, nor the all too 'realistic' politician who knows only what is, can serve as the model for socialism.[60] For the essential is "not retention of purity at any price . . . but conquering the situation and retaining purity at once . . . a preservation of the idea at the height of difficulty, in confusion."[61]

Perhaps the most tempting approach to Buber's history of the utopian urge is a critical analysis of his sources and of the conclusions he draws from them. It would also be the least fruitful. Buber's brand of intellectual history is highly schematic, subjective, at times impressionistic.[62] The evidence often cannot support the weight of the concusions and the relevance of certain citations to the argument that he makes is questionable.[63] The importance of his work, however, lies not in its strict historical accuracy or scholarly methodology but rather in the utopian vision that Buber extracts from history (at times 'imposes' would be more descriptive) and in the critical comments of a contemporary Utopian on the diverse personalities that fill the pages of utopian history. We shall, then, attempt to follow Buber's presentation of the utopian idea with our attention focused not primarily on facts but on interpretation, evaluation, and development.

Buber regards the history of utopian socialism as the record of the urge to actively and fundamentally "restructure" society in the "here and now"—this in opposition to the views that consider restructuring as secondary to change in leadership or as coming in the indefinite future as a result of impersonal forces. "If this is correct," Buber asserts, "it should be possible to demonstrate, in the history of utopian socialism, the line of evolution taken by this element"—an evolution in which "each step occupies its own proper place and is not interchangeable."[64] Buber's study conceives of utopianism as an *ens realissimum* developing historically from potentiality to actuality.

The "forerunners," Saint-Simon, Fourier, and Owen, provide an indispensable yet only fragmentary advance in this evolution. Saint-Simon and Fourier each contribute a "single constructive thought" and these are loosely amalgamated— though not synthesized—in the thought of Owen. Saint-Simon is credited with introducing the revolutionary idea of

"restructure." It is not merely a question of authority changing hands but of a fundamental change in the nature of
authority itself; of an alteration that will "permeate the
whole inner structure of society." For in the "régime industriel," government will be replaced by administration and no
leadership will be required "other than that provided by the
social functions themselves."[65] Government as a "distinct
and special class" will give way to a "unitary" order in which
the "natural leaders of society itself, the leaders of production," will conduct the affairs of society in the name of the
"producers."[66]

But Saint-Simon has approached the problem with the
broad strokes of olympian vision and is consequently lacking
in "the conception of genuine organic social units out of
which this restructuring can be built."[67] Fourier's concerns,
by contrast, are immediate and human and hence it is the
actual unit of social organization that monopolizes his
attention. The notion of the jointly producing and consuming, small, self-sufficient community is Fourier's great contribution to utopian history. Yet Fourier's contribution is
marred by his excessive involvement with the specifics of
organization, and one misses in his work any overarching
utopian vision which connects individual units into higher
associations and "universal harmony."

Fourier's position is badly wanting in other areas as well.
Among other things, the continuing gap between rich and
poor that Fourier envisages renders the new *phalanx* not
much superior to present society.[68] The imposed uniformity
that would make each *phalanx* an exact replica of every other
totally omits the crucial elements of human will and free
development—the life breath of social experiment. What
results is a "mechanical fantasy" that has aided the development of utopian socialism largely by being transcended.

But Buber's most fundamental criticism lies buried implic-
itly in all that he says even if it is never expressly articulated.
L'Attraction Passionelle, which constitutes the core idea of

the *phalanx*, results in an automatic "concord of instinct and activity" without any real meeting between individuals. For all Fourier's talk of "communalizing," there is no concern with community. Dialogue is squeezed out by organization. The happy harmony that Fourier prescribed is an escapist kingdom of heaven that does not even begin to suspect that communal life is not merely a product of attractive and synchronized work schedules, that paradise cannot be poured out of concrete, that communal life is nothing if it is not a deep bond between man and man.

With the astuteness that comes from experience, Robert Owen, the businessman-Utopian, rejects the contrived "technics" of Fourier's blueprint and the abstractions of Saint-Simonian history, preferring to focus on the "empirical solution" to the problem.[69] This leads him to the conclusion that

> . . . the transformation of society must be accomplished in its total structure as well as in each of its cells: only a just ordering of the individual units can establish a just order in the totality.[70]

While accepting the small agricultural unit as the building block of a restructured society, Owen, in contrast to Fourier, is preeminently interested in the fundamental requirements of communal life, relegating the intricacies of organization to secondary status. These pivotal requirements—joint property and expenditures, united labor and equal opportunities—are to result in "mutual and common interests" among all members. It is not nearly so important that property be exclusively common or that expenditures be rigorously equal as it is that there be a pervasive spirit of communality, of "common housekeeping." The underlying conception of Owen's plan, Buber declares, is precisely this: that from common possession and enjoyment, from "mutual give and take," will arise a commune with the "appropriate participation of all members in one another," with "real bonds between individuals." This type of communal village is the new structural unit in Owen's vision of a restructured society.[71]

Restructuring that follows this pattern is clearly not to be achieved all at once. "Owen," Buber writes,

> is thinking of the new society, as growing out of the old and renewing it from within. At the same time various stages in the evolution of the new society will have of necessity to exist side by side.[72]

Owen has caught sight of the idea of "restructuring" in the "here and now." "This is the foundation of socialism."

Building upon this foundation, Proudhon takes a giant stride forward. Because he is opposed "to all utopias whose essence is political organization and a social credo," that is, all-encompassing structural and philosophical systems, Proudhon "continued the line of development" that began with the "forerunners."[73] The questions he sets for himself are the genuinely utopian questions of social restructure and responsibility to the present moment. Restructure, as in Saint-Simon, involves a "radical alteration of the relationship between the social and political order . . . the emergence, in place of a political regime grafted upon society of a regime expressive of society itself."[74] And there must be no belief in the "dominion of fatality" to bring about these changes. For this, "only the creative, restructuring powers that reign in the depths of man can avail."[75]

Proudhon's portrait as it emerges from Buber's hand displays unmistakable twentieth-century existentialist characteristics.[76] He is the resolute opponent of all systems, the champion of human will, the man who recognizes yet bears the pitiless "contradictions" and "antinomies" of reality. His thought is marked, in Buber's appraisal, by a "fundamental relationship to social reality," that sets about dealing with social problems without the crutch of doctrine or the faith in absolutes. Proudhon accepts no certainties about the future and assuredly no inexorable processes that lead out from the present to the golden age of tomorrow. Historical principles that might provide sure ground for a program of activity cannot be "adequately summed up in any system of ideas," and even if they could be, it would not help, for in no age is "any one principle all-powerful." What then is left for the committed Socialist like Proudhon? Only to steep oneself with "strength and courage," to "bear the strain" of reality with "all its contrasts and contradictions," its coexistent theses and antitheses, and to seek a way out without sacrificing any of the conflicting elements in the resolution.[77]

Utopia, for Proudhon, was therefore not a system, but the ideal of a structurally renewed society. To a degree greatly surpassing Saint-Simon, Proudhon understood the need for restructure in a non-technical sense. For while Saint-Simon had been interested above all in the transformation of the state—so that it would follow the lines laid down by economics—Proudhon starts with the renewal of society and the alterations that are its necessary concomitants. "The 'industrial constitution' of Saint-Simon does not signify a new structure," while Proudhon's "federalism" does.[78]

Above all, it is centralization, that "monstrous parasitism," which Proudhon considers the great enemy. No matter whether this concentration of power carries a capitalist or a socialist label its effect is the same—"to devour all corporative, regional and private freedom." Centralism surely has the advantage of uniformity and discipline, but, following the antisystematic bias which Buber stresses, Proudhon writes that ". . . the world, society and man are made up of insoluble problems, contrary principles and conflicting forces. Organism means complication, and multiplicity means contradiction, opposition, independence." To reduce multiplicity to an artificial unity means that "the individual no longer belongs to himself in such a system; he cannot feel his worth, his life, and no account is taken of him at all."[79]

Structural renewal involves the decentralization of authority and the establishment of small and moderately sized groups composed of freely associating individuals. Only "the simple tasks of general initiative, mutual assurance and supervision" need be left to the central authority. For the smaller units "need no direction in a great many of their activities; they are capable of governing themselves with no other inspiration than conscience and reason." These units— "the local community or common living on the strength of [their] own relationships"—associate with each other on the basis of "reciprocity of service, 'mutualism', growing into a federation of federations."[80]

But Proudhon has not escaped authoritarian centralism only to be lost in an atomized individualism. "What he opposes to the state," Buber writes in language highly suggestive of his own, "is not the individual as such but the individual in organic connection with his group, the group being a voluntary association of individuals." This principle of "free association" creates a group in which people "can preserve their freedom in the very heart of society." Yet despite this Rousseauian vision of all associated and all free, Buber feels that Proudhon's fear of 'association' (by which he meant planned, centralized associations like Louis Blanc's national workshops) prevented him from adequately exploring the composition of these vitally important new social units. Proudhon fails to answer the essential question: "How must the units be constituted so that they can federate into a genuine popular order, a new and just structure?"[81]

Enter Kropotkin. More clearly than any of those who preceded him, Kropotkin perceived the structure of the "new society" and the units that would be its component elements. The "new social form . . . will be composed of a number of societies banded together for everything that demands a common effort."[82] It will be marked by federations of all sorts which will meet the economic, spiritual and artistic needs of the people, crossing national and perhaps even

continental boundaries when necessary. And down to the
"smallest of units—the street, the house-block, the district,
the parish," it will work to create "permanent contacts
between everybody for the thousand and one common interests."[83] Moreover, the new social unit "fitted to serve as a
cell for the formation of a new society," must aim at the
"fullest development of individuality" and "personal initiative." To accomplish this, Kropotkin combines decentralization with the integration of agriculture and industry. In place
of the dehumanization wrought by the division of labor and
excess specialization, he sets the principle of labor integration, which, following Fourier's idea of work alternation,
envisages "a village based on field and factory alike where
the *same* people work in the one as in the other alternately."[84]

But it must not be thought that the new society will be one
of fixed and immovable forms. It will, in Kropotkin's vision,
"transform itself incessantly for it will be a living organism
in development," "ever-changing" and "never finally constituted." This new order "cannot be imposed," or programmatically produced; it lives only from the spontaneous,
deeply willed aspirations of all who collaborate for a restructured society.

> It is not a question of manipulating an abstract principle but
> only of the *direction* of realization willed; of the limits of
> realization possible in this direction in any given circum-
> stance—the line that defines what is demanded here and now,
> becomes attainable.[85]

Kropotkin has come quite near the essential utopian
vision, but the path to utopia has one final obstacle to
overcome before it reaches its destination. This is the crucially important relationship between revolution and regeneration. It is indeed true that social reconstruction depends
upon revolution, but, tragically, it "will always result in the
exact opposite of what most honest revolutionaries strive for
unless [the positive goal] has so far taken shape *before* the

revolution that the revolutionary has only to wrest the space for it in which it can develop unimpeded."[86] Kropotkin did not sufficiently recognize that

> . . . revolution is not so much a creative as a delivering force whose function is to set free and authenticate—i.e., that it can only perfect, set free, and lend the stamp of authority to something that has already been foreshadowed in the womb of the pre-revolutionary society; that as regards social evolution the hour of revolution is not an hour of begetting but an hour of birth provided there was a begetting beforehand.[87]

This critical step—the appeal for an "immediate beginning" in the here and now—was taken by Landauer.

To enter the world of Landauer is to enter the antechamber to Buber. The atmospheres are palpably similar, their intellectual roots an entwined network, even their styles—vigorous, passionate, tending to the rhetorical—exhibit much that is common. On the subject of socialism they shared the view that revolution is purely 'negation', the sweeping away of the tenacious apparatus of an impeding regime. Revolution is entirely unable, even in its most comprehensive and tumultuous forms, to bring the "affirmation," the "positive goal," any closer. Regeneration, decentralization, community, mutuality, that is, the social as opposed to the purely political side of the struggle for a new society, are both the final aims and the indispensable precursors of a successful revolution.

At a number of previous points we have had occasion to speak of Landauer so it is not necessary to present here any more than the specific contribution to the utopian ideal with which Buber credits him. This contribution, Buber writes, can be summarized in a single "heavy-laden" word: "spirit." By "spirit" Landauer intends not

> . . . spiritual reality merely as the product and reflection of the material world, as mere "consciousness" determined by social "being" and explicable in terms of economic-technical relationships. It is rather an entity *sui generis* that stands in close

relation to the social being, without, however, being explicable at any point in terms of the latter.[88]

Spirit, or rather its absence, is the cause and crutch of the old order, its presence the bond of the new. "Where there is spirit there is society, where there is spiritlessness there is the state. The state is the surrogate for spirit."[89] The mission of the revolutionary movement is to rekindle and inspire, to cause people to be "born anew,"[90] to "wring" from a slothful people "something that has always been present," to awaken them to the possibilities of the hour. United and renewed by spirit, these revolutionized individuals establish a dynamic reality that slowly gnaws away at the state from within until it displaces it through a final confirming revolution that inaugurates an era of experimentation and socialist construction. It is a labor of Sisyphus, but any less exacting, less basic transformation cannot but end in failure.

The preceding pages have dealt with more than a century of intellectual history from Waterloo to Weimar. Yet they have never really strayed from Buber himself. His imprint is distinctly visible on every page. The interpretation and selection reflect at least as much on the author as they do on the personalities discussed. Indeed, *Paths in Utopia* is most fruitfully approached as a phenomenology of Buber's mind set into history. Piece by piece, idea by idea, Buber's social philosophy takes shape through the historical medium of the utopian tradition, until, with Landauer, it emerges relatively complete.[91]

What then has Buber added to this tradition? I believe there are two significant elements. His elaboration of 'community' (a hitherto sociological and historical concept in Tönnies and Gierke) and its central role in socialism contributes considerable substance to the small unit that stands at the heart of the utopian-anarchist position. The life of dialogue and its quintessential case, the *I-Thou* relationship, breathe a "soul" into what was often a mechanical body politic. It lends significance to social living, transcending the claims of efficiency and functionality, and contributes a new and deeply meaningful criterion for Socialists to consider aside from economic success or even the abstractions of justice.

Political justice, however formally defined, involves the apportioning of desirable resources according to relevant criteria. This entails, by implication, separate units each claiming their share of these resources. The entire notion of justice rests upon the multiplicity of claimants, upon opposing claims to the same 'good', upon conflict. Distributive justice implies legitimate arbitration between claims, but it cannot touch the separateness of the claimants, the sealed ego boundaries out of which each claim arises. A socialism whose exclusive principle is social justice cannot pass beyond this fragmented condition. Justice cannot create community.

Buber's achievement lies in defining socialism in terms other than justice. Socialism, Buber insists, seeks to harmonize human affairs not only by giving each individual his due but by piercing the insularity of individuation and creating community. It is not primarily in the just *division* of labor and resources that socialism excels but rather in its quality of communal *union*, its ability to create openness, mutuality, and fraternity. Socialism is the interhuman become public ethos.

Justice is, in fact, a derivative of the interhuman in that it rests on the recognition of human inviolability (no deprivation without good reason), a recognition that can dawn only through relation. The disposition to justice is always in the plural case. Community does not, of course, cancel the justice principle, but justice becomes more and more an inner drive rather than an abstract doctrine to the degree that the other's *Thou* is perceived. Moreover, justice as a principle is an extrinsic quality and hence it may be instituted programatically. Community as an intrinsic disposition can be prepared for but never decreed. Establishing community requires both grace and will, the flowering of the interhuman into brotherhood.

A second contribution of significance is Buber's introduction of the existential outlook into the realm of social experiment. Without reiterating all that has already been said on this score let it simply be noted that the interplay of ideal and real, all that permits Buber to bestride the two generally inimical points of view, existentialism and utopian socialism, give his work particular interest for the present when purity and cynicism glare at each other across an unbridgeable abyss.

4

The Prophet and the Apocalypse

Only the present is real and what men do not do now, do not begin to do immediately, they will not do in all eternity.

Landauer

ALTHOUGH Buber devotes relatively little space to dealing expressly with Marx,[1] there is very little in his thought that will not gain in perspective by being seen in counterpoint with the thought of the great German revolutionary thinker. This is not surprising since the Judeo-Germanic culture in which Buber matured was pervasively influenced by Marx and the Hegelian tradition,[2] to say nothing of the socialist circles in which he traveled. And even if Buber's thought is often profoundly antagonistic to Marx's in both tenor and substance, there is more than an accidental parallel in general structure and foci of concern.

Buber himself indirectly calls attention to this kinship by attributing Marx's 'eschatology' to Jewish sources. "Karl Marx too, the Rhinelander of Jewish origin, was nothing but a translator of the Jewish faith in the future and will to the future. With consummate aptitude he translated it into the language of a pantechnical age . . ."[3] Indeed, Buber's attraction to Marxian formulations is visible in his early presentations of Zionism when he was prone to frame the question in terms of the "Jewish Proletariat."[4] Marx, in Buber's eyes, is a fellow traveler who, starting from authentic Jewish beginnings, took a false path in utopia.[5]

Differences between the two thinkers begin at the most basic level of philosophical anthropology. Buber identifies the "essence of man" with relation, "the capacity inborn in men to enter into meeting with other beings."[6] "To be a man means to be *the* being that is over-against (*gegen uber*)." Buber continues:

> ... what is peculiar to man is that one can ever and again become aware of the other as this being existing over-against him, over-against whom he himself exists. He becomes aware of the other as one who relates to him out of his selfhood and to whom he relates out of his selfhood. By virtue of this characteristic reserved to him, man has not simply entered into being as one species among other species—only just so much more manifoldly endowed—but as a special sphere.[7]

The "humanum," the "great superiority of man before all other living beings" is that he is able "to come into direct contact with everything that he bodily or spiritually meets ... Man can grasp all that encounters him on his life-way as a being existing in itself beyond his own interests."[8] When men fail to achieve this meeting, that is, "where this self-being turned toward the partners over-against me is not lived, the sphere of man is not realized."[9]

Marx, in his *Economic and Philosophic Manuscripts of 1844*, also deals with a type of human nonrealization but it is markedly different from that of Buber. Although Marx in later life disdained formulations such as "the essence of man," here, in his early writings, the term and parallels to it are quite freely used.

"Productive life," writes Marx epigrammatically, "is species-life."[10] "In the mode of life activity lies the entire character of a species-character of man ... Conscious life activity distinguishes man immediately from the life activity of an animal."[11] It is "labor, life activity and productive life," that is, the consciously active, creative, and transformative posture vis-à-vis nature that sets humans off from the animal kingdom. Human self-realization involves setting one's stamp on nature, actively converting and shaping it to human dimensions. Through the energy called forth in this process a person creates himself, "he develops his slumbering powers and compels them to act in obedience to his sway."[12] In this way an individual comes to realize what Marx calls his species-being. Nonrealization, or in the Marxian vocabulary, "alienation," occurs when "labor is external to the laborer—that is, it is not part of his nature—and the worker does not affirm himself in his work but denies himself. . . .By degrading free spontaneous activity to the level of a means, alienated labor makes species-life of a man a means of his physical existence," that is, it denies his "essence."[13]

Take as an example the respective postures of Marx and Buber toward an object of nature—a tree. The Marxist observes the tree as a material body with distinct properties and specific potentialities that can be creatively converted to human use as a table, a wood carving, or an element in a landscaping design. By means of *praxis* the tree that previously stood in independence, or perhaps in defiance of human design, now reflects our desires; it has become integrated into the human world. To practice freely this kind of directed activity is to construct a "humanized nature" and simultaneously to bring the human powers to fulfillment.

Buber would demur at this position. For the

> . . . primary relation is not the technical relation common to man and beast, above which man then rises, but that man's specific primitive technique, the invention of independent tools suited to his purpose and able to be used again and again, has become possible only through man's new relation to things as to something that is inspected, is independent and lasting.[14]

Animals are unable to grasp the world as "other," as "existing for itself. " The environment in which they move is not a detached habitation but merely the inescapable and unquestioned context of their activities. They are unable to grant the permanence and independence to nature requisite in forming tools, that, by virtue of their separate existence, await recurrent use. Only a human

> gives distance to things which he comes upon in his realm; he sets them in their independence as things which from now on continue to exist ready for a function and which he can make wait for him so that on each occasion he may master them again, and bring them into action.[15]

Labor and creation are derivatives, a second stage that presupposes the ability in the first instance to set the world at a distance, to perceive it as "over-against." What remains irreducibly human, the substratum of all activity, is the world of relation. True though it may be, as Marx feels, that human beings desire to "imprint" themselves on things, "to use them even to possess them,"[16] this is only a consequence of relation—the term consequence bearing two meanings. First, that relation is the prerequisite of all human activity and second, that it is precisely the relation with an object that impels humans to set their imprint upon it. A work of art, for example,

> is neither the impression of natural objectivity nor the expression of spiritual subjectivity, but it is the work and witness of the relation between the *substantia humana* and the *substantia rerum*, it is the realm of the 'between' become a form.[17]

While setting at a distance is what makes "man possible," it cannot "yield the essential answer to the question, how is human life realized." As opposed to the Marxist, Buber contends that the life of human beings is not exhausted by the sphere of "transitive verbs" that "have some *thing* for their object," or by "experience" that "extracts knowledge" from nature. "For what they bring him is only a world that consists of It and It and It, of He and He and She and She and It." And although the world of *It* "is not evil" and "without *It* a human being cannot live . . . whoever lives only with that is not human."[18] Distance may provide "the human situation," but only relation "provides man's becoming in that situation."[19]

To return to our neglected tree, one may consider it from many aspects; as a still-life "picture," as "movement" and "growth," as a representative of a "species," or of natural laws, and certainly as an object for transformation and use. But none of these postures passes beyond the setting at a distance, beyond experience and activity. But it may happen that "as I contemplate the tree I am drawn into a relation"[20]— a relation that transcends the particularities of distinct features and uses, the accidents of time and place— the relation of an *I* to a *Thou*. From relations such as these— toward nature, people, and God—one's humanity "unfolds." The human *differentia* that was noted in its most elemental form as setting at a distance, has now become, raised to its highest power—the *I-Thou* relationship—the bearer of human fulfillment. In a word, if Marx characterizes man as the maker, *Homo Faber*, for Buber he is both in his basic nature and at the height of his capacities the relator, the "man of dialogue."

From this parting of the ways, the separate routes of each thinker stretch out by implication and application to the entire network of their thought. In both cases the "end" is immanent in the "beginning." Alienation and materialism grow out of the concept of *Homo Faber* just as Buber's existentialism and "narrow ridge" issue from the idea of man as "over-against."

One basic result of the divergent anthropological analyses is a difference of approach regarding human "becoming," his autogenesis. For Marx, as has been noted, a person becomes human through objectifying his will, through work, that is, transformative work creates human awareness of themselves as distinct from animals,[21] produces changing needs and develops means of fulfilling them, and effectively creates the intellectual framework that suits a particular set of material premises. Human species-being emerges and unfolds *pari passu* with one's work.

For Buber, entering into relation is the act through which a person constitutes himself. By the dynamics of relation the *I*, the "unchanging partner" comes to recognize itself as separate and distinct. "Man becomes an *I* through a *Thou*."[22] But not only does self-recognition come through relation, "genuine meeting" is itself the means by which "human life and humanity come into being."[23] Meeting molds our consciousness to make us aware of others in their otherness and of our social nature; it sets the stage for the arts, culture and national groupings. Ultimately, through grasping the wholeness of all otherness, a person's mind is directed to God, where "the parallel lines of relations meet."

Buber's ambivalent attitude toward labor and productivity sheds light on this position as well as on a share of its shortcomings. Parallel to Marx's notion of an independent natural world that people proceed to bring under their control, Buber sets the idea of an *Urdistanz* that is overcome in relation. Activity, however free and creative it may be, is not capable of overcoming distance, inasmuch as activity inevitably uses, manipulates, and experiences, is purposeful, calculating, and detached.

> A purely technical relation cannot be an essential one, since it is not the whole being and the whole reality of a thing one is related to which enter into the relation but just its applicability to a definite aim, its technical suitability. An essential relation to things can only be a relation which regards them in their essential life and is turned towards them.[24]

Characteristically, when Buber pleads for the humanization of work, the essential thrust of his argument is for the reestablishment of meaningful *relations* between atomized workers, between people and their tools and produce. To be sure, the question of meaningful labor, as Buber enthusiastically poses it, is entirely in the spirit of Marx.

But is it (the place of work) irrevocably an alien place? Must henceforth through all the world's ages the life of the being who is yoked to business be divided in two, in alien "work" and home recovery? More, since evenings and Sunday cannot be freed of the workaday character but are unavoidably stamped with it, must a life be divided out between the business of work and the business of recovery without a reminder of directness, of unregulated surplus—of freedom?[25]

Buber's answer is very much his own:

No factory and no office is so abandoned by creation that a creative glance could not fly up from one working-place to another, from desk to desk, a sober and brotherly glance which guarantees the reality of creation which is happening— *quantum satis.*[26]

Rationalization need not be rejected but "let it introduce the living man into its purpose and calculations, he who longs to stand in a mutual relation with the world."[27] The aim is then "to fill business with the life of dialogue," to fulfill the "longing for an order of work in which business is so continually soaked in vital dialogic as the tasks to be fulfilled by it allow."[28] Moreover, apart from his relation to fellow laborers, "a worker can experience even his relation to the machine as one of dialogue."[29] He may draw "the lifeless thing into his passionate longing for dialogue, lending it independence and as it were, a soul."[30]

One may better understand this 'exotic' position by focusing on the role of "man the creator" in Buber's thought. First, it is indicative of Buber's cast of mind that when he does speak of man as the creator, it is primarily in reference to the artist,[31] the "elite" among creators. Free creativity as an element crucially important for the non-artist receives only scant mention. He recognizes fully that "man wants to make things," that "what is important is that by one's own intensively experienced action something arises that was not there before."[32] Creativity, or as Buber prefers to call it, "the

originator instinct," is unique among other human attributes. For

> ... here is an instinct which no matter to what power it is
> raised, never becomes greed because it is not directed to
> "having" but only to doing; which alone among the instincts
> can grow into passion, not into lust, which alone among
> instincts cannot lead its subject away to invade the realm of
> other lives. Here is pure gesture which does not snatch the
> world to itself but expresses itself to the world.[33]

Nevertheless Buber cautions:

> ... there are two forms indispensable for the building of
> human life, to which the originator instinct, left to itself, does
> not lead and cannot lead, to sharing in an undertaking and to
> entering into mutuality.[34]

The originator-person in the act of creation is severed both
from the world and from others. As creator, a person is a
solitary being. To enter the world of creation is to set all
meetings and relationships that have risen and matured
between the creator and nature adrift in the mind's eye, cut
off from their moorings in reality. It is the confined world of
the intensely personal, of inner space, where open relationships are condensed into driving, idiosyncratic inspiration,
where the mystery of the "other" becomes an experienced
subjective cipher of usable experience toward a specific end.
The originator-person "stands wholly without bonds in the
echoing hall of his deeds."[35] For

> ... no matter how directly, as being approached and claimed,
> as perceiving and receiving, the artist experiences his dealings
> with the idea which he faces and which waits embodiment, so
> long as he is engaged in his work spirit goes out from him
> and does not enter him, he replies to the world but does not
> meet it anymore. Nor can he foster mutuality with his work:
> even in the legend Pygmalion is an ironical figure.[36]

Buber's contention that creative work "does not and
cannot lead to sharing in an undertaking" is likely to raise

the rejoinder of the Marxist: "Does not Marx derive the social nature of man precisely from his being a *Homo Faber*?" Insofar as humans cannot transform nature unaided, they are social beings. Human species-being "presupposes" a social nature.

> Activity and consumption both in their content and their mode of existence are social: social activity and social consumption; the human essence of nature exists only for social man—as his existence for the other and the other's existence for him—as the life element of the human world; only here does nature exist as the foundation of his own human existence.[37]

The argument goes yet further. The paradigm case that Marx offers for future human relations is taken from the relation between the sexes, and here Marx's language seems, indeed, to prove his deep appreciation of a person's social nature.

> From this relation [the sexual] man's whole level of development can be assessed. It follows from the character of this relationship how far man has become and understood himself as, a *species-being* a *human being*. The relation of man to woman is the *most natural* relation of human being to human being. It indicates, therefore, how far man's *natural behavior has become human*, and how far his *human* essence has become a natural essence for him, how far his *human nature* has become *nature* for him. It also shows how far man's needs have become *human* needs, and consequently how far the other person, as a person, has become one of his needs, and to what extent he is in his individual existence at the same time a social being.[38]

Sexual relations, in Marx's discussion, are spontaneous, necessarily reciprocal, directed to the other not as the object of my desire but as a coequal partner, indeed, they seem quite reminiscent of Buber's *I-Thou* relationship.

But there is one difference and it is fatal to the comparison. Man's social nature, according to Marx, once rooted in his creative transforming character, cannot transcend its origin, that is, his social relations will be colored and fashioned by the activity that is both its source and concomitant. Once man's social nature, its form and content, are seen as emerging from his "essence" as an object-creating being, his relationships to others will necessarily be stamped with this same purposefulness. Teamwork is the key word, not relation. People are united in a task rather than in a brotherhood that exists for and of itself.

Marx's discussion of sexual relations is, at first glance, inconsistent with this analysis inasmuch as the participants seem to relate to one another in an "essential" manner not adumbrated by *Homo Faber*. A closer look will, I believe, belie this impression. Marx writes in the aforecited quotation that for the "humanized" individual the other person has become "one of his needs"—an elevated need perhaps, even a characteristically human need, but a need all the same. Despite the deeply satisfying quality of this relationship and although the partner is not reduced to a crass object, the ultimate motive remains use and satisfaction. The relation is *reciprocal* but not *mutual*.[39]

The Marxist is likely to reject the above distinction as a fruitless quibble, but to Buber, the ability to say *Thou* has momentous consequences. Man's social nature understood in its functional sense, Buber concedes, is explicable in terms of *Homo Faber*; but his ability to see the other as a *Thou* must—if we accept *Homo Faber* as our framework—either be dismissed as grandiose *schöngeisterei* or be approached as mystery.

> The being of the world as an object is learned from within, but not its being as a subject, its saying of *I* and *Thou*. What teaches us the saying of *Thou* is not the originator instinct but the instinct for communion.[40]

To speak the *Thou* one must leave instrumentality behind.

Only if someone grasps his hand not as a "creator" but as a fellow creature lost in the world, to be his comrade or friend or lover beyond the arts does he have an awareness and share of mutuality.[41]

But even if one grants that Marx does not rise above a view of relation colored somehow by function, Buber is doubly remiss in underestimating the role of free creative activity as a prime and irreplaceable ingredient in the complete life. Indeed, Buber seems to have ignored his own warnings against simplifying the complex wholeness of human life[42] by setting relation above man's myriad potentialities like a sun in whose light they all shine.

The realm of *I-It* is not merely "not evil" or necessary for human life; it may very well include that positive, meaningful, and essentially human energy that people expend on the world, fulfilling thereby their powers and potentialities. If it is the "sublime melancholy of our lot that every *Thou* must become an *It* in our world," it would be singularly melancholy indeed if only the fleeting breakthrough to the *Thou* infused our lives—whose greater parts are lived under the sign of *I-It*—with substance and significance.

I-It need be redeemed by nothing but *I-It* itself. The *I-It* world of work and experience can be overcome, made holy as it were, not only by cancelling its *I-It* character but by recognizing in the domain of *I-It* some of man's most rewarding, most 'human' moments. To seek the meaning of *I-It* or its failures by the light of *I-Thou*[43] is to miss the great possibilities of *I-It* itself—that is, to forsake the potential of the greater part of our lives.

The sharp line that Buber draws between *I-Thou* and *I-It*—the one workaday, uninspired, pragmatic, the other singular, consummate, unconditional—divides human life too sharply. Man as creator and as relator are cleft asunder into unbridgeable kingdoms with separate sovereigns. Buber is certainly right when he claims that *I-Thou* cannot survive the dense atmosphere of the ordinary bustling world, but this warrants the conclusion (one that Buber does not make) that the latter requires standards of its own. Ironically with all of Buber's profound concern for the "real" person and the "here and now," he has not provided criteria with which to sift and evaluate the bulk of human affairs. *I-It* remains monolithic and undifferentiated grey.[44]

One striking parallel between Buber and Marx is terminological: *dialectic* and *dialogue*. Philosophically, however, the terms serve to underline differences and with them as starting points, certain essential divergences in outlook become apparent.

"The life of dialogue," Buber explains, "is no privilege of intellectual activity like dialectic." For while dialectic is an exacting and exclusive discipline, dialogue "begins no higher than where humanity begins."[45] Feuerbach, reacting against the highly intellectualized dialectic of Hegel, writes in the same vein: "True dialectic is not a monologue of the solitary thinker with himself, it is a dialogue between *I* and *Thou*."[46] Dialogue, then, is an exercise of the whole self, open to all, directed outward; dialectic, a cerebral activity conducted by the initiated in the privacy of their own intellects.

Although Marx's use of the dialectic brings "the actual individuals, their actions, and the material conditions of their lives" into consideration appreciably more than the abstruse speculations of Hegel, it is still far from achieving that immediacy and involvement with the lived moment of the "real" person that is the hallmark of Buber's thought.[47] Marx vitiates man in his concrete singularity into the representative of a class who participates as an abstraction in a dialectical process, the inner logic of which carries him along. If one may speak of a dialectic in Buber at all, it is a highly personal and concrete affair that is lived, even suffered, with no resolution but that of paradox. While in Hegel and Marx the *Aufhebung* of battling 'thesis' and 'antithesis' into 'synthesis' sets the former pair to rest, for Buber resolution means nothing but an unflinching acceptance of the appeals of both claimants that acknowledges the cogency of each without seeking relief in simplification. If 'synthesis' has any meaning in this context, it is only a fierce personal honesty, the courage to make oneself the battleground of contending ideas.

While Buber was among the many who carried on a lifelong dialogue with the ghost of Marx, unfortunately he does not seem to have been aware of Marx's early writings[48] or of the many scholarly works that appeared after their publication; hence—like the Social Democrats—he identified Marxism with the more mechanistic, nondialectical approach of Engels.[49] The Marxian revolution as Buber (and Landauer) saw it was primarily a technical transformation to which the subject of personal renewal was an embarrassing postscript that could find no permanent place and was constantly pushed off further and further into the future. In this context the unity of theory and practice could mean no more than a coordination of tactics with philosophy. The conclusions of philosophy—the results of detached thought—must be converted into an efficient program of action which the proletariat would proceed to set into motion. Nowhere in this process is there room for personal regeneration; class consciousness is merely a disposition to follow the imperatives of philosophy. The proletariat emerge from the revolutionary struggle wiser to the wiles of the bourgeoisie but not appreciably changed in character. Given this premise, it is not surprising that Buber considered the ardent Marxist claim for a new post-revolutionary society a true instance of utopianism in the bad sense, a "leap of faith," a "belief in miracles."[50]

Modern scholarship has amply demonstrated that the unity binding theory and practice in Marx is not merely cognitive but rests on a new consciousness considerably more fundamental than Buber imagines. This new consciousness is identified with a thoroughgoing self-emancipation that provides the main revolutionary drive—without which, as Buber himself predicts, the revolution will be "stillborn." The organizations that foster this self-emancipation

> . . . change the worker, his way of life, his consciousness of himself and his society. They force him into contact with his fellow-workers, suggest to him that his fate is not a subjective, particular and contingent affair but part of a universal scheme of reality. They make him see in his fellow-proletarians not competitors for work and bread but brothers in suffering and ultimate victory, not means but equal ends.[51]

Not only do the material conditions of bourgeois capitalism undergo changes that prepare for revolution; the proletariat, Marx claims, prepare the revolution within themselves—the human subjective side of revolution—and this is quite indispensable to success.

Nevertheless, Buber would still find Marx's version seriously wanting for he could not accept limiting the potential for renewal to only the proletariat. Insofar as Marx, the champion of *Homo Faber*, sees the new proletarian consciousness emerging from revolutionary activity framed by a particular material surrounding, it is clear why only the proletariat are to be so affected. In Marx's words: "The change in human nature which produces communist consciousness on a mass scale can occur only in the practical activity of making revolution,"[52] an activity reserved for the proletariat. For Buber, renewal is the inalienable *human* prerogative, the unreserved response of any and every person to the Voice that calls him, *teshuva* (repentance or return) in religious terms—hence it must be coterminous with mankind.

Regarding the nature of the unity that binds theory and practice, Marx and Buber express much that is common. While there is a distinctly more personalist, voluntarist tone to Buber's version of the concept—human decision is far more important than material conditions—Marx, too, is clearly convinced of the need for philosophy to find both subjective and objective expression in the proletariat. Buber writes that the Hasidic rabbis internalize their teaching to the point where they are not only the "apostles" of Hasidism "but its working reality. They are the teaching."[53] The *philosophy of realization* is such that it "has no room for a truth remaining abstract, hovering self-sufficiently above reality, but . . . every truth is bound up with a demand which man, the people, Israel, are called upon to fulfill integrally on earth."[54]

For Marx, it is the proletariat who, under the influence of revolutionary associations, become the "working reality" of socialist principles. The insight gained in revolutionary activity transforms the oppressed worker into a humanist.[55] The proletarian subject and the future communist object become one and identical. They, too, by the example of their lives, their nonexploitative relations to their fellow workers, "are the teaching." For those who "are afraid lest their ideals be desecrated by coming in to touch with profane reality," who think they honor the idea "by relegating it to the starry heaven of imagination," Marx has nothing but scorn.[56]

What separates Marx and Buber most profoundly in this regard (one might even generalize and say the Marxist and the Existentialist) is the unwillingness on the part of the latter to grant the permanent, settled, once and for all unity of theory and practice.[57] Roughly parallel to theory and practice in Buber's thought are utopia and existence and we have seen repeatedly how dynamic and unconquerable is the tension between them. If Buber would grant that "it is not enough that thought should seek to realize itself; reality itself must force its way toward thought," [58] he would add his doubts that thought and reality could ever come to harmonious final rest. Convergence of subjective and objective forces, even in optimum conditions, can guarantee no more than a fragile unity that requires constant, painstaking surveillance and adjustment. Even in the most propitious of circumstances, Buber would not grant human happiness as a datum but acknowledges freely the continuous possibility of personal and existential problems.[59]

The age-old philosophic pairs—'spirit' and 'matter', 'is and ought'—are neither irrevocably cleft in two nor subject to thoroughgoing resolution as with Marx. The demands of theory and practice, of utopia and existence, intersect in the human person—the being who is conditioned but rises above conditions, who is confined by reality but capable of vision. His is the "ever anew" Promethean struggle to lift reality to vision—a struggle that of itself will never come to rest.

One further observation: According to Marx, the subjective side of revolution is of a mass nature, that is, through revolutionary associations, class consciousness seizes the mass of the proletariat. Theory could not be unified with practice were this not so.[60] The transformation of men, in Buber's thought, is, by contrast, a deliberate, one-by-one process that cannot be accelerated by mass movements. Each person is charged to begin with himself. In religious terms, "when he lets this awareness (of the Divine address) be choked off by the group, he is denying God the actual reply."[61] Besides, actual regeneration cannot be planned or organized like a political party. People do their best, but regeneration is a meeting of will and grace.[62]

The precipitous addition of great numbers, although it may swell a movement's ranks and its importance in political terms, is a perilous undertaking that may just as easily lead to the swamping of ideals and the substitution of breadth for depth. There is too much that identifies the masses seized by party slogans with the irresponsible, short-sighted mob for Buber to lend credence to claims about the "new man" who undergoes inner transformation in the revolutionary struggle. Only a political movement that expresses the inevitably slow movement of human renewal is revolutionary in the deepest sense.[63] "True community and true commonwealth will be realized only to the extent to which Single Ones become real and out of whose responsible life the body politic is renewed."[64]

Clearly, the traditional Marxist argument against religion as the 'opiate', that is, the refuge from responsibility for immediate meliorative action, is not applicable to Buber. There is not the slightest sign that he regarded faith as a refuge from responsibility to act or as accommodating people to the unpleasantness of their lot. "Man's being created in the image of God," the young Buber had written, "I grasped as deed, as becoming, as task."[65]

> That one accepts the concrete situation as given to him (by God) does not in any way mean that he must be ready to accept that which meets him as "God-given" in its pure factuality. He may rather declare the extremest enmity toward this happening and treat its "givenness" as only intended to draw forth his own opposing force.[66]

Faith is, in truth, the only source for action that will not suffer from sterility and exhaustion when the initial burst of enthusiasm has spent itself. It is a self-refilling well of energy that weathers the bitterness of frustration, the routine of every day, and, what may be most difficult, the loss of challenge that accompanies victory.

Interestingly, Buber attacks the Marxist with their own weapon, claiming that their closed system provides an organized mass escape from responsibility by presenting blue-printed answers to the intractable questions of political behavior.

> Current Marxism, as it generally meets us in reality, threatens the duty of personal responsibility. It has become, in fact, one of the escape-systems from concrete responsibility of our time. This escape is many-sided and systematically organized, with old and new *Weltanschauungen* employed in order to make it credible.[67]

The system is all the more damaging since it provides the proletariat with a false sense of security in the future and consequently lets their guard fall to the innumerable dangers of the present. It is no surprise, given the absolute optimism of a determinist eschatology, that questions of means and ends are of distinctly subordinate status. The prospect of an assured future is not designed to make the proletariat alive to the dangers of cynicism and "temporary" opportunism.

Here again Buber is doing battle more with the Social Democrats and Engels than with Marx. The multifaceted, highly subtle dialectic Marx employs makes it impervious to such broadside arguments. Questions of "inevitability" are necessarily complicated by the interplay of subjective and objective forces. Marx explicitly rejects pure mechanical materialism as expressed by the French encyclopedists or by Owen.[68] No revolution can ever carry the guarantee of success even if it possesses all the material and human conditions for success. All that Marx would grant is that the unfolding of the future is the culmination of the possibilities existing in the present.

But if it would be unfair to debate with a dessicated version of Marx, there is, nevertheless, something to be said for Buber's line of criticism even in regard to a more faithful reproduction of Marxist philosophy. If the term 'inevitability' cannot be of specific application and if proletarian errors and wrong turns may be granted, there still remains in the background an undeniable confidence in eventual victory. And while it is also true that proletarian will and self-emancipation are indispensable elements for successful revolution, can one conceive of Marx seriously entertaining the possibility that this new consciousness would not emerge? It is this security born of a closed system that Buber finds repellent. The bias was undoubtedly confirmed when "current Marxism, as it generally meets us in reality" acted with what Buber felt was complacency and lack of self-examination in a dreadfully complicated era.

Historically and theologically, Buber writes, there have been two views of redemption that have contended for humanity's allegiance. The one he calls *apocalyptic*, the other *prophetic*. The 'prophetic', as the term implies, is modelled after the biblical prophet, while the 'apocalyptic' finds its clearest expression in the various eschatological Jewish-Christian works that appeared in the late Hellenistic period.[69] These alternative postures clearly illustrate what stands between Buber and Marxian socialism.

The prophetic voice speaks to people out of the urgency of the real moment, placing before them the "stern alternatives" they confront: what is to be done, at this moment, now. "It is always intended for particular men, to induce them, as directly as if they were hearers, to recognize their situation's demand for decision and act accordingly. "[70] The prophet's call for decision issues from the depth of his own personal decision—"he is borne by his task . . . the spirit moves him; not only his organs of speech but the whole man is taken up into the service of the spirit. The body and life of the man become a part of this service and by this a symbol of the message."[71] And this call for decision unmistakably entails the belief that human decision is an effective lever on the future. Man,

> . . . the unique being . . . is created to be a center of surprise in creation. Because and so long as man exists, factual change of direction can take place toward salvation as well as toward disaster, starting from the world in each hour, no matter how late.[72]

The prophetic call, although it so repeatedly suffers rebuff and defeat, fails in only one "hour of history, but not so far as the future of his people is concerned. For his people preserve the message as something which will be realized at another hour, under other conditions, and in other forms."[73] This is so because the prophet does not believe

> . . . that he possesses an abstract and general, a timeless concept of truth. He always receives one message only for one situation. This is exactly why after thousands of years, his words still address the changing situations in History.[74]

By contrast, the apocalyptic writer

... has no audience turned toward him; he speaks into his notebook. He does not really speak, he only writes; he does not write down the speech, he just writes his thoughts—he writes a book.[75]

Nowhere "does there stir the prophetic breath of actually happening history and its fullness of decision." He writes to a world in which human action is no more than frenzied purposeless movement.

Everything here is predetermined, all human decisions are only sham struggles. The future does not come to pass; the future is already present in heaven, as it were, present from the beginning. Therefore, it can be 'disclosed' to the speaker and he can disclose it to others. His innermost question is not concerned with what poor man shall undertake but why things happen to him as they do.[76]

Apocalyptic credos arise

... wherever man shudders before the menace of his own work and longs to flee from the radically demanding historical hour, there he finds himself near to the apocalyptic vision of a process that cannot be arrested.[77]

But the seductive appeal of the apocalypse is not exhausted by the "end of days" type of soothsaying; it is found in any of the systematic, methodical attempts to compress reality into a fixed configuration, to make of philosophy a catechism: the closed system.

No teaching finds it so difficult to preserve its strength as one which places the meaning of life in the working reality of the here and now and does not tolerate man's fleeing before the taxing infinity of the moment into uniform system of Is and Ought; the inertia soon proves itself the stronger and coerces the teaching.[78]

Marx stands out as the "chief example" of the "modern apocalyptic" thinker. Following his view of Marx, Buber claims that in his "announcement of an obligatory leap of the human world out of the aeon of necessity into that of freedom, the apocalyptic principle alone holds sway."[79] Buber continues characteristically:

> Here in place of the power superior to the world that effects the transition, an immanent dialectic has appeared. Yet in a mysterious manner *its* goal too, is the perfection, even the salvation of the world. In its modern shape, too, apocalyptic knows nothing of an inner transformation of the world and cooperates in it; it knows nothing of the prophetic "turning." Marx could, indeed occasionally (1856) write, "the new forces of society"—by which the *pre-revolutionary* society is meant—"need new men in order to accomplish good work," although according to the materialist interpretation of history, new men can only arise from the new post-revolutionary conditions of society. . . Three years later Lassalle could write with justification that linking brazen necessity to necessity it passes over and obliterates just for that reason the efficacy of individual resolutions and actions.[80]

On just this point, however, a basic objection may be urged against Buber. Historically, the obliteration of "the efficacy of individual resolutions and actions" has had a result quite the opposite of what might be expected. Far from undercutting the motive power of action, the imminence of the "end" has in fact been a shot of energy that stirred people to their very best efforts. Similarly, and this is quite pertinent to Marx, an apocalyptic proclamation is not simple future telling; it calls upon each person to realize the dawn of the new day, to hasten that which is well-nigh upon us. As one writer puts it:

> The apocalyptic "must" does not imply the kind of necessity characteristic of the neutral "must" usually ascribed to the laws of nature, but is coined in the strongest anticipation of the end of history in the actuality of faith.[81]

Nowhere has action displayed so much devotion as where the end is assured.[82]

This is all true but also quite beside the point. Buber is very much aware of the activity that the apocalyptic principle encourages.[83] But it is not in passivity that the apocalyptic is deficient but precisely in its action that derives from something other than personal responsibility. Although people scurry in anticipation of the "end," their movement is not prompted by inner compulsion but is borrowed from and agitated by the power of an event that looms ever larger on the horizon of the future. Having been a close observer of the Russian and German revolutions, Buber could not have spoken of Marxian passivity, but he was convinced that because their "responsibility" to the future was mediated through a doctrine which claimed this same future for itself, responsibility amounted to little more than a tautology, the inner echo of a closed system. Responsibility, in the prophetic sense, means that one's decisions and actions and, of course, the decisions and actions of communities of men, are heavy with consequence, often decisive in determining the shape of things to come. There is no future already written requiring only to be unrolled, because the human person is God's partner in history and not merely the midwife to an impending age. Responsibility—the kind that matures into compelling inner decision and striving realization—cannot grow through the mediation of ideology, or systems, or from the apocalyptic 'must', but only from a living, fearless encounter with the world.

The division of messianic activity into prophetic and apocalyptic principles is not a chance phenomenon in Buber's thought but of a piece with his most fundamental convictions. The opposing views of history inherent in these two principles—the one causal, deterministic, and systematic, and other largely voluntaristic—accord with and derive from the *I-Thou* and *I-It* relationships. More precisely, the prophetic and apocalyptic principles are, in one sense, the *I-Thou* and *I-It* relationships projected into philosophies of history.

The Marxian (apocalyptic) philosophy of history, follow-ing Buber's interpretation, sees man as the creature of history, framed by the evolution of economic activity and assigned an active but only auxilliary role in the drama. Under the sway of causality the individual is an unequal partner in relation with the forces of production. His move-ments, will, indeed consciousness itself, are dominated by the material conditions of class and historical epoch. This is the unchallenged kingdom of *I-It* where the conquering advance of *objects* has overrun people and reduced them to obedient *subjects*. The materialist position impresses people into its service by, in effect, denying them the ability to do anything else.

Buber contends, however, that the possibilities inherent in *dialogue* are ignored by this formulation. Dialogue is based upon a coequal subject and object that impress themselves on each other without at the same time overpowering their opposite. In effect, this constitutes a rejection of the claim of both idealism and materialism in favor of a tense mediate position. Neither the *I* nor its object encompass the entire relation. Neither is the *I* lost in the *Thou* nor the *Thou* reduced to a function of the *I*'s subjectivity. Both relate and withstand. Translated into more conventional philosophic language this means that people are shaped by the reality they encounter but are also capable of withstanding, indeed, transcending it.

The human person is both the creature of casuality and the creature sui generis, living simultaneously inside and inde-pendent of history. To study the "whole" person is to reject all those disciplines that shut out the human being in all his complexity—that consider him simply as a "bit of nature," a historically determined being, or on the other hand, a totally free agent. The human person, the creature of dialogue, is set into history but not totally subsumed under its categories.[84] Decision is therefore neither an abstraction of man communing with himself nor the hollow ritual of doing the inevitable. The human power of decision is firmly set into the concrete historical moment without forfeiting thereby its independent nature; the "whole" person lives as a uniquely endowed being within the confines of history.

Marxian socialism, by willingly accepting the *I-It* relationships as exhaustive, is condemned to live under its imperious rule. Having sealed all the exits—better yet by denying there are any—the Marxist necessarily reduces the power of decision to the role of a restricted functionary in a shut-in world. But for Buber, the world of *I-Thou* with its momentary breakthroughs, in which people reach beyond to meet otherness—nature, humanity and God—illumines potentialities that in daily existences are scarcely visible. It points to hidden powers that enable one to withstand and overcome the dictates of causality. The *Thou* who stands "over-against" me, neither purely as my object nor yet as the shaper of my consciousness—real, concrete, within a definite context yet outside the bonds of causality—is the prototype for the potentialities of human action in history.

> The unlimited sway of causality in the *It*-world, which is of fundamental importance for the scientific ordering of nature, is not felt to be oppressive by the man who is not confined to the *It*-world but free to step out of it again and again into the world of relation. Here *I* and *Thou* confront each other freely in a reciprocity that is not involved in or tainted by any causality.[85]

To meet the *Thou* is to glimpse into the world of freedom, "Only those who know relation and who know of the presence of the *Thou* have the capacity for decision." [86] Although the *Thou* cannot cancel the world of causality — one must constantly return to it—the power of relation "invades creation," freeing each person to struggle in the province of causality itself.

It is interesting to note, if only parenthetically, that Buber's position on good and evil revolves around just this point.

Evil is essentially resignation to the dictates of causality. The evil person is swept along by causality, making no move to assert himself and his formidable powers. "If there were a devil he would not be the one who decided against God, but he that in all eternity did not decide."[87]

Apart from the consequence for causality, the *I-Thou* and *I-It* relationships and the ideas that derive from them diverge also in regard to epistemology. Insofar as the world is one of objects and order, it is amenable to systematization. Hence, a philosophy that limits its field of concern to *I-It* will quite likely be a systematic one, with clear premises, neatly arranged argument, and methodical conclusions. It may even claim for itself the title "scientific." By contrast, the *I-Thou* relationship defies all such systematization since, by its very nature, it cannot involve an exchange of information, or for that matter anything concrete. It is "pure meeting," through which no specific substance can be transmitted, no contents secured, and no programmatic conclusions derived. The *Thou* can never be ordered. Thus the *I-Thou* relationship also sets Buber off from any symmetrical network of ideas like those of Marxism. "Pure meeting" can offer no rigorous propositions or universally valued precepts; like the prophets it can speak from the moment into the moment, tentatively, honestly, with "holy insecurity." Truth can never become definitively codified but must always remain "an attitude towards, an inquiry into, a struggle for."[88]

Of all the criticisms that Buber levels at Marx, the most persistent and fundamental is that, because he was too single-mindedly concerned with revolution, its economic underpinnings, its political consequences, its technical progress, he lost sight of its real goal—the renewal of society. In his disciples, both Leninist and Social Democratic, this shortcoming becomes a glaring defect that produces in the one case a totalitarian regime and in the other a dissolution of ideology.

Of the three modes of thinking in public matters—the economic, the social, and the political—Marx exercised the first
with methodical mastery, devoted himself with passion to the
third, but—absurd as it may sound in the ears of an unqualified Marxist—only very seldom did he come into intimate
contact with the second and it never became a deciding factor
for him.[89]

With certain variations, Buber carries this line of criticism
to the entire range of Marxist history, from the writings of
Marx himself to the Soviet forced collectivization of the
peasants. Marx's thought, Buber comments, while at times
very close to the "restructuring viewpoint" discussed in the
previous chapter, is nevertheless marred by an "ambivalent
attitude" that saps the strength of this commitment. On the
one hand, his various pronouncements on the Cooperative
movement, the Paris Commune, the "sloughing off of the
political husk,"[90] come in for warm praise by Buber, who, at
one point exclaims: "Never did any 'Utopian' socialist express himself more radically."[91] Marx sees the enormous
potential of the Cooperative movement as a model for future
organization, as pointing to the "proper way" to rebuild
capitalist society. His ardent regard for the Paris Commune
as well, indicates the depth of his concern for decentralization, federalism, and the primacy of the social over the
political principle. Both the Cooperatives and the Commune
are tentative but highly significant advances that prepare the
road leading out of capitalism to the socialist future. Both
indicate how "the parasitic excrescence of the state" might
be dissolved. Both point to a great social transformation
based on free spontaneous association, strictly accountable
representatives, and maximum local autonomy. Buber concludes that "a federalism of communes and Cooperatives
. . .is thus acknowledged by Marx as genuine communism."[92]

Yet even though Marx accepted the "essential components
of the commune idea," he fatally undermined it by never
seriously considering how this might be squared with what

Buber identifies as his basic "centralist" orientation and his "political" outlook. Marx remained ambivalent because despite his "occasional" allusions to social renewal, he had "no inner relation to the idea." Consequently

> . . . he could not make up his mind to foster those elements [of renewal], to promote them and sponsor them. The political act of revolution remains the one thing worth striving for; the political preparation for it—at first direct preparation, afterwards the parliamentary and trade unionist preparation—the one task worth doing, and thus the political principle became the supreme determinant.

This was so to the extent that

> . . . every concrete decision about the practical attitude to such restructural elements as were actually present, in the process of formation or to be constituted anew, was reached only from the standpoint of political expediency. Naturally, therefore, decisions in favor of a positive attitude were tepid, uncoordinated and ineffectual, and finally were always cancelled out by negative ones.[93]

How a thinker of Marx's stature and sophistication could so manifestly contradict himself, the one moment praising federalism the next defending statism; at one point genuinely committed to the establishment of the social principle and at another dominated by the "tactical propagandistic" attitude that is part of the political principle, Buber never adequately explains. It is also notable that a good part of Buber's evidence rests on Engels and the Social Democrats, those "held to be most knowledgeable in Marxist affairs."

Of Marx himself there are only a handful of citations that Buber adduces and they do not adequately sustain his case. The deepest insight into "Marx's ambivalent attitude to the questions of internal transformation of society" is afforded, Buber claims, by his well-known correspondence with Vera Zasulich on the subject of the Russian *Mir* and the possibility that it might be the germ cell of Russian socialism. [94] Marx's "equivocations" on the subject (particularly in his drafts) Buber takes as a symptom of his basic indecision about social restructuring. Had Marx been seriously interested in social renewal, Buber seems to be saying, he would have accepted the *Mir* and encouraged his correspondent to set all her strength to freeing and developing it. He hesitated because revolution in itself was a rival goal in his mind that, in the final choice, won his support. Buber's argument, which is as surprising as it is unwarranted, concludes that "here as elsewhere the determining factor is clearly the political element: the fear lest constructive work should sap the strength of the revolutionary impetus."[95]

Actually, Marx very carefully examined the prospects of the *Mir*, stressing both the points in its favor (its universality and deep traditions) and those against it (the isolation of each unit) and concluded, in the actually drafted reply, that the *Mir* had great potentialities for Russian social regeneration but that it needed to be freed (apparently by revolution) from the corruption into which it had fallen.[96] He gives no clear answer, not, as Buber feels, because he is lacking "insight into the significance of social restructure" but precisely because he is cautiously weighing these very possibilities for regeneration. To make restructure a realistic goal, the *Mir* had to present concrete, not imagined or romanticized, prospects of being able to shoulder the burden of a new society. The question as Marx answers it, is analytic-historic and not at all a matter of social regeneration versus revolution. Marx does, in fact, find the *Mir* in its contemporary form too infirm and corrupted to be, of itself, the center of a movement for social renewal. Yet he points to the very significant role that it could play were the obstacles to its functioning removed by revolution. Thus if there is any truth to Buber's claim that Marx feared the *Mir* lest it divert revolutionary energy, it is that the *Mir*, decayed anachronism that it was, would be the object of great but futile efforts that could end nowhere but in disappointment and with the neglect of other vital and more fertile areas for revolutionary activity.

Very much the same is true in regard to the argument that Marx's opposition to social restructure is evident in his criticism of the various "doctrinaire experiments, exchange banks and workers' associations" which

> having given up the struggle to overthrow the old world despite all the means at its disposal, prefers to seek its own salvation behind society's back, privately, inside the narrow framework of its existence, and which will thus necessarily come to grief.[97]

Here again, what motivates Marx is not any bias against or uncertainty about social restructure per se but doubts regarding the method of its accomplishment. Certain types of experiments are, in Marx's eyes, destined to "come to grief" because of their proclivity to ignore what he regards as the realities of economic development and because they choose to derive their programs from pure ideals. What really stands between Buber and Marx is, then, not the value of restructure but rather the tactics for its realization. Marx, basing the development of socialism on the forces of production inherent in capitalism, rejects all experiments irrelevant to this framework. Buber, the enemy of determinism, sees potentialities for restructure present at virtually all points, requiring, above all, human decision for their implementation.

A second contention of Buber, closely related to the first, is that "Marx always remained a centralist at heart" and in the final analysis subordinated the federal and decentralized to the statist and centralized. The evidence against this argument is very strong,[98] and the single citation that Buber adduces hardly justifies his conclusion. He points to a comment contained in a letter from Marx to Engels about the tendencies of the French representatives at the General Council of the International.

Proudhonized Stirnerism. Splitting up everything into little "groups" or "communes" and then making a "company" of them but not a state.[99]

Buber concludes "by implication," that "it is here that the undercurrent of State Centralism creeps unmistakably into Marx's ideas," and that Marx "holds fast to the State as such."[100]

Once again Buber has mistaken a tactical comment for a statement of basic policy. Marx opposes any premature communalistic activity because it ignores and can never solve the fundamental questions posed by the state. For the state to be overcome it must first dialectically reach its full development. Decentralization and federalism can take place only after centralization and undivided rule have exhausted all their possibilities. Expecting renewal to emerge en masse from communalistic experiments is, as Marx writes in the aforementioned letter, like Fourier's belief that by demonstrating his "experiments "to us the rest of the world overwhelmed by the force of their example will follow suit."[101]

What Buber takes to be the ambivalence of Marx toward social restructure are, in actuality, two separate movements of the dialectic. The first moves toward the full development of the possiblities of capitalism, involving the growth of the centralized monolithic state; the second—which the *Aufhebung* of the first—toward its dissolution and replacement by decentralization and local autonomy.

Nevertheless Buber is justified in pointing to Marx's unwillingness to participate in the constructive work of restructure that is in fact possible in the here and now. If in his *Inaugural Address* Marx could praise the Cooperatives, he made no move to encourage their growth.[102] He relies on the historical dialectic to accomplish what Buber sees as the burden of human responsibility. In this sense, it is legitimate to point to the Leninists, if not as the orthodox disciples of

Marx, at least as an indication of what may happen to a doctrine that allows relatively little room for positive restructuring activity in the here and now, preferring to allow history and revolution to take on the full responsibility for the future.

Lenin, Buber argues, is a product of this "divided spiritual inheritance" of Marx: "Socialist revolutionary politics, without socialist vitality."[103]

Having dedicated himself totally to the victory of the revolution, Lenin lost sight of its real goals. The *Soviets* that might have become the germ cells of a new society are dealt with as the "battle-organs" of the revolution. The various "agricultural cooperatives" likewise become merely the "bulwark" of the new regime. Here social restructure has truly become a purely "tactical-propagandistic" matter. Stalin makes the point painfully clear when he says: "From the standpoint of Leninism the collective economies, and the *Soviets* as well are a weapon and nothing but a weapon." And Buber replies: "One cannot in the nature of things expect a little tree that has been turned into a club to put forth leaves."[104]

5

Rome, Moscow, and Jerusalem

Those who would treat politics and morality apart will never
understand the one or the other.

John Viscount Morley

E.H. CARR, the noted English historian, clearly disturbed
by the growing tendency of political individuals to divide
into camps of "Utopians" and "Realists," presents a typology that by now should be quite familiar.

> The two methods of approach—the inclination to ignore what
> was and what is in contemplation of what should be and the
> inclination to deduce what should be from what was and what
> is—determine opposite attitudes toward every political prob-
> lem.

The Utopian believes in the possibility of more or less
radically rejecting reality and substituting utopia for it by an
act of will. For the Realist, reality presents a *fait accompli*
that one is "powerless to change." He deprecates the role of
will and maintains "that the function of thinking is to study
a sequence of events which it is powerless to influence or
alter." Carr concludes that "the characteristic vice of the
utopian is naiveté; of the realist sterility."[1]

Utopia, in Buber's thought, as has been noted frequently,
is a *particular* aspect of the Absolute: the Absolute projected
onto society. Political "realism" as well is only one expression of a far more inclusive ideological position. The opposition between utopia and reality to which Carr alludes is, for

Buber, a single manifestation of a generic phenomenon, on the same order as the tension between ethics and necessity, between godliness and organized ritual, even, in a sense, between *I-Thou* and *I-It*.[2] "Occidental dualism," the severing of the realm of the spirit from the realm of the world—the latter to be approached not as response-eliciting challenge but as fact—is a general condition of which Carr has elaborated only one aspect. It affects Western man in far more than just the areas of politics and diplomacy; it has, Buber laments, entered the very texture of his perceptions.

Carr extends his argument to cover some ramifications of this typology, notably for this work's purpose, the antithesis between the Left and the Right.

> The radical is necessarily utopian, the conservative realist. The intellectual, the man of theory, will gravitate toward the Left just as naturally as the bureaucrat, the man of practice, will gravitate toward the Right.[3]

Buber, too, in a 1928 address, sets the question into a similar framework:

> The world political situation of our time is . . . marked by two focal points, Moscow and Rome [Fascist Rome]. If the first, Democracy without Demos, that is without a truly constituted people, applies itself to neither the idea nor the reality with responsibility; the latter sets up one against the other, a false service to the idea and a false service to the reality.[4]

In these rather cryptic words lies hidden the vital nerve that branches out to animate the corpus of Buber's political writings. Moscow and Rome represent the antithetical poles of—not so much Left and Right—as utopia and existence. Typically more schematic and hortatory than scholarly, Buber's antithesis of Moscow and Rome is an attempt to clothe the two paradigm models with historical concreteness without at the same time giving up the flexibility and wide applicability of an 'ideal type' in favor of particular historical phenomena. The concept becomes tangible enough to be of service for historical analysis but not so specifically associated with a single phenomenon that its purity as a model is impaired.

Moscow is the imperious rule of the idea hollowed out of all real human content.

> In Moscow the living idea is replaced by the principle. The living idea always possesses form, the form of what can and ought to issue out of certain potentialities of certain people and groups of people. The principle reduces the idea to formlessness: In place of particular people and groups, concrete in their popularity, culture and destiny, we confront the abstraction—man, the citizen, the proletarian—in place of the body, a skeleton, in place of a search for the way with its real decisions, the prefigured route. Moscow is the sovereignty of the principle moderated only by the opposition of reality; and even after it is decided to take this opposition into consideration, to fuse it, so to speak, with the principle itself, it becomes, to be sure, modified in content 'for the time being', but it does not cease to be, according to its demand and character, the formless principle.[5]

The utopia of Moscow works out of a blueprint. If exigencies force a change of plan, a new plan, a new blueprint, is quickly drawn up; but no more than in its predecessor is there any "contact of life" between the idea and the reality. Utopias of this sort—stilted, chained to stereotypes, ritualistic—often eventuate in realities that have only a formal resemblance to the original idea. Moscow, that was to announce the "leap into the era of freedom," has instead become "the Leviathan masquerading as the Messiah."[6]

There may be no special messianic politics.[7] Messianic yearnings may indeed be mingled with political activity but never, as is the case of Moscow, in the form of an exceptional *vade mecum* detailing the procedure leading to utopia. Socialism, to be sure, is a kind of messianic activity, but it is simply the open-hearted, creative response to the challenge that emerges from reality itself. If a "drop of messianic consummation" must be mingled with all political ventures, it is not by some singular radically new category of activity but only by a hallowing of the here and now. "We cannot prepare the messianic world, we can only prepare for it."[8] There is, in effect, no difference between activity designed to maximize the possibilities of this hour and activity aimed at the messianic age.

Here, a subtle but highly important distinction must be introduced. Despite the passion with which Buber may deplore the severing of the idea from the reality in which it must function, and despite the force with which he enjoins a living dialogue between the Absolute and the demands of the political hour, he carefully insists that the two must not be confused or identified with each other. Politics, which involves the desire to achieve certain concrete ends, is marked by the critical fact that success may be attained and recorded. Religion remains "even in man's highest experiences of the mortal way, that which simply provides direction; it never enters into historical consummation." History, in its religious sense, "is what takes place on the journey from origin to perfection and this is registered by other signs than that of success." The "successes" of religion are subjective, highly fragile and finally, unverifiable. If we think we see instances where religion does seem to have registered impressive victories, as in the Christian Middle Ages, Buber reminds us that in such cases it is no longer religion that prevails but the politics of religion; and here although it seems that "the Word is victorious . . . it bears its fruit in the *corruptio seminis.*"[9]

'Success' and 'failure', the criteria of politics, are hopelessly inadequate terms when the subjects to be described are, for example, th prophets or religious martyrs. Religious history is written not only in the visible, notorious successes but often in hidden defeats.[10] The Absolute may find its most exalted embodiment in the despised and unnoticed, while the "world-historical" nations monopolize headlines and history books.[11] Were a history of the world written along standard lines to be set alongside a history of the Absolute in the world, they would prove to be very different works. The successes of politics are registerable but not necessarily real; the successes of religion are real but not necessarily registered.

Since they are fundamentally different from each other, there cannot be, given the unredeemed nature of the world, any complete synthesis of the two. To attempt to introduce the strict demands of the Absolute into political life is either to abdicate the world of politics or to renounce one's obligations to the Absolute, to be, in Arthur Koestler's terms, either "yogi" or "commissar." Such an inflexible adherence to absolute principles is typologically an offshoot of the category of Moscow.

Plato's philosopher-king, ruling by virtue of his interior relation to the truth, constructing and ordering a model state directed only by consideration of reason, operates by the principle of Moscow. The guardians of *The Republic* possess only the unconfronted, detached idea. Their wisdom results from deliberate isolation from just those passions, contingencies, and relations that are the hallmark of the world of Caesar. Their truth is attained by "liberation" from the "shadow-world" of the concrete, situation-bound reality of men. Mathematics, the stripping of the corporeal into the purest of abstractions, is the archway into their world of truth. And this truth, once attained, decides with seeming ease and definitive accuracy the great questions of social policy. "Plato is the most sublime instance of that spirit which proceeds in its intercourse with reality from its own possession of truth."[12]

A different form of this approach has already been noted in Kierkegaard's shunning of the political world for the isolated purity of the "single one." Politics demands compromise, concession, defilement; therefore it is no place for the seeker of God.

A far more complex example is presented by Gandhi. Notably, he was the leader of a movement that had immense political influence and died a political casualty of India's struggle for independence. Nonetheless, his religious principles—notably *Satyagraha* or "truth-force"—never truly confronted the exigencies of public life or the realities of a mass movement in an essential way.

> So far as Gandhi acts politically, so far as he takes part in passing parliamentary resolutions, he does not introduce religion into politics, but allies his religion with the politics of others.[13]

Moreover, whenever Gandhi tries to make of religion a political force, it is only a religion of uncompromising purity that he knows. If, in the confrontation, the religious principle must undergo modification, Gandhi quickly becomes a non-political man. In the struggle with the "serpent of politics," religion must either emerge uncompromised or it must abandon the struggle entirely. The "tragic character" of Gandhi's greatness, Buber tells us, is not a matter of "inner contradiction"—his commitment to purity at all costs was fearless and consistent—"but that of the contradictions between the unconditionality of a spirit and the conditionality of a situation."[14]

Gandhi straddled two worlds without their ever meeting within him. He feared the mass movement he created—he said of it: "They [the English] do not know that I fear it still more than they do themselves. I am literally sick over it. I would feel myself on surer ground if I were spit upon by them;"—he was convinced that only as a "minority of *one* voice," in the purity of hopeless isolation, could he have the courage to withstand all adversity. "This is for me," he concluded, "the only truthful position."[15] Buber admires both Gandhi and his position, but he cannot "follow him."

> The way in which Gandhi again and again exercises self-criticism, going into heavy mortification and purification when the inner serpent shows itself powerful in the movement, is worthy of the purest admiration.[16]

But as sublime and formidable as Gandhi's position may be, it is not "the way of response"; the real voice of the moment's urgency is choked off by Gandhi's single-minded dedication to the call of the Absolute.[17]

The matter is further complicated by the relationship between religion and success in Gandhi's thought. For while Gandhi will not avail himself of any of those tactics that one terms 'political', he nevertheless hopes for what is unmistakably a political victory. He seeks political success through religious means. The intractable entanglements involved in such an undertaking are highlighted for Buber by Gandhi's comment that Indian *Swaraj* (independence) would be attained "in one year" if only the Indian people showed discipline, self-denial, readiness to sacrifice, capacity for order, confidence, and courage. And again, at a later date, Gandhi wrote that "if India wants to become free, it can only do so with God's help. God loves the truthful and nonviolent." But Gandhi misses the antinomy involved in linking religious means to political ends. For, as Buber points out:

> God's love is not measured by success. How God's love works is His affair. One may be certain of the truthfulness and nonviolence of the love of God, but not of the attainment of *Swaraj* in one year. "In one year" is a political word; the religious watchword must read: Sometime, perhaps today, perhaps a century. In religious reality there is no stipulation of time, and victory comes, at times, just when one no longer expects it.[18]

This confusion of roles that is endemic to persons of spirit concerned with politics is at least partially attributable to that manner of thinking to which we have given the short-hand label: 'Moscow'. Because they tend to keep their moral preachments separate from the situations for which they are intended, the world of God separate from the world of Caesar;[19] because they speak from one self-enclosed world into another, there is the constant danger of inapplicable standards, hybrid terminology, and, most seriously, of irrelevance. Buber's "narrow ridge," although it assuredly does not make the problem itself any simpler, cuts through the confusion raised by the duality of conflicting criteria, to make of the religio-political judgment a single, intensely demanding but humanly complete act. The person of spirit "may not forget that if his work is to be done in public life, it must be accomplished not above the fray but in it."[20] For if religion withdraws from politics, "it evades its task, despite all hosts and sacraments of incarnation." But, on the other hand, if

it sinks into that sphere, then it has lost its soul. Gandhi, as no other man of our age, shows us the difficulty of the situation, the depth of its problematic, the manifoldness of the battlefronts, the potency of the contradiction, which is encompassed by paradox and must be endured in every hour.[21]

'Rome' signifies the hegemony of the actual over the idea.

In Rome instead of the contemplation of reality, with its profound perspective and the constant, sudden upsurge of the *Imprévu*, there is a recognition of one salient, conspicuous part of reality that is identified with the whole—namely, the human will to power, lust after power, pleasure of power, and the cares of power. That state is seen as an arrangement of power-having and power-seeking which is mastered by the desire for power that proves itself appropriate to the moment. By means of the social bonds that are created through the apportioning of power, the ideologically founded bonds are overcome. The genuine contemplation of reality is always reverential before it, even when one feels called upon to change it; "actualism" is without reverence; it is unwilling to truly fight and overcome, only to momentarily manage the given. The sovereignty of "actualism" in Rome is camouflaged rather than mitigated by means of a decorative and effective latching on to an obsolete tradition.[22]

At its most cynical and manipulatory, 'Rome' finds archetypical representation in the "leader." With Mussolini, for example, ideas that stand "over-against" reality and in critical tension to it are superseded by the myth that serves no function other than to facilitate the leader's control over political power. Whatever the ideas or ideologies propounded, they have no intrinsic value—as a goal to be reached, as a critical tool with which to evaluate—they are useful only insofar as they mobilize the masses. "It is not necessary that the myth have reality content," only that it permit a despairing people to believe in and follow the leader who treads with such apparent confidence where others see no path.[23] Not only does the idea as imparter of direction disappear, whatever fragment is retained by the intellectuals finds itself fundamentally compromised. For they become "quick and obedient pups in the service of the ruling powers; retrieving ideologies in place of the slogans thrown to them."[24]

The leader goes beyond Machiavelli, "who believes in the state and in power only for the sake of the state," because he believes only in himself. If

> Lenin fashioned because he had a vision; Mussolini undertook time and again to fashion what he had just contrived. Lenin strove for power because he strove to promote his cause as no other could, and because he could provide it with this service only if he ruled. Mussolini wants to rule because he does not want to serve.[25]

"For us," Buber cites a directive of Hitler, "leader and idea are one, and each party comrade has to do what is commanded by the leader who embodies the idea and alone knows the final goal."[26] And Buber comments: "The leader embodies the idea, but there is no idea."[27]

But if the idea is absent in 'Rome', may one not at least expect that reality be seriously considered by those who live at its mercy? The answer here can be only a very partial yes. For just as 'Moscow', despite its ostensible commitment to the socialist ideal, has no interior relationship to the idea as a living, situation-tested inspiration, so 'Rome', for all its close scrutiny of the actual, is interested in reality only as presentness, as a series of tricky variables requiring manipulation if one is to retain the upper hand. Here there is no response to the moment, only its efficient management. Reality presents no roughhewn challenge calling out to the full range of a person's energies, only a gaming situation for the shrewd and unprincipled—the practitioners of Machiavellian *virtù.*

Examples of 'Rome' are, if not quite so pernicious as Fascist Italy and Nazi Germany, so much a part of contemporary politics that there is hardly any need to adduce particular cases. The general amorality and bankruptcy of vision in political life, Buber laments, are so widely taken for granted that there is scarcely any effort made to disguise opportunism. The "end of ideology" in the West may well signify a general acceptance of "actualism" as the dominant mode of political perception.

Buber concludes:

> In this way the ideological and anti-ideological dictatorships stand facing each other. In each of them there is concealed a genuine power—in the one that of belief in the socialist idea, be it even distorted and deformed; in the other, the recognition of the importance of the covenant with concrete reality, be it perceived even superficially and as without substance.[28]

A denuded utopia and a deficient reality carve up the world between them. Each operates within the self-enclosed sphere it posits, seeing the part as the whole and even the part incompletely. Is this, however, inevitable?

In one regard perhaps it is. Those who choose to see only the reality will end by falling short of even this limited goal. For reality as an unexamined fact is necessarily a flat, one-sided presentness. Reality is a becoming as well as a given. Without a vision of its capacities, without the idea as a die for its future, reality lacks perspective and depth. "Genuine reality," Buber might say, is related to by the whole person. Reality, in its breadth of challenges, dilemmas, and opportunities, elicits the broadest of human responses; but remove the leaven of potentiality and it becomes dimensionless, not related to but controlled, not by the whole person but by the will to power. Quite the same is true of the idea standing alone. Without the animating flesh and blood of real life-situations, it will become, willy-nilly, a dogmatic abstraction. And as an abstraction it, too, forfeits any claim to the whole person.

Still the question returns. Does the choice between 'Rome' and 'Moscow' exhaust the alternatives? In Buber's words: "Does there exist a Jerusalem?"

We shall, in the concluding chapter, deal more specifically with the real historical Jerusalem and the great expectations that Buber had for it. Here, 'Jerusalem' signifies, above all, an approach, a manner of viewing and dealing with political problems. It is easy to regard 'Jerusalem' simply as a reasonable compromise between fact and idea. But that would reduce a demanding and dynamic synthesis to a well-worn platitude of common sense. 'Jerusalem' is anything but common. It is a rare interaction of vision and realism, in which neither element is diluted or lost.

A number of examples are in order. The revolutionary, Buber argued in a memorial speech for Gustav Landauer, does not declare

"I must here use force, but I do not want to do so" [this would be, depending on the outcome of the dilemma, either a form of Rome or of Moscow];[29] but "I have taken it upon myself to use as much force as is necessary in order that the revolution be accomplished, but alas for me and for it if more force is used than is necessary."[30]

The latter formula contains, as the former does not, two integrally connected demands that must answer jointly for any given situation.

Again, when Buber writes to Gandhi in defense of the Jewish settlement in Palestine, he rejects Gandhi's counsel of pacifism, explaining that he cannot support a position that permits good to be undone by evil and stand by idly.

For I cannot help withstanding evil when I see it is about to destroy the good. I am forced to withstand the evil in the world just as the evil within myself.I can only strive not to have to do so by force. But if there is no other way of preventing the evil destroying the good, I trust I shall use force and give myself up into God's hands.[31]

As these examples signify, the person of Jerusalem "lives on the knife's edge." But it is in the instant of decision—when, solitary, without reduction or escape confronting the demands of the moment *and* of eternity—that the cutting blade is felt most sharply. Although the position of one's group or party may be significant to him, he acts alone.

Only one thing matters, that as the situation is presented to me I expose myself to it as the Word's manifestation to me, to the very ground where hearing passes into being and that I perceive what is to be perceived and answer it. He who prompts me with an answer in such a way as to hinder my perceiving is the hinderer (Satan), let him be for the rest who he will.[32]

In its worst form, allegiance to party or group can make of otherwise scrupulously honest and compassionate people, practitioners of deceit, betrayal, even murder, without a trace of "inner conflict," of "wounds and scars." Nevertheless, this does not mean that one's group has no claim to loyalty—

Buber is, of course, an ardent supporter of nationality, closely-knit communal life and interhuman responsibility. It does entail, however, that no group can answer for or assume guilt for any person's actions. 'Jerusalem' is composed of "single ones" for whom the responsibilities of community life are serious and exacting. "I believe," Buber declares,

> ... that it is possible to serve God and the group to which one belongs if one is courageously intent on serving God in the sphere of the group as much as one can. As much as one can at the time; *quantum satis* means in the language of lived truth, not "either-or," but "as-much-as-one-can." If the political organization of existence does not infringe on my wholeness or immediacy, it may demand of me that I do justice to it at any particular time as far as, in a given inner conflict I believe I am able to answer for. At any particular time; for here there is no once-for-all: in each situation that demands decision the demarcation line between service and service must be drawn anew—not necessarily with fear, but necessarily with that trembling of the soul that precedes every genuine decision.[33]

The decision that is of 'Jerusalem', therefore, approaches the political individual in the full force of its demands and the full weight of its contingency. "You let the cruel reality of both sides inflict itself on you without reducing it. You, theatre of war and judge, let the battle be fought out unchecked."[34] There can be no relying on established precedents to make the boundaries between the two conflicting claims more easily assignable.

> Sometimes, striving to be just I go in the dark until my head meets the wall and aches and then I know: "here is the wall I cannot go further." But I cannot know it beforehand otherwise.[35]

Although Buber runs into quite a significant paradox in trying to maintain, in the face of critics' probing, that these ethics of 'Jerusalem' are not elitist,[36] he acknowledges, indeed he stresses, the importance of the "teacher" in pointing out to the people the demands of genuine decision. As opposed to the "leader,"

> we call a teacher of the people a man who recognizes both the eternal truth and the present reality; the man who measures one by the other and teaches justice to the people: to recognize both, the truth in its lofty outstretching and reality in its sharp contradiction and to measure one by the other.[37]

Weighing and measuring, advancing and retreating, the person of 'Jerusalem' seeks to locate in each hour the farthest point of legitimate advance—"the line of demarcation."[38] It is this elusive line of demarcation that is the concrete, operational goal of Buber's thought. In its day-to-day pinpointing lies the great work of 'Jerusalem'.

One of Buber's closest associates has singled out this line of demarcation as his most significant contribution to political thought.[39] The present work is dedicated to the truth of that proposition; nevertheless there is a tendency to simplify the interaction of existence and utopia implicit in this "line," into adages like "as much as you can," "try your very best," and "the better is the enemy of the good," and to leave it at that. These are homespun bits of wisdom but hardly the paramount contribution of a major philosopher to thought. To see the line of demarcation in tactical terms only, as a policy of doing your best, is like concentrating on the line of scrimmage in a game of football without considering the goals at both ends of the field. The line of demarcation becomes significant only in perspective—as the shifting meeting-point in an ongoing clash of two total commitments. In itself it is of little moment; it is invested with importance by the magnitude of the forces involved in determining its location.

The more rigorous and systematic reader of Buber will inevitably, at one point or another, be bothered by the question of "sanctions." Allowing for all the authentically

wise things that Buber has to say about the human condition
and the need, at times, to compromise principles, even to
accept evil, what in the last analysis justifies it? What
sanction permits the person of 'Jerusalem' to make concessions to that which he plainly recognizes as evil? What
justification can Buber have when he enjoins the person of
spirit who faces clashing political demands "not to proceed
on principle," and to act "not in order to keep [his] soul
clean of blood," which he terms "a vain and wretched
enterprise?"[40] Is it a type of Kierkegaardian "suspension of
the ethical," a relative scheme of means and ends, or simply
a justification from necessity?

If one takes the last suggestion first, necessity alone must
be disqualified since it is a form of 'Rome', the submission to
the dictates of reality. As to a possible justification by some
kind of hierarchy of means and ends, Buber, as we shall see,
expressly rejects any doctrine that absolves iniquitous means
because they serve a desirable end. Suspension of the ethical,
although here Buber is more ambivalent, is likewise very
clearly not his point of departure because of the impossibility
of ever being certain that it is really the Absolute that has
demanded the sacrifice.[41] As the question is pursued further,
it becomes more and more knotty and less given to clear-cut
resolution. If, for example, one were to say, as has been
suggested, that for Buber no principle "is valid beyond the
power of human beings to realize it,"[42] one would run
headlong into another unavoidable—*why*? Why do moral
imperatives cease to be binding at a given point? Why should
moral precepts derive their binding force from anything
besides their intrinsic validity?

The intransigence of the problem should alert the ques-
tioner to the fact that somewhere in the course of the inquiry
he has taken a wrong turn. Actually, the difficulty stems
from the question itself because searching for systematic
criteria is entirely foreign to Buber's method and will yield
nothing but frustration and irrelevant answers.

Were Buber pressed to justify the use of force, or the need for compromise, he would emphatically disown any scheme that purported to give blanket answers or even specific hypothetical solutions to moral-political dilemmas. Sanctions must be sought in the inexhaustible, actually experienced, situation-bound world where real dilemmas arise and demand solution, not in a hypothetical constructions that fit this or that moral system. There are no general criteria that are valid, independent of real encounters with real situations. In the very final analysis, the justification lies in lived-life and lived-life alone. As Buber very characteristically writes,

> That meaning is open and accessible in the actual lived concrete does not mean it is to be won and possessed through any type of analytical or synthetic investigation or through any type of reflection upon the lived concrete. Meaning is to be experienced in living action and suffering itself, in the unreduced immediacy of the moment.[43]

And if the question is asked yet again—But what confers on lived-life or the "immediacy of the moment" the power of justification?—there can be no answer but the "holy insecurity" of the person, who stands before the awesome choices that present themselves and with the whole of his self attempts to answer. It may be annoyingly elusive for those accustomed to moral systems more readily tamed into consultable symmetry—"no teaching finds it so difficult to preserve its strength," as has already been noted, "as one which places the meaning of life in the working reality of the here and now and does not tolerate man's fleeing before the taxing infinity of the moment into a uniform system of Is and Ought,"[44]—but Buber will have it no other way.

One of the more unsettling lessons of political history is that "Machiavellianism" is a phenomenon not limited to unscrupulous power brokers, but very often characterizes just those who are most ardently committed to ideologies of social reform, political freedom, and national independence. If the ends, so the logic runs, are so overridingly desirable, then temporary lapses into opportunism are quite justifiable.

With the growth of modern social and political movements that claim to be grounded in absolutes of varying kinds, the classic question of means and ends becomes far more involved and dangerous. In addition to the familiar temptations of effective but immoral means to accomplish commendable ends, there now looms a "suspension of the ethical,"—not merely the desirability of the end outweighing the inequity of the means but a temporary abrogation, a dispensation as it were, from ethical responsibility—that is particularly seductive to those most aflame with ideals. "Time and again," Buber recounts,

> . . . when I ask well-conditioned young souls, "Why do you give up your dearest possession, your personal integrity?" they answer me, "Even this, this most difficult sacrifice, is the thing that is needed in order that . . ."[45]

But the question of obedience to the call for sacrifice "is preceded by the problematics of the hearing itself." "Moloch," Buber reminds his readers, "imitates the voice of God," so that where the "suspension of the ethical is concerned, the question of questions, which takes precedence over every other is: Are you really addressed by the Absolute or by one of his apes?"[46] This question is all the more pressing, since with the "death of God," that is, with the decline of the capacity to conceive, to sense, that which one is unable to confront visually or bodily, there no longer exists the possibility that a glimpse of the real Absolute will put the "apes" to flight.

The more standard question of means and ends receives, in Buber's hands, a compellingly straightforward treatment. "I cannot conceive anything real," Buber declares,

... corresponding to the saying that the end 'sanctifies' the means; but I mean something that is real in the highest sense of the term when I say that the means profane, actually make meaningless the end, that is, its realization.[47]

The revolutionary must be acutely aware that "what is realized is the farther from the goal that was set, the more out of accord with it is the method by which it was realized." The "insuring of the revolution," for example, "may only drain its heart's blood."[48]

For Buber this is a particularly significant point since genuine social restructuring—'Jerusalem'—in his view, is essentially a transformation in people, a renewal of their spirit. Success in reorganizing institutions, leadership, even ownership, he insists, must inevitably come to nothing if people remain unchanged. And while it might be argued—if formal reorganization were the desired end—that the irrefutable and visible success in ends justifies whatever means are required, there clearly can be no such case made for a teaching that sets its primary accent on the creation of "new men." Where the renewal of people is at stake, there can be no question of success through means that are antithetical to the goal. For it is inconceivable that a spirit of brotherhood can be cultivated through brother killing or that honesty can be promoted through deception. The preparations for a new human reality are the molds that determine its shape. In this sense, one can understand, in its full significance, Buber's arresting axiom: "No way leads to any other goal but to that which is like it."[49]

But Buber is not content to reject the justification of expedience; he goes considerably further. The complementary thesis that morality is good politics or at least that morality and successful politics must stand together in the long run, he claims is valid as well. While it is true that "politics of the moment do not accord with ethics," politics of a broader scope, a politics of permanence, that intends to survive not only the crises of the present but to strike enduring roots against the incessant batterings of reality, must plant itself squarely in the soil of ethics.[50]

This bold thesis is problematic on a number of grounds. If, when Buber writes that morality is good politics, he means that somehow a moral policy will find reward in the divine scheme, then he has come perilously close to that confusion of politics and religion of which he accused Gandhi.[51] But granting that this is not Buber's meaning, there remains yet a more difficult problem. How can this proposition be squared with Buber's oft-repeated contention that the successes recorded in history are predominantly not genuine successes, while the small voice of authentic accomplishment is most often unnoticed, disdained, frequently even brutally silenced?[52] If the moral is also the politic (and vice versa), this assertion is thrown into serious question. The pervasive themes of the Lord's "suffering servant," whose pure moral and political counsel suffers inevitable failure, and of the people of Israel, who to some extent are the "suffering servant" writ large, are difficult to sustain if, in the long run, morality is politically effective. Even if it is finally conceded that morality is, in fact, in the best interests of successful long-range politics, Buber's touching, quasi-biographical, highly self-conscious portrait of the prophet or teacher whose advocacy of moral awakening goes unheeded,[53] renders the issue largely academic. For if the moral policy, as good as it may be, is continually disregarded, its political efficacy is irrelevant.

Quite apart from the matter of internal consistency, Buber's thesis is very hard pressed to justify itself as a useful description of political realities. If Buber meant his dictum to apply only to Arab-Jewish relations (his comments in this regard are all in the context of Middle Eastern politics), to wit, just dealings, mutual recognition, dialogue are the only policies that will bring to realization the goals desired by both peoples, then his point is valuable, perhaps even prophetic. But if Buber intended his statements as more generally applicable rules of thumb—as the unqualified language strongly suggests—one must count it a dictum of only very limited usefulness. For although treacherous dealings over a considerable period may occasion reprisals, revolutions, or international isolation, history generously offers at least as many counter-examples in which injustice has triumphed with utter impunity.

"Hope for This Hour" is the suggestive title for the parting address that Buber delivered at Carnegie Hall at the end of his 1952 American lecture tour.[54] He outlined for his audience the underlying human problems upon which the Cold War rested and the possible grounds for hope that they might be overcome. Not the world wars or the Cold War, he summarized his argument a few months later, have "produced this crisis; it is, rather, the crisis of man which has brought the total war and the unreal peace that followed."[55]

"The crisis of man" that convulses our time refers to the decomposition of the normally tenuous strands of trust that bind people to one another; in Buber's words, "existential mistrust." There has always been and probably will always be a certain type of mistrust between people, but our age has made it so much a part of its ordinary perceptions that it is taken for granted that it cannot be otherwise. Symptomatic of this condition and reinforcing it as well, are the doctrines of Marx and Freud that attempt to unmask human motivation and to see in it the subliminal workings of either class interest or of unconscious drives. It is no longer a question of insincerity of willful deception—of which all realistic people are rightly wary—but an inexorable and permanent condition from which there is no escape. "One no longer fears that the other will voluntarily dissemble, but one simply takes it for granted that he cannot do otherwise." Rather than openly judging his words in themselves,

I listen for what drives the other to say what he says, for an unconscious motive say, or a 'complex' . . . My main task in my intercourse with my fellow man becomes more and more, whether in terms of individual psychology or of sociology, to see through and unmask him.

What is fundamentally at stake here is no longer the other's honesty or uprightness but the "inner integrity of his existence." This uncompromising game can only end in reciprocity, "as the unmasker himself becomes the object of unmasking."[56]

The very first casuality of the game is dialogue. Where trust has been eroded, the channels of dialogue are blocked. If the other is so comprehensively questionable, open and direct dialogue becomes virtually impossible; "the abysses between man and man threaten ever more pitilessly to become more unbridgeable."[57]

On the level of public life and the affairs between groups and nations, this devastating mistrust feeds the "political principle" by creating fears that are groundless and by inflating real differences to the point where they appear impassable. Only a strong regime, the strongest in fact, can protect against the nefarious intentions of the adversary. As people seek security against the threat of perceived danger from others, more and more authority is invested in the political province. The legitimacy of this authority becomes almost an article of faith. The state, as institutionalized fear and distrust, "not infrequently . . . fosters a perspective which allows differences of interest to appear as radical opposition. The accumulated power of mastery thrives on drawing profit from a—so to speak—latent exceptional condition."[58] Ironically, everywhere the corrosive power of relativism is keenly felt, but the state that exists in visible plurality stands absolute and without rival.

If Hobbes had made the state a "Leviathan," that reduced the realm of God to a part of the realm of Caesar, he at least acknowledged the unconditional superiority of God, be it only in matters of individual conscience and as the fount of truth. Two centuries closer to the present day Hegel did away even with this small remnant of independence from the world of Caesar. The state is the "ethical idea" itself, and there can be virtually no appeal beyond it. This position is the antechamber to the twentieth century.[59]

Where can this self-perpetuating and self-reinforcing cycle be broken?

The answer, Buber avers, surely does not lie in dismissing the illuminating insights of Marx and Freud, although their provinces of usefulness do need to be demarcated. People often perceive and speak through the filters of their social and psychological peculiarities, and insofar as this is true it must be reckoned with. Purity does not mean innocence. But the "human remainder" needs to be carefully cultivated, for it is the "hope for this hour." To confirm the other without either unmasking or accepting his conviction, to "wish to trust him, not blindly indeed but clear-sightedly"—here is where the dialogical immediacy between persons can be revived. Dialogue will be more discriminating, but by the same token it will be more authentic and sober. Only insofar as this more comprehensive realism is adopted, "can a genuine dialogue begin between the two camps into which mankind is today split."[60]

But what, Buber asks, gives us the right to hope that this may happen? The deepening crisis of confidence seems irreversible, and nowhere is there any beginning that might be pointed to as a sign of the future. Even "the debates between statesmen . . . no longer have anything in common with human conversation: the diplomats do not address one another but a faceless public."[61]

"Yes," Buber replies, "this must be said again and again, it is just the depth of the crisis that empowers us to hope." The glimmer of human awakening comes at the darkest hour. "This power begins to function when one, gripped by despair, instead of allowing himself to be submerged, calls forth his primal powers and accomplishes with them the turning of his very existence."[62] "I believe despite all," he affirms, "that the peoples in this hour can enter into dialogue, into genuine dialogue with one another . . . Only in this way can conflict while certainly not being eliminated from the world—be humanly arbitrated and led toward its overcoming."[63]

Finally, who can undertake to lead humanity into this era of dialogue? No one single identifiable or coherent group.

> There is, it seems to me a front—only seldom perceived by those who compose it—that cuts across all the fronts of the hour, both the external and the internal. There they stand, ranged side by side, the men of real convictions who are found in all groups, all parties, yet who know little or nothing of one another . . .[64]

These individuals who have overcome the mistrust in themselves, who have "no authority save that of the spirit," who are acquainted with the true needs of their own people and appreciate those of other peoples as well, form a scattered but faithful army that will come together out of the hostile camps and lead the dialogue between them.

In answer to those who criticized the "abstract" and vaguely idealistic arguments of his Carnegie Hall address, Buber clarified but nevertheless reconfirmed these very views.[65] He had indeed appealed beyond politics, "its perspective, its speech, and its usages," directly to the "genuine concrete" of the actual lives of actual people, attempting thereby to present an alternative to the "impotence of politicism." "Enmeshed in the political machinery we cannot possibly penetrate to the factual." The "encrustation of catch-words" and rhetoric make for a thick and immobilizing "political fictitiousness." "Enclosed in the sphere of the exclusively political, we find no means to relieve the present situation; its 'natural end' is the technically perfect suicide of the human race."[66] Again Buber stresses that' there are still some singular persons who have escaped total politization, and if they

> ... will begin to speak to one another, not as pawns on a chessboard but as themselves, partakers of human reality, a tiny seed of change will have been sown that could lead to a transformation of the whole situation.[67]

Nowhere else in his writings does Buber rely so completely, so uniquely, on pure exhortation and on the stubborn belief that crisis breeds solution. And certainly nowhere else does he reject politics so completely. These essays are also rare and extreme among Buber's writings in their attempt to cut through enormously complicated problems—often problems of real substance and undeniable density—with a breathtaking act of will.

Throughout his long and crisis-filled career, Buber tried to expose himself to the claims of both the ideal and the real. But it must be said that it was consistently the weight of the ideal that threatened to overturn the delicate balance. True, he never tired of reiterating his commitment to the "genuine concrete," the "here and now" and "actual life"; but these are frequently dramatic abstractions, emotionally charged formulae that are invoked to the extent that realism is repudiated. His early mysticism and utopianism, the yearning to soar unhindered, never really left him, and periodically they break through his defenses and will away the reality. In such cases one may be deeply moved, one may count him a man of extraordinary spiritual passion, but one cannot follow him.

But this type of thinking does not predominate. Precisely because of his early flirtation with utopian *hubris* and because of his awareness that this tendency endured within him, Buber was on his guard against spiritualizing politics, against

high-mindedness overreaching itself. He very typically takes
strong exception to the view that:

> Life allows itself to be permeated by religion, politics does
> not. A life that was to be permeated by religion would no
> longer know politics. Only the permeation of life with the
> yeast of the religious can one day deliver us from the serpent
> of politics that holds us ensnared with its cold coils.

If that were so, Buber argues, it would virtually mean "to
abandon public life to damnation here and now."[68] The
person of 'Jerusalem' is not content to transcend real political
issues by simply appealing for spiritual reawakening; this
implies the irredeemability of public life. Wherever the "line
of demarcation" between the desired and the possible may
fall, it must be within the political sphere itself.

What is surely most remarkable in Buber is the stubborn
optimism that he refuses to abandon—that he truly sits
astride both the tragic sense of failure that has been the
inevitable lot of the spirit and an irrepressible hope that
"nevertheless" the world will hear. Is it a perspicuity that is
lost upon us who are paralyzed with politics, is it a form of
stubborn delusion, or is it the unshirkable burden of the
Lord's suffering servant?

6

Jerusalem and Zion

Does there exist a Jerusalem?

Buber

NOWHERE is the synoptic integration of Buber's thought so apparent as in his Zionism. Here, virtually all the strands of his variegated thinking converge to present the fullest interplay of his ideas in their broadest framework. The philosophy of dialogue, communitarianism, utopian socialism, the biblical-prophetic vision, messianism, nationalism, education, merge here into a loosely bound, intellectually homogeneous but unsystematic totality. The various methodological and personalistic traits that mark Buber's approach—the dynamic of the existentialist and utopian viewpoints, the narrow ridge, the line of demarcation—appear as well, with great drama and revealing immediacy.

A few biographical particulars are highly relevant. Buber's association with Zionism, which spanned a period of more than sixty-five years, began in the closing years of the nineteenth century in the youthful Zionist circles of Berlin. From the very outset, as has been noted,[1] his was a dissenting voice. So much so that at one point, after a particularly sharp disagreement, Herzl wrote Buber asking that he try to "find his way back to the movement." But Buber persisted in his opposition. The series of 'unorthodox' (in every sense) addresses which he delivered between 1909 and the end of the First World War and which established his reputation as a

137

spokesman for the younger generation were at least as much elaborations of his singular Zionist perspective as they were *Reden über das Judentum*.[2] For this was and remained the distinguishing theme of Buber's Zionism: it would either derive its spiritual content and goals from prophetic messianic Judaism or suffer the fate of all other self-regarding, exclusivist nationalisms of the present time.

Buber's isolation in the Zionist movement was most clearly evident when, against the background of Arab violence toward Jewish settlers in Palestine, he addressed the Twelfth Zionist Congress in 1921. His admonitions against the rise of unrestrained Jewish nationalism were accepted with the kind of irritation and bitterness that generally greet moral preachments directed at people of action during the tense moments of political decision. The Sixteenth Zionist Congress of July-August 1929 at Zurich, was held under the sign of impending riots in Palestine that, in fact, exploded with hitherto unmatched fury the day following the close of the Congress. Buber appealed for "concrete" action to bring about an understanding between the Jewish settlers and the Arab population, but, according to at least one observer, his address was already marked by a tone of resignation.[3]

But the isolation and powerlessness that Buber suffered in the Zionist movement were overshadowed by the catastrophic events that followed the Nazi rise to power in January 1933. The various accounts of this period unanimously attest to the heroic efforts at education and spiritual resistance that made Buber a focal point of the Jewish community in its most desperate hour.[4] If one may speak of isolation at all in regard to these years, it is only the isolation the Nazis attempted to impose upon him in the face of his obviously effective attempts to rally the Jewish youth.

When, in 1938, his position in Germany was no longer tenable, the sixty-year-old Buber made the long-awaited move to Palestine. The change could not have been more drastic. From being the uniting symbol of German Jewry's resistance, he became a member of a small group on the very fringe of the Zionist movement that won only grudging tolerance at very best. From the leader and teacher who addressed a message of hope and national pride to his people, he became an often venomous critic and debunker of Zionist nationalism and goals.

The twenty-seven-year period that Buber lived in Israel can be conveniently divided in two: the first until the establishment of the State of Israel in 1948, and the second comprising the subsequent years until his death in 1965. What separates the two periods is not any change in policy but an alteration of circumstances that compelled different approaches to the same problem. Whereas until 1948, Buber's main goal in Zionist politics had been the cultivation of Arab-Jewish cooperation to culminate in a bi-national state, with the founding of Israel he turned to those possibilities that the new circumstances offered.

It is not my intention to recount here the full history of the development of Buber's Zionist thought.[5] All that is important for the present purposes is a framework into which the various ideas and pronouncements can be set. It is still less my intention to make any general judgments on the various positions that Buber or his opponents took in the many disputes that shook the Zionist movement during his lifetime. As these lines are being written in Jerusalem, the issues of Zionism are as alive as ever and very little would be added by partisan polemics. Above all, our aim here shall be to correlate Buber's Zionism with the rest of his thought and to present a picture of the "philosopher of realization" in the world of politics.

The first two decades of the twentieth century witnessed an intensification of nationalism in most of the Western world. National loyalty tended to replace or overshadow other forms of loyalty, whether to church, to family, or to locality. The Jews of Europe who emerged from ghetto life into the mainstream of Western thought at this time were deeply affected by the rise of nationalism, and Zionism, although it reflected the peculiarities of the Jewish experience, must be set into the context of this historical process.[6]

Yet with all that Jewish nationalism owed to the historical moment in Europe, Buber does not accept it in its prevailing forms and simply annex it to his own ideas. After being digested by Buber, nationalism, like all else he dealt with, emerges as a characteristic product thoroughly marked by his unmistakeable intellectual style.

"Every great culture that embraces more than one people," he writes in *I and Thou*, "rests upon some original encounter, an event at the source when a response was made to a *Thou*, an essential act of the spirit."[7] In less mystical language Buber writes, at approximately the same time, that the "concept 'people' [*Volk*] always implies unity of fate [*Schicksalseinheit*]." This unity "presupposes that in a great creative hour throngs of human beings were shaped into a new entity by a great molding fate they experienced in common."[8]

Seen from the perspective of "conscious and active difference," that is, when a *people* "grows aware that its existence differs from that of other peoples . . . and acts on the basis of this awareness," it has become a *nation*. This formative self-consciousness that sets well-defined goals in place of simple feelings of community and kinship issues from a decisive social or political transformation. The birth of the Roman Republic and the French Revolution[9] exemplify such transformations—each event providing a distinct orientation and particular mission for each people.

So understood, Buber places great positive value on the phenomenon of nationality. Following Moses Hess's assertion that "anti-national humanitarianism is just as unfruitful as . . . anti-humanitarian nationalism,"[10] Buber rejects the alternatives posed by the contemporary "struggle between nationalism which denies the spirit of the people and assimilation which denies the body of the people."[11] It is not simply literary caprice that led Buber to characterize his thought as "Hebrew Humanism." The adjective "Hebrew," is inserted "to prevent the misunderstanding that I am concerned with some sort of vague humanity at large."[12]

Abstract rootless humanitarianism and internationalism deny a prime source of human creativity and variety. A nation cannot free itself of its "historic responsibility" without simultaneously endangering its "innermost fruitfulness."[13] Only out of the polyphonic richness of the many nations, each striving to "shape its reality in the light of its own truth,"[14] can universalism—the harmony of numerous voices—escape the shallow, undifferentiated "good intentions" of a colorless internationalism.

Besides the consciousness of a particular task that nationhood imposes, it also provides the necessary context for its realization. Again Buber follows the lead of Moses Hess:

> As to effecting the unity of life and theory, it is only possible with a nation which is politically organized; such a nation alone is able to realize it practically by embodying it in its institutions.[15]

And Buber elaborates:

> The secret of the *nation* is that only in and through the nation can this distinction [between theory and practice] be converted into the fullness of life. Though something of righteousness may become evident in the life of the individual, righteousness itself can only become wholly visible in the structures of the life of a people. These structures enable righteousness to be realized, functioning internally within the various groups of the people, and externally in the people's relations to other nations; to function in abundance and diversity and with regard to all possible social, political, and historical situations. Only life can demonstrate the absolute and it must be the life of the people as a whole.[16]

Paradoxically, it is also the nation that is the laboratory of universalism.

For only an entire nation, which comprehends peoples of all kinds, can demonstrate a life of unity and peace, of righteousness and justice to the human race, as a sort of example and beginning. A true humanity, that is, a nation composed of many nations, can only commence with a certain definite and true nation.

The universal must be constructed out of healthy distinct units of particularity.[17] If "in the relations between various sections of this people, between its sects and classes," a nation can serve as a model of nationhood, it is simultaneously serving as a commencement of

> . . . a true fellowship of nations, a nation consisting of nations. Only nations each of which is a true nation, living in the light of righteousness and justice, are capable of entering into upright relations with one another.[18]

Moreover, the nation presents the best natural conditions for social renewal and the socialistic "life of community."

> The true connection between Nation and Socialism is discovered here: the closeness of the people to one another in mode of life, language, tradition, memories of a common fate—all this predisposes to communal living, and only by building up such a life can the peoples of the earth constitute themselves anew.[19]

Just as Buber identified the "social principle" with freedom and spontaneity, and the opposing "political principle" with coercion, in the present context, he juxtaposes the nation and the state. Nations historically represent creativity, states the ever-present attempt to force this fertile originality into the constraints of order.[20] By providing a common social and cultural matrix, nationality becomes a decisive component, both in the construction of socialist society and in furnishing that vital spirit which gives it life.

But as salutary as the benign potentialities of national feelings may be, there are few things so aberrant or destructive as these same national feelings that have deteriorated into exclusivist, self-glorifying nationalism. While each nation is called upon to preserve its particular point of view and to cultivate its own way of life—Buber deplores the growing indistinguishability of nations—this is subordinated to the great unity of mankind and must be designed to serve it.[21] Self-affirmation "in the face of the world" is a healthy and necessary phenomenon, but it requires simultaneously the affirmation of the other, his uniqueness and his due. To lose one's sense of balance, to blur the boundaries between one's rights and those of others—these are the hallmarks of aberrant nationalism.

Nationalism in its advanced form "regards the nation as the supreme principle, as the ultimate reality, as the final judge."[22] It recognizes no authority besides or above itself and being the holiest of ends it sanctifies all means that lead to its aggrandizement. It does not consider itself merely as a unique irreplaceable voice in the chorus of nations but as its soloist; the others lending only supporting accompaniment. This "progression" from *people* to *nation* to *nationalism* marks the movement in the psychological realm from spontaneity to self-consciousness to hyper-self-consciousness. As Buber writes:

> Being a people may be compared with having strong eyes in one's head; being a nation, to the awareness of vision and its function; being nationalistic, to suffering in connection with a disease of the eyes from the constant preoccupation with the fact of having eyes.

> In a people assertiveness is an *impulse* that fulfills itself creatively; in a nation it is an *idea* inextricably joined to a task; with nationalism it becomes a *program*.[23]

Still it should not be inferred from the foregoing that Buber finds no value whatsoever in nationalism and is anxious to discard it in all cases. Nationalism, like the state, is symptomatic of shortcoming. If the state points to a lack of natural community and functions as a substitute for it, nationalism attests to an incongruity between the task of a nation and the means at its disposal for achieving it. It acts as a signal of disease. Nationalism is, in fact, "nothing but an expression of the anxiety, weakness, and infirmity of a people. No strong, healthy people has known such a growth on its national feeling."[24] If this weakness, be it in regard to political unity, to independence or to territorial security, is remedied, then having fulfilled its purpose, nationalism will naturally lose its *raison d'être* and disappear. The danger appears, however, when nationalism somehow manages to establish itself as "*the* permanent principle," "when it tries to do more than overcome a deficiency." In such cases, "it no longer indicates disease, but is itself a grave and complicated disease."[25]

The history of nationalism, for Buber, is parallel to that of the state in that both of them originate with the breakdown of the secure "closed cosmic system" that typified united Christendom of the Middle Ages. People

... grew more and more specialized and at the same time isolated, and found themselves faced with the dizzy infinity of a new world image. In their desire for shelter, they reached out for a community structure which was just putting in an appearance, for nationality.[26]

Even if united Christendom was no "Kingdom of God," but only of a far inferior version—*Sacrum Imperium*—nonetheless

... there was still an authority which could moderate and make peace, which was above the self-glorification and will to dominate of the nations and the rule of the 'princes' was transcended by a spiritual power actual enough not to allow them to become 'gods'.[27]

But with the disintegration of Christianity, first institutionally, and then even as an effective moral force, the national groupings in which isolated individuals took their shelter, became, in the absence of any common restraining force, laws unto themselves. The shelter from uncertainty which they sought in the nation became in the course of time the only unshakeable certainty they knew.

Zionism, despite its similarities to nationalism in general, is on many counts a unique phenomenon. Most significantly, Zionism combines national existence with an interlocking community of faith. Of all the ancient peoples in whom faith and nation constituted a unity, only Judaism survived the combined thrust of Christian universalism and the fragmenting effect of the secular nation-state. Not until the Emancipation, when Jews began to enter the mainstream of European intellectual life, does the erstwhile unity—particularly its "faith" aspect—come under attack. But in sharp contrast to the position which sees Zionism as a secular national substitute for a no longer viable Judaism—as the severing of the concepts of people and community of faith—Buber approaches Zionism precisely as the potential fulfillment of the task of Judaism. Zionism is Judaism striving for realization.[28]

Before the Jews became a community of faith, they had already become a *people*, in virtue of a mighty shaping event—the Exodus from Egypt. No longer were they merely an aggregation; they had attained, through this great collective experience, to "that stage of self-evident unitedness that justifies the name *people*."[29] Nationhood came to the Jews when, through the revelation at Sinai, they were forged into a community of faith; when they saw themselves united in the light of a common "Center." Rising above simple self-consciousness, Israel became the carrier of a historic mission; it stood charged with chosenness, that is, the responsibility to establish the "Kingdom of God" on earth, to transform a community of faith into a community of deeds.

It is not fortuitous that the inception of nationhood and of the faith community emerged simultaneously from the identical catalyzing experience. The contemporaneity of birth portends a mission in common, a relationship of mutual dependence that cannot be rejected without at the same time renouncing the uniqueness of the Jewish experience and its source of creative energy. Faith and nation, for Buber, are to each other in approximately the same relationship as mind and body. Faith provides the direction and goal, nation the material framework; it is the "Center" about which the nation takes its stand. Faith requires nation to escape the lofty prison of abstractions, to embody itself concretely in a living reality; nation is dependent upon faith to supply purpose for what might otherwise be an inert mass of people.[30]

The challenge that confronts the people of Israel is to bridge the distance between the two and convert faith and nation into a single uncompounded unity. Ethics will be not only an inspiring idea but a visible quality expressed concretely in social institutions. Politics and religion will give up their claims to exclusive sovereignty over the profane and the holy. Politics, the amoral play of power, and religion, the sacrosanct "upper story of humanity," will converge in the seamless reality of the community of deeds. Only in the nation, in fact, can faith find full expression. And climbing still higher, we catch a glimpse of the pristine ideal—the Kingdom of God. Here, laid out before us, is a shimmering anarcho-theocratic vision of the actual rule of God without intermediaries, without theocrats. The sovereignty of God is far more real and effective than the rule of people, for it is authority without coercion and obedience without threat. The reality of God's kingship is earnestly recognized—not merely as an edifying theological metaphor. Each person in his or her own life and work absorbs and embodies this rule so that it becomes a living reality. Faith percolates into every part of the people's existence and activity, suffusing them so entirely that the community of faith and nationhood become virtually indistinguishable. Israel, the *faith-nation*, is to be the point of intersection between idea and reality.[31]

But Israel's task does not end here. The chosenness of Israel finds expression in its unique mission to the world. It is to be the spark that ignites the renewal of mankind and "Jerusalem," the source of that new social alternative that shall serve the world as a model. Israel is charged to become the radiating "Center" of a reconstituted world.[32]

Although failure is virtually unavoidable for even the most ardent pursuer of this vision, it is far from the chief danger that faces Israel. The main threat lies in the ever-present seductive power of "normalization," the rejection of chosenness—becoming, as the Israelites said to Samuel, "like all other nations."[33] While the precariousness and vulnerability of Jewish life in the Diaspora impelled many Jews to seek security through shedding their uniqueness, so long as Israel lived as a "ghost people," severed from its land, the danger of shirking uniqueness was an individual phenomenon limited to outright rejection of Jewishness.[34] The founding of the State of Israel has set the matter into a new—but still very old and biblical—perspective. Normalization in this context means conspicuously exploiting the national symbols while renouncing the responsibilities they entail; becoming just another political entity in the mediocre mainstream of political life—corrupted by its vices and partner to its goals. If Israel must begin with the particularities of its own experience so as to concretely embody its faith, the true prophetic-Zionist goal transcends nationhood in a vision of universal renewal.[35] For Buber then, the critical question for Zionism is: will Israel shoulder its chosenness, seeking its security precisely in its unique responsibilities, or shall it fall victim to the enticements of "normalization" and following the road of least resistance, turn its face on historical duty?[36]

But as with the utopian-socialist vision, it needs to be emphasized that Buber is presenting an ideal and not a program. Perhaps more clearly than anywhere else, Buber walks the line of demarcation in his Zionist activity. It is again a question of the proper boundaries, of advancing when advance is possible, and falling back when there is no other choice. So long as the spur of messianic fervor stands behind Israel's actions, compromise is legitimate. If, however, concessions issue from the desire to avoid obligations, to bury responsibility under the ballast of nationhood—flags, guns, and national anthem—then Zionism's right to exist is undermined.

Stepping down a few rungs from the unconditioned ideal, how does Buber see Zionism in more programmatic terms? One would do very well to begin by asking why the Zionists chose for their movement an old, biblical, poetic-rhetorical term like 'Zion', instead of some more popular, current expression like Judah, Israel, or Jerusalem. For Buber, the choice of 'Zion' is critical. More than being just a convenient label for a certain national movement, synonymous with simple Jewish nationalism, Zion conveys both the substance and program of a movement that is atypical. It is notably of very ancient vintage, "a continuation and restatement of an age-old religious and popular reality adapted to the universal form of the national movements of the nineteenth century,"[37] and not merely a "new invention" created in the aftermath of the French Revolution. But in a more profound sense, Zion points to the many sidedness of the Zionist idea. Zion, in its simple sense, is a place—either the hill of the Jebusite fortress captured by David (today to the south of the walled city of Jerusalem) or more loosely Jerusalem itself. "It is significant," Buber writes, "that this national concept was named after a place and not, like the others, after a people, which indicates that it is not so much a question of a particular people as such but of its association with a particular land, its native land."[38] Moreover, Zion is not only a place, it is also an idea; the idea of redemption and rebirth that animated the prophets, the idea of the millennium. Zion signifies both the Kingdom of God and the responsibility of the people of Zion to establish this Kingdom in their own land, the land of Zion. Composed of three distinct elements—the idea, the people, and the land—Zionism is charged with their integration. The land must be rebuilt by a people come alive through the power of an ideal.

The connection to the land, although made light of by Buber's non-Zionist sympathizers, is no mere symbol or incidental peculiarity. "It is a symbol because it is a reality," Buber wrote to Gandhi. "Zion is the prophetic image of a promise to mankind: but it would be a poor metaphor if Mount Zion did not actually exist."[39] For no symbol can have "authentic existence in the spirit if it has no authentic existence in the body. In order that Israel may become the first fruit of the divine harvest, it needs a real land as well as a real people."[40] Even the most dedicated attempt to realize the mission of Zion outside the framework of a live and functioning nation on its own soil cannot long endure.

Some promising experiments in founding just community life in the Diaspora—notably Hasidism—came to grief on just this point. The Hasidic experiment failed

> . . . because it did not aim for the independence, for the self-determination of the people; or to state it differently, because its connections with Palestine were only sporadic and not influenced by the desire for national liberation. Political corruption which invaded the Hasidic movement was the result of this deficiency.[41]

The operative principle in the life of these small, dependent communities could not be the actualization of justice; this requires an "autonomous national entity, autonomous national institutions," that are possible only "with the return to the Holy Land." In their absence, the principle of "brotherly love," vaguer, not given to concrete objectification, contingent upon the will of others, is the only bond upon which the community could rest.[42]

Moreover, even "a hundred adopted homes without one that is original, make a nation sick and miserable." Even though "the well-being and achievement of the individual may flourish on step-motherly soil, the nation as such must languish." "We need our own soil," Buber insists to Gandhi, "in order to fulfill it: we need the freedom to order our own life: no attempt can be made on foreign soil and under foreign statute."[43]

Not any "soil" will do—it must be Israel. The most despised of peoples and the most desolate of lands are wedded to each other for a "unique" and "incomparable" mission. Neither "the people without the land nor the land without the people" can consummate its purposes. The land, Buber suggests in a mildly mystical vein, appears in this relationship

> ... not as a dead, passive object, but as a living and active partner. Just as to achieve fullness of life the people needed the land, so the land needed the people, and the end which both were called upon to realize could only be reached by a living partnership.[44]

Furthermore, this land "has begotten our particular makeup, our characteristic energies, our personalities," and only this land "will renew them, will be able to beget them anew." And Buber adds poignantly: "A child who has suffered shock can be calmed only by his own mother; we, whose innermost lives have been convulsed by shock a thousand thousand times," can find repose only in the motherland.[45]

But as is so often the case with Buber, the land, the material, the existent, cannot stand by itself; alone it is merely a fact, a given. To settle and rebuild Palestine is only one-half the equation; without the shaping power of a guiding ideal it becomes merely a technical achievement. If it is true that "Israel would lose itself if it replaced Palestine by any other land," it is no less true that "it would lose its own self if it replaced Zion by Palestine."[46] The pervasive and underlying theme of dynamic union between the real and the ideal surfaces here once again. "The ideal of Zion is rooted in deeper regions of the earth and rises into loftier regions of the air, and neither its deep roots nor its lofty heights . . . must be repudiated."[47]

The simultaneous affirmation of both the soil and the idea is the special province of the people. Both soil and idea in themselves are immobile; the people as a dynamic catalyst constitute the bonding element. Notably, the synthesis to be so achieved by the people's active agency ends by including the people within itself. For the people contains elements of both body and spirit—being both a concrete nation and the embodiment of a certain consciousness or faith—and in the process of effecting the synthesis between land and idea their own inner duality is overcome. The regeneration of the people is thus conditioned upon their confronting the reality of the land with the imperatives of the idea. The new person created in this way, the *Halutz* (pioneer), is a unique synthesis of the idealist, tiller of the soil, Jewish nationalist, and, Buber claims (despite their denials), perpetuators of the biblical faith.[48] They are in every way the pivot of the Zionist movement, living exemplars of the striving for unity between theory and practice.

But what is it that qualifies the Jews, above all others, for this great world-historical task? Prima facie, Buber's unflattering portrait of Diaspora Jews would seem to rule them out as the agents of redemption. They lack precisely the wholeness of life that the union of idea and reality—that is, redemption—entails. As a people they are "onesided in development," suffering from "barren intellectuality" and "a detached and somewhat intellectual holiness," while taking "no part in the production of goods."[49] They exemplify most radically the dualism between life and spirit, between the national ideal and the national reality. They are, in short, the most unredeemed of people.

Paradoxically, however, the depth of the Jewish tragedy is also the secret of its promise. In an argument that contains remarkable parallels to the young Marx's description of the

dialectical self-emancipation of the proletariat, the young
Buber writes:

> This then, is, and continues to be Judaism's fundamental
> significance for mankind: that, conscious as is no other
> community of the primal dualism, knowing and typifying
> division more than any other community, it proclaims a world
> in which dualism will be abolished, a world of God which
> needs to be realized in both the life of individual man and the
> life of community: the world of unity.[50]

Out of its position as the archetype of duality, Israel most
clearly recognizes the "archehuman," the "universally human," and becomes "the most distinct embodiment, the
exemplary representation of one of the mind's most supreme
elemental ideas,"[51] that is, the wholeness of redemption.

The third factor of Buber's Zionist synthesis, the idea—
upon which we have touched only very lightly to this point—
is where he parted company from most of his associates
within the movement. If one were simply to strip away some
of the more characteristic expressions which dominate
Buber's presentation to this point, one would be left with the
skeleton of a Zionist program that would be acceptable to
most Zionists. The Jewish people, the program would run,
devastated for two millenia at the hands of various oppres-
sors, needs its own ancestral home in order to prevent the
tragedy's recurrence, to recover from its traumatic suffering,
to normalize its life as a nation. The Zionist, when faced with
the further question: "but to what end?" is not a little
unnerved. "Are not these ends sufficient?" he retorts indig-
nantly.

No! Buber replies—a movement like Zionism cannot find
its sole justification in that it helps people.[52] From his earliest
years in the Zionist movement, when he campaigned for
education toward aesthetic-cultural renaissance, to an 1918
letter to Franz Oppenheimer in which he asks for his aid in
preventing the growth of "*Umgeist*" in Palestine,[53] to his last
years spent in adult education, Zionism meant for him above

all a movement of national and social renewal. Most of his polemics with other Zionist leaders center on just this point: is a "Jewish state" the goal of the Zionist movement? True enough, Buber asserts, the purely "spiritual center" that Ahad Haam and others supported, fails to meet the felt needs of a wander-weary people.[54] "I do not fail to appreciate," Buber writes, "the great historical significance of the Jewish state."[55] Alone, however, it is a pyrrhic victory.

From the very outset, Buber's attack was directed against those who felt that the main efforts of Zionism should be on the diplomatic front. Herzl, as a prime example, tirelessly traveled from one political leader to another, trying to secure support for his idea of a Jewish National Home. But, Buber argues, this is to mistake formal recognition for actual accomplishment. Diplomacy may be indispensable for acquiring confirmation of an already present reality, but it can be only an adjunct to the real task of creating it. Without a movement to establish a renewed Jewish settlement in Palestine, a community surviving on the strength of its own inner commitment, diplomatic machinations are tantamount to building a house—from the second floor up. Diplomacy, like revolution in Buber's utopian-socialist thought, may clear away obstacles, but it cannot create a new reality.[56]

The "political Zionists'" error, Buber contended, began at the most basic level, that is, their general conception of the Jewish state. Here again, Herzl's *Der Judenstaadt* and *Altneuland*[57] are typical. Jewish nationalism, so Buber interprets Herzl, is a reaction to anti-Semitism; *nationalism* in the exact sense of Buber's typology. Were anti-Semitism to vanish, so would Zionism. There is, in Herzl, no positive content to the Jewish settlement in Palestine. He fails to see the great chain of history reaching back to Sinai that sets the entire movement into perspective. From his shallow, liberal, unhistorical viewpoint, the land only needed to be secure and the Jewish problem was well on its way to solution. Given this assumption, diplomatic maneuvering was the obvious tactic. So long as the land was made available—from whom and under what conditions was of little importance—the rest was simply a matter of course. Questions such as national renewal or Zion's singular mission were quaint but hardly relevant. Herzl's purely political approach to Zionism reflected a noble humanitarian venture that was entrapped in the present because it had neither roots in the past nor a sense of mission for the future. This was "the tragic shortcoming of Herzl's nature," that although he spoke as a leader of Jews, he was far removed from Jewishness, and although he was critically instrumental in realizing the fondest of Jewish dreams, he had little inner sense of the animating Jewish vision.[58]

Max Nordau, Herzl's first lieutenant, expressed the impatience of the majority with Buber and his circle when he disqualified the educational-cultural work they supported as "only theoretical." For Buber, however, it was anything but a theoretical luxury. "Rebirth" was the purpose of Zionism. Zionism without a national renewal meant creating yet another *Galut* (Diaspora) but this time in the land of Israel. The land and the language, as Buber summarized the majority's program, are not ends. Of course,

> . . . without the language there can be no success but still it depends on what is said in the language. Without the land there can be no success but still it depends on how the land is lived in. To think that the land and the language will, of themselves, bring everything to be appears to me like Bakunin's belief that the autonomous revolution needs no direction or teaching, rather the whole of mankind will teach itself.[59]

If Zionism does not encourage a deep-reaching process of individual and national regeneration, it is "an empty word." "Do not rely on Palestine," he warned. "Zion will not arise in the world if it is not prepared in the soul."[60]

In later years, faced by the growing hatred between the Jewish and Arab communities in Palestine, Buber was willing to sacrifice the autonomous Jewish state to bi-nationalism precisely because what mattered above all else was preserving the conditions in which renewal might take place. A Jewish state could survive in the political atmosphere of the 1940s only at the price of its inner purpose. His position vis-à-vis the Arab community was not only—or even mainly—a question of social humanitarianism but rather an attempt to preserve Zion "in the soul" (in this case by respecting the justice of the Arab claim) so that it might still be realized in the world.[61]

On the occasion of his first visit to Palestine in 1927, Buber formulated the relationships of the three component elements of Zionism in a manner that was, despite the differences in terminology, quite consonant with the tripartite typology presented here. He speaks of the development of the Zionist idea as the progression of three stages: *Staatzionismus, Kulturzionismus,* and *Wirklichkeitzionismus.*[62] Now it has been shown on a number of occasions how Buber's historical progressions are, in effect, nothing more than his own position examined through the unfolding of its various immanent components.[63] In this case, *Staatzionismus,* lowest of the way stations on the road to the complete idea, corresponds to the element that was earlier identified as the land. It implies a domination over the land that is meant to bring the "political Zionists" to mind. *Kulturzionismus* is the realm of the spirit. It implies a Zionism rooted in the detached idea and corresponds to the position of Ahad Haam and perhaps to the young aesthete Buber as well. The third term, *Wirklichkeitzionismus,* represents the Zionist idea in its fullness. Here, the idea and the land, through the agency of a realizing people, grow into unity. It implies a meeting of the ideal and the real in the here and now of lived life.

But if this species of revolutionary Zionism is truly based on *Wirklichkeit,* as Buber insists it is, why will it escape the fate that *Wirklichkeit* has visited upon all other revolutions? Buber, after all, is profoundly aware of the perennial failure that overtakes even the purest of intentions. Yet Zion may well be different.

Even while he calls upon the young to "resist" the inevitable forces that conspire to strangle renewal,[64] he nevertheless argues that Zion presents a unique opportunity for success. If it offers a virgin and totally malleable land to the sculptor of renewal, as did early America, it offers something even more important—the great prophetic tradition of a just society. America, while certainly not built in an intellectual vacuum, can claim no such preexistent, unified or widely influential body of guiding precepts.[65]

More significantly yet, the revolution of Zion will not be forced to choose between the Scylla and Charybdis upon which most revolutions are shipwrecked. The effectiveness of Western revolutions is undermined because in "existing institutions both the decayed roots of sovereign rule and the seeds of community" coexist. The result is that revolution pulls both out of the ground, which means that the healthy growth in need of care is destroyed along with whatever should be destroyed. In the absence of continuity or tradition, the revolutionaries "yield to a self-glorifying intellectualism," trying "to build everything anew out of cerebral concepts." Or, on the other hand, the revolution, "fearing either the task of new creation or impairment of the young growth . . . shies away from setting to work on the decaying material."[66] The result in either case is a stillborn revolution; in the one case because with the past abolished, the present has no inner sustaining power, and in the other because the retained past will soon overcome the present.

Zion is uniquely endowed in that it does not have "to rebuild an already existing structure" and face the consequences of either too great or too small a break with traditional historical patterns. It begins with a material tabula rasa. But its tradition, its memory, carries "the exalted commandment to establish a genuinely communal . . . settlement." This is, then, the ideal merger of circumstances: a fallow, waiting land and a philosophy of realization that is as yet unfulfilled. True, Buber cautions, "we must separate the pure and eternal aspects of this tradition from the impure and temporary," but this, we may infer, does not present the serious dangers inherent in Western revolutions.[67]

Here as well, the struggle against countervailing forces will be made less severe because of the land's relative isolation. There will be few of the myriad social pressures that confront a budding human experiment trying to function in the midst of a hostile society.[68] The experiment will have virtually unlimited freedom of endeavor, full scope of choice, and full weight of responsibility.

But beyond the circumstantial advantages lies the heart of the matter: the enormous viability of *Wirklichkeitzionismus*. It is neither uniquely a reaction to pressing needs, as Herzl had envisioned, nor a lofty idea like the "cultural home" that has no essential relation to hard fact. The singular force and staying power of *Wirklichkeitzionismus* lie in the wedding of the purest of ideals to the most trying of realities.

When Buber speaks of *Wirklichkeitzionismus* he has in mind particularly the pioneering settlers, the Halutzim, who, having left the traditional Jewish civilization of Europe, came to Palestine with thoughts of totally renewing themselves both as people and as Jews through a radically new socialized form of life. Upon their arrival, they confronted a resisting land that thwarted any but the soundest and soberest of intentions. Here, the fastidiousness of doctrinaire purism, the airs of café socialism, the tendency to extravagance and faddishness, perished in short order. The socialist forms that gradually grew out of this collision of intentions and necessity are the "Jerusalem" that Buber so admired and the source of his hopes for the Jewish settlement in Palestine. Plekhanov is said to have remarked that the Jewish Socialists of the Bund were all Zionists afraid of seasickness. Whatever the justice of this comment, for Buber Zionism and socialism were integrally united in the person of the Halutz.[69]

In the popular mind, these social forms have a single shorthand label: kibbutz. The truth is, however, that there exists a great deal of diversity within the general form, ranging from community ownership and use of only the most vital and expensive machinery to complete community involvement in virtually all phases of collective and individual life. The searching experimentation with new forms and ideas that led to this diversity and the fierce ideological pride and competition among them, point up the vitality of the movement and prompted Buber to hope that it would survive where others had failed.

> New forms and new intermediate forms were constantly branching off—in complete freedom. Each one grew out of the particular social and spiritual needs as these came to light—in complete freedom, and each one acquired, even in the initial stages, its own ideology—in complete freedom, each struggling to propagate itself and spread and establish its own proper sphere—all in complete freedom. The champions of the various forms each had his say, the pros and cons of each individual form were frankly and fiercely debated— always, however, on the plane which everybody accepted as obvious: the common cause and the common task, where each form recognized the relative justice of all other forms in their special functions. All this is unique in the history of cooperative settlements.

And Buber adds by way of conclusion:

> What is more, nowhere, as far as I can see, in the history of the socialist movement were men so deeply involved in the process of differentiation and yet so intent on preserving the principle of integration.[70]

True though it may be that the Jewish village commune "owes its existence not to a doctrine but to a situation . . . to certain problems of work and construction" that dictated collective efforts, it is equally true that ideals were not just an afterthought, "something to be added that would justify the accomplished facts." The key to the "non-failure" of the kibbutz and presumably the grounds for hope in its future lie in the spirit of the founders in whom "ideal motives joined hands with the dictates of the hour." Out of this union a tentative but tenacious social form emerged.

> The important thing is that the ideal motive remained loose and pliable in almost every respect. There were various dreams about the future: people saw before them a new, more comprehensive form of the family; they saw themselves as the advance guard of the Workers' Movement, as the direct instrument for the realization of socialism, as the prototype of the new society: they had as their goal the creation of a new man and a new world. But nothing of this ever hardened into a cut-and-dried program. These men did not, as everywhere else in the history of cooperative settlements, bring with them a plan, a plan which the concrete situation could only fill out, not modify; the ideal gave an impetus but no dogma, it stimulated but it did not dictate.[71]

Buber sensed that the Halutz, like the Hasid, embodied a striking renewal of the human spirit. This renewal was neither theory nor program but real life.[72] In his life the line between idea and reality was virtually imperceptible. The common meal, the decision on budget, housing, or work were, in the deepest sense, ideals which had become life. The sublime inspiration of even such giant figures as Goethe, Thoreau, or Tolstoi, was, by comparison, intellectual, self-conscious, incomplete. For the Halutz was no longer the "man of spirit" such as characterized the West and especially the Galut, where humanity was known and sought after, but a spontaneous "man of life" in whom humanity "was lived with the simple perfection of one in whom renewal has entered the blood."[73]

The Halutz then was far from being an ordinary pioneer. He had not come to settle and build a new territory but to restore an old land and to materialize an age-old idea. Neither would his pioneering role terminate when the land had been reclaimed. As opposed to other movements of national liberation, the role of the Halutz was not to end with the one-time sacrifice that would succeed in liberating his country from foreign domination and setting free his people's particular genius. His was a "permanent revolution," a total revolution that committed itself to the building of a new life, a new people, a new environment. This could not be accomplished through a coordinated series of historical actions of even the most sacrificing and courageous nature but only through the continuous, day-to-day grappling with the regeneration of his people.[74]

Permanent revolution skirts the fringes of the eschatological, and Buber does indeed approach the kibbutz with an awe worthy of the millennium. This is understandably so—since the kibbutz is the crowning linchpin of his thought, where all its separate components fuse into a single form. Buber's socialism is incarnated in the self-sufficient community-cooperative that joins with others like itself to form a *consociatio consociationum*. His Zionism, too, comes to full expression only in these pioneering nationalists who incorporate a dream as well as a reality into their lives. The biblical-messianic vision, Buber claims, was, despite its secular dress, the ultimate impetus for their efforts, and so the kibbutz represents, as well, a contemporary case of the prophetic spirit at work.[75] Similarly, the educative role of the kibbutz as a "center" brings into play the philosophy of education through encounter and example that Buber advocated.[76] 'Renewal', 'communitarianism', 'dialogue', and the rest of the terms that can be strung together to complete the fabric of Buber's thought are all intimately connected with and refracted through the kibbutz.

Beyond the affinities of policy, method, and purpose, Buber was attracted to a certain ethos that surrounded the Halutzim. This spirit, although quite difficult to capture precisely, expressed itself generally in a desire to view social problems in terms of the widest, most generically human considerations. Being part of an elite that came from all classes, the Halutz was above class. As part of a movement for general renewal, he disdained small-minded, factionalist, party politics. His was a *movement* not a *party*. And although the Halutz was part of a highly select elite, he was concerned above all with service to the community.[77]

These spiritual qualities, together with what Buber regarded as the three fundamental guidelines of the Halutz's program—productive work on the land, the common life of community, and federation into a community of communities[78]—and all this under the sign of the dynamic meeting of idea and reality, fed Buber's eager sense of hope with the presentiment that here at last was a spark that might ignite first the renewal of the *Yishuv* (Jewish settlement) and then go on to become a universal phenomenon. In the spirit of Isaiah's prophecy, Buber writes that "the renewal of the world and the renewal of Zion are one and the same thing, for Zion is the heart of the renewed world."[79] And to continue the progression: the Halutz is the heart of a renewed Zion. "The land is built around him and the people is built around him."[80] Renewed and revitalized, the land and the people of Israel are to be the source of universal emulation and inspiration.

> The people of Israel is called upon to be the herald and pioneer of the redeemed world, the land of Israel to be its center and the throne of its King.[81]

It is exceedingly simple to ridicule the romanticized and overdrawn elements in the picture of the Halutz which Buber presents. It is even simpler to make light of Buber's expectations from the perspective of the present. Still, anyone who has been exposed to the kibbutz, met its people, or sensed its spirit cannot doubt that something truly extraordinary took place (and to some extent is still taking place) here.

Without entering the polemical arena in which kibbutz ideology and practice are still highly controversial matters, one judgment may be made with relative certainty. If Buber could go no further in the forties than to describe the kibbutz as a "signal non-failure," there has not taken place since then that positive movement which would warrant the verdict "signal success."

Some of the dangers that the kibbutz (as well as any other communitarian group) would have to face successfully in order to survive and influence its surroundings were enumerated by Buber on various occasions. These constitute in some sense a catalogue of the ills that beset the cooperative movement today. First of all, Buber warned that the kibbutz could not survive as an isolated phenomenon and still retain its position as the seed of social renewal. "If there arise around her cities that are thoroughly without spirit, the spirit of kibbutz will disintegrate as well."[82] To a significant degree the kibbutz is now involved in just such a struggle, trying to preserve its values (and members) from the enveloping allure of the city's consumerism and materialism.

A great deal of the difficulty involved in this struggle lies, paradoxically, in the success that the kibbutz has had in raising standards of living and competing with the city. For if the advantages of kibbutz are perceived in material terms, that is, what it can provide in terms of housing, work opportunities, or the carefree life, then each person is compelled to make a calculus of pleasures and pains and decide accordingly. Only if there is something more, a mission linked to history, a purpose that transcends short-term conveniences, can the kibbutz retain its uniqueness and exert influence on the community at large. This is the basic substance of Buber's second warning. "The Halutz who lacks the historical perspective is likely to arrive at a technical naturalism . . . the ethos of such a 'self-sufficient' world is ephemeral because it is not continually nourished anew by an ultimate bond with Being."[83]

Another factor that threatened to erode ideals was the large immigration the Yishuv and the kibbutz had to absorb during the Nazi period and in the aftermath of the war. These new immigrants were not the young idealists who leapt into the malaria swamps or the desert with a vision of the future, but a huddled, frightened mass who had escaped to a haven from oppression. The problem was intensified and complicated when in the space of a very few years, in the early and middle fifties, another very large influx of immigrants, this time from North Africa and the Middle East, with very different cultural and technological perspectives crowded into Israel. How to welcome them but nevertheless preserve the Halutzic spirit was among the knottiest of problems the kibbutz had to face.[84]

As a result of the weakened position of the kibbutz and its semi-defensive posture vis-à-vis the community at large, Buber sensed that a compensatory politicization of its role was taking place. This made federation a creature of political organization rather than a natural, geographic or mutual interest union, more a function of party solidarity than a reflection of the free dynamic of association. The same challenges threatened to convert the "solidarity despite differences" that unified the founders into a self-preserving particularism, an egoism of the group, that would make of each successful kibbutz an exclusive joint stock company, jealously guarding its own privileges against all others.[85]

Yet, from the time in the twenties when he first focused upon the potentialities of the Jewish cooperative movement in Palestine as a new social alternative,[86] to the very last months of his life, Buber never lost hope in the possibilities and the hidden strength of the kibbutz. At the age of eighty-two he was still able to declare, "Despite all, I dare to believe."[87]

The "line of demarcation"—or as Buber expresses it in a more literary-existential spirit, the "narrow ridge"[88]—is not a comfortable place. On this lonely and often unpredictable way, losing one's footing is an ever-threatening danger. It calls for the exhaustingly constant exercise of discernment and tact, while blocking access to the beckoning beaten path.

Buber's involvement with Zionist politics is an attempt to live such a teaching, and it presents a number of concrete examples of the way the theory was translated into practice.

From his earliest days in the Zionist movement, there surfaces occasionally a momentary expression of dissatisfaction with the literary-aesthetic character his thought was assuming. Ironically, the first of these takes the form of a thankful retrospective glance in which he disavows the vaguely utopian and romantic beliefs he held in the past—and all this at the inception (1901) of his mystical period.[89]

His formula "*Gegenwartsarbeit*,"[90] exhibits more élan than understanding of constructive work and though it is a portent of the reality-centered orientation to come, it reveals Buber's weakness for abstract 'salon' realism.

More than a quarter of a century later (1928), Buber addressed a league of Left Zionists on the necessity of building a socialist Palestine.[91] Judging from the tenor and substance of the address, his audience contained uncompromisingly idealist elements who opposed cooperation with bourgeois Zionists, refused assistance from them, and rejected all forms of private initiative in Palestine. Buber begins by identifying himself as a "Jewish socialist whose point of departure is reality and not ideology."[92] It must be recognized, he adjures his listeners, that there is no chance of building the type of all-or-nothing socialism they champion, given reality as it is. The line of demarcation must be drawn to include all those things possible at this moment and to work for the future inclusion of what remains beyond our power today. To those who rejected bourgeois financial support, Buber answers that one cannot live honestly with the Zionist idea without realistically surveying the actual situation and the ways to its overcoming. The youth, he continues, has

> . . . found fault with our speaking of money, our needing it; and the money is not ours. As if we could implement the work

of construction without money, or as if we could receive any other money besides just this. If the youth, even now, in this difficult hour, want to live in the clouds, they forfeit their task to their people. They must see the difficulty of the situation and that it cannot be evaded.[93]

Private enterprise too must be accepted, if only it harmonizes the profit motive with the national good.[94] And Buber concludes with a singularly compelling encapsulation of his thought that bears repeating:

> We do not choose our situation, we are entangled in it, and now we need to show that we are up to it. Not the preservation of purity at any price is what matters, but mastering the situation and the preservation of purity together. What matters is to preserve the idea just where it is most difficult to do so—in confusion. True purity is not innocence. The real trials of life do not take place outside of life, but rather in the bustle and tumult, where it seizes you, where it takes your breath away, and where you nevertheless can prevail . . . In every hour utopia must confront—a confrontation of life with topia. This is the authentication in entanglement: as much as you can in every hour.[95]

Seven years prior to this conference, Buber had taken an active part in the Twelfth Zionist Congress in Carlsbad. Aside from the two addresses he delivered[96] and the *Kongressnotizen*[97] that followed, he authored a draft resolution on the Arab-Jewish conflict that came in the wake of a number of bloody incidents in which Jewish settlers lost their lives. His draft began with a restatement of the Zionist resolve to build a Jewish settlement in Palestine despite the violence against them and ended with a passionate declaration that the Jewish national will was not and would not be directed against any other nation. In the event, his draft was rewritten, condensed, and partially altered.[98] Deeply shaken by the changes that were made Buber withdrew from Zionist politics for a number of years, devoting himself instead to "questions of general human significance."

Writing many years later, in an open letter to his close friend Judah L. Magnes, Buber recalls the episode and gives a striking picture of the difficulties facing the man of spirit embroiled in the backrooms of political intrigue. He tells how his draft resolution was brought to the drafting committee that had to pass on the final version of the text offered the Congress.

> At this point something took place, that for professional politicians is as routine and simple as can be, but it frightened me to such a degree that until today I have not freed myself from it. In the drafting committee that was composed for the most part of old friends of mine, one small revision and another small revision and another were proposed. Each one, ostensibly, had no decisive importance and all of them were explicitly argued on the grounds that the resolution had to be edited in a form that would be acceptable to the Congress.

His objections were set aside with the words,

> Do you want only a gesture, or do you want the Congress to accept the principle of Jewish-Arab cooperation, to make the issue its own issue and fight for it? If this is what you want, you must agree to these small changes.

Not wanting to be left with a touching but ineffective gesture, Buber ultimately yielded to the asked-for changes.

When the final version was at last completed, he was struck by its beautiful but perfunctory sentences, from which it seemed to him the heart and soul had been removed. Still, he agreed to present it to the Congress. "But I felt then," he writes to Magnes,

> ... that my role as a 'politician', that is, as a man who participates in the political activity of a group, had ended. I had started with the matter, and it was upon me to bring it to conclusion; but as for something new in which I would again be forced to choose between the truth and the realization—this was forbidden to me.[99]

Fifty years after the fact, it is difficult to understand the great moral crisis that Buber faced. A comparison of the two versions of the draft does not really make clear the insurmountable problems they posed to his conscience or justify his withdrawal from Zionist politics. True, there are differences between the versions. But for the most part they are not substantial. Buber's version is characteristically fervent and literary, while the final draft is businesslike and rather prosaic in style. They exemplify admirably the differences between an impassioned manifesto and a political resolution. Apart from the explicit reference to the "unscrupulous Arab leaders," to whom Buber had referred only obliquely, and a mention of the Balfour Declaration that Buber had omitted, the final draft contains all the points of the original version drafted by Buber. And although it might be argued that the general impression made by the two drafts is different—the final version having a more belligerent tone—at least part of this is due to the translation into political terms of an emotive message and the naming of the parties to the conflict explicitly.[100].

The stark choice between "truth" and "realization," that Buber saw, is very fundamentally opposed to the spirit of his teaching and must be reckoned as the most significant departure from the "narrow ridge" of his political career. He descended into the real world of political give and take and found it incompatible with preserving his own purity. The advice he gave to the dogmatically idealistic Left Zionists [101] went unheeded by Buber in the moment of crisis. The precariousness of the "narrow ridge" is attested to by its author himself.[102]

Far more typical, however, was Buber's position regarding Jewish statehood. Nowhere, in fact, was the teetering balance of the "narrow ridge" more finely poised than in the events that directly led up to and followed the foundation of the State of Israel in 1948. The situation in the middle forties had deteriorated rapidly. Barely a day passed without headlines announcing some bloody act of terrorism or reprisal. Jews were just beginning to learn the full story of the Nazi holocaust, and they reacted with feelings of profoundest determination that they would finally have their own national home. The Arabs, confronted by the prospect of mass Jewish immigration and frightened that they would lose their numerical superiority, hardened their position and resolved not to permit any Jewish advances. Very few were in the mood for compromise.

Still, there were those who worked in this volatile atmosphere to accomplish the eleventh-hour miracle. There had been a series of associations for promoting Arab-Jewish rapprochement dating back to 1925 and the general idea of bi-nationalism can be traced back to a 1921 essay of Ahad Haam,[103] but never before had the issue been more burning or tragedy more imminent. Most active among those seeking to avert the looming catastrophe was the group known as the Ichud or Union.[104] Founded in 1942 by Judah L. Magnes, President of the Hebrew University, the Ichud was dedicated to a program of bi-nationalism and to the construction of a joint Jewish-Arab economic base on which a bi-nationalist society could be founded. Buber was highly active in the Ichud, contributing articles,[105] speaking publicly, testifying before committees of inquiry,[106] and perhaps most important for him, cultivating personal contacts with Arabs of all types.

Characteristically, what mattered primarily to Buber was not the international diplomatic arena where white papers on partition or parity of population reflected some passing interest, but a concerted effort to build up an enduring dialogue between the two peoples out of the life-contacts fostered by integrated economic activity. While real differences between Jews and Arabs plainly existed, they were not nearly so irresolvable as the political hysteria, fostered by the various parties and demagogues on both sides, made them appear. The matter-of-fact reality underlying the political turmoil presented problems that, in an atmosphere of mutual respect, could be honorably worked out. "More often than not conditions are affected by the mass intoxication with fictions, without which, it seems, most people can no longer go on in a dreadfully complicated world." Nurtured by "fictitious" political ideas, an "emotional surplus" transforms difficult problems into impossible ones. Politics, far from reflecting the problem itself, is responsible for its aggravation.[107].

Only if the "realities of life" are "given a chance to force the walls of political fictions" can the immediacy of real human speech begin to do its work. The inverted image, in which a political "superstructure" dictates to the socio-economic "infrastructure," must be righted. The primacy of "economics over politics" needs to be asserted and through the expansion of joint ventures, which will bring thousands of Arabs and Jews together in the immediacy of real life, the dialogue necessary for living side by side will begin.[108] Buber agreed wholeheartedly when Magnes wrote: "It is fatuous to think that good will can be engendered through abstract formulas. Good will can come through life . . . ."[109]

It was often charged against Buber that the bi-national solution suited his tastes very well because he had neither appreciation for the land nor sympathy for the dream of an autonomous Jewish people in it.[110] This of course was quite untrue.[111] It was not with ease or with joy that Buber relinquished his ideal of an all-Jewish Palestine. But, he began with the conviction that "neither people can get in Palestine all it wants and both people will have to make concessions." [112] In order to prevent the inevitable bloodshed and to prevent—even in the eventuality of a Jewish victory— a fortress Israel living by its military prowess in hostile Arab encirclement, [113] Buber was willing to forego the ideal of total independence in favor of bi-nationalism. It was all reality would allow. And it was enough, provided that the national rights of the Jewish community were guaranteed and an autonomous national existence was possible.[114]

Less public, but in Buber's eyes at least of equal importance, were the personal, daily contacts he went out of his way to cultivate with the Arabs of Abu Tor—the largely Arab neighborhood of Jerusalem in which he lived. Even in the very last months before the outbreak of hostilities, Buber and his wife made a point of very conspicuously walking the streets of Abu Tor and keeping alive the warm relationships they had developed with their Arab neighbors. As the prospect of war grew closer and closer, all of the Jewish inhabitants of Abu Tor left their homes and took sanctuary with family or friends in the Jewish quarters of the city—all, that is, except for Buber. He stubbornly refused to leave, ignoring pleas of the Jewish authorities that he do so immediately. He continued his walks, assuring those he met that so long as was possible he would remain, and insisting that his presence meant that the hope of dialogue was not dead. Finally, with war just hours away, an armored car of the Jewish military came into Abu Tor and removed Buber and his family to safety. In the haste of departure they were unable to take with them either their large collection of paintings and sculpture or the enormous library [115] accumulated over the years. During the fighting, his home was guarded against pillaging by some of his Arab friends until he returned during the cease-fire and finally removed his belongings.[116]

Prior to and during the war Buber wrote what are surely the most vitriolic polemics of his career. He aimed his attack against the nationalists in particular and more generally against all those who, in his view, were narrow-mindedly complacent about the justice of the Jewish position. The reader can sense the almost deliberately provocative tone and timing Buber chose in his last-ditch attempt to shock the Jewish population into an awareness of the moral issue as he saw it. Perhaps most outstanding is the short article he wrote in 1948 shortly after the Arabs opened the attack on the newly proclaimed state. "Enough! Let us put an end to falsities," Buber cried. "The truth is that *we* began the attack 'peacefully', when we began to trickle into the land."[117] Nearly a decade earlier, speaking of German anti-Semitism, he turned on those whom he felt had adopted Hitler's methods and used them for the Zionist cause, with a paroxysm of unparalleled bitterness: he who follows such a teaching "does Hitler's work in the land of Israel because he desires that we worship the god of Hitler after calling him by a Hebrew name. And he who does Hitler's work will be swallowed up together with him."[118] Returning to very much the same theme in the spring of 1948, he again went to the limit of his ability to provoke:

> This Zionism profanes the name Zion; it is nothing more than one of the coarse nationalisms of our day that recognize no authority above the—imaginary—interest of the nation. I would say that it reveals itself as a form of national assimilation that is more dangerous than any individual assimilation; for the latter did not corrupt any but the individuals and families that were assimilated, while national assimilation disintegrates the seed of Israel's selfhood.[119]

After words of this kind, it would naturally be expected that their author refuse participation in the fighting, even renounce his ties with the movement gone astray. Understandably, there were those who reacted in just this way. But Buber, struggling on the tightrope drawn taut between the oppositions of a cruel hour, had no such recourse. In an retrospective mood he reflects:

> A half-century ago when I joined the Zionist movement for the revival of Israel, my heart was complete. Today a tear runs through it. A war over political structure is liable to change, at any moment, into a war over national existence. Therefore I cannot do otherwise but take part in it with my own existence, and my heart trembles today like the heart of every man of Israel. Still, even in the face of victory I will not be able to rejoice, because I fear that a victory of the Jews may well mean the downfall of Zionism.[120]

The war itself was "the most grievous of the three"[121] that Buber lived through. Zionism had not proved itself up to the demands placed on it. But still his people were engaged in the agony of war. If the ideals of the past had been violated and the prospects for the future were dim, the present compelled his close association with and support for the fighting men of the young state.

When the war came to an end, Buber once again returned to his role of critic, gadfly, and educator. He condemned the 1956 Sinai Campaign as an adventure in the service of imperialism, called for equality of treatment and rights for Israel's Arab citizens, and for efforts to relieve the sufferings of the Arab refugees. He also became deeply involved with adult education, particularly for those thousands of immigrants from North Africa and the Middle East.[122]

Among Israelis, he was quite an unpopular figure a *Propheta in Patria*; his name, more often than not, bringing a sour smile to their lips. And paradoxically, while this name became a household word in the West, it was largely ignored, even unknown, among the youth of his own country. Still in 1958, the octogenarian wrote:

> The form of the Jewish Republic that was born out of the war, the State of Israel, I accepted as my country. I have nothing in common with those Jews who take it upon themselves to dispute the factual form of Jewish independence. The commandment to serve the spirit must be fulfilled, from now on, in this country and from inside it. Still, he who will serve the spirit truly and with all his heart is commanded to attempt to set straight that which has been distorted until now; he is commanded to toil to restore and clear the road to mutual understanding with the Arab people, a road that is at present covered by rubble.[123]

Conclusion

Martin Buber is a writer with whom it is difficult to compromise. His philosophical personality is such that the reader either becomes so completely engaged with the substance and style of the message that there is a virtual suspension of all critical detachment; or the cool cutting edge of reason, unwilling to drop its defenses against the onrush of stirring human sentiment, dissects, examines, and otherwise undermines the message. To the detached reader, his engaged counterpart seems accepting, impressionable, unsophisticated. The engaged reader for his part, judges his critical colleague, cynical, niggling, impertinent.

The greater part of the research on Buber falls into one of these two categories. A significant number of serious works go through hundreds of pages with no word of doubt, to say nothing of criticism. The tone ranges from reverent to hagiographical. Buber's works are edited into inspirational snatches, his biography told with much pious I-and-Thou-ing, his prophetic visage emblazoned across countless book covers. Critical works, by contrast, pay no heed to Buber's authentic wisdom or to his penetrating insight to which open-hearted readers cannot help but respond. Their approach, although often pointing to clear deficiencies in Buber's thought, misses the real issues by a wide mark. The fragmented version of Buber they present lacks any of the magnetic humanity that breathes life into the original. They truly miss the forest for the trees.

Buber himself recognized the dangers of both approaches. He rejected the title "prophet" that was so often thrust upon him, while castigating his 'detached' critics for their curiously lifeless analyses. What Buber asked of his readers was only that they allow themselves to be addressed personally and respond with no less of their 'selves' than he gave to the appeal. To lose oneself so thoroughly that dialogue is no longer possible, violates the first principle of real relation: there must be both *I* and *Thou*; dialogue requires that one relate but yet withstand. On the other hand, detachment deliberately cuts itself off from the source of understanding. There are, to be sure, two parties to the relationship but they do not speak to one another. Here, then, is the reader's "narrow ridge"—to become a real partner in a dialogue, neither malleable to the point of passivity, nor recalcitrant to the point of resistance; to become a "single one" facing a "single one."

At least part of the problem involved in approaching and interpreting Buber is the difficulty in distinguishing between the man and the thinker. The thought *was* the man. The tension between existence and utopia, for example, was as much a personal phenomenon as an intellectual matter. There is virtually nothing in the thousands of pages of published writings that can be said to be 'academic' or simply 'scholarly'. Buber's goal, the goal of an advocate rather than an observer, was to convert, not to convince.

Normally, with philosophers whose thought presents itself as detached from the author, arguments and contentions may be cooly assessed and disinterestedly scrutinized. Buber, however, is so integrally involved with his work that this normal process is no longer adequate. Buber's own spiritual passion speaks through his words in a way that lends force to his writings, not explicable simply in terms of the ideas themselves. The voice of the man is heard above the written word. His moments of real greatness are moments of great humanity. And this is perhaps the secret of the matter: Martin Buber was a rare phenomenon among professional philosophers—he was a greater man than he was a thinker.

Notes

1   The Origins of a Philosophical Temperament

1. *See*, for example, Georg Gerster, *Trunken von Gedichten* (Zurich, 1953), p. 143.

2. His main contributions to Jewish scholarship were his editions of the *Midrash*, a large body of allegorical, ethical, exegetical material on the Bible. Buber's own concerns with Hasidic legend and Jewish "myth" are very much in the spirit of his grandfather's work.

3. Chaim Weizmann, *Trial and Error* (New York, 1949), pp. 86-87. Although Weizmann's judgment may be somewhat harsh, it indicates something of Buber's character at the time. He writes: "I was often irritated by his stilted talk which was full of forced expressions and elaborate similes, without, it seemed to me, much clarity or great beauty . . . in a sense it may be said that Feival [a close associate of Buber] gave to Zionism, losing himself in it, and Buber took from it, using it as his aesthetic material."

4. Ahron Eliasberg, "Aus Martin Bubers Jugendzeit," *Blätter Des Heine-Bundes* (April 1, 1928), no. 1, p. 4. He was prone to "Jewish Anti-Semitism," writes this contemporary, often using the term "echtjudisch" in censure. For interesting pictures of Austrian intellectual life at that time *see* William M. Johnston, *The Austrian Mind: An Intellectual and Social History 1848-1938* (Berkeley and Los Angeles, 1972); Hans Kohn, *Karl Kraus, Otto Schnitzler, Otto Weininger: Aus dem judischen Wein der Jahrhundertwende* (Tubingen, 1962); William McGrath, *Dionysian Art and Populist Politics in Austria* (New Haven, 1974) and *Critique*, August-September, 1975 (dedicated to *Vienne, Début d'un siècle*).

5. *See*, for example, "Uber Jakob Boehme," *Weiner Rundschau*, vol. V, no. 12 (June 15, 1901), pp. 251-53. His doctoral thesis of 1904 (which is an unpublished manuscript in the Martin Buber Archive, Hebrew University, Jerusalem) also deals with Christian mysticism of the Renaissance period. On his dissertation and the entire mystical phase of Buber's youth *see* Paul R. Flohr's excellent unpublished Ph.D. Thesis, *From Kulturmystik to Dialogue: An Inquiry into the Formation of Martin Buber's Philosophy of "I" and "Thou"* (Brandeis University, 1973) *passim*, as well as Flohr's "The Road to *I* and *Thou*: An inquiry into Buber's Transition from Mysticism to Dialogue," in Fishbane and Flohr, eds., *Texts and Responses: Studies Presented to Nahum N. Glatzer* (Leiden, 1975), pp. 201-25.

6. *See* George L. Mosse, *Germans and Jews: The Right, the Left and the Search for a "Third Force" in Pre-Nazi Germany* (New York, 1970), esp. ch. 4. *See also* Mosse's *The Crisis of German Ideology; Intellectual Origins of the Third Reich (New York, 1964);* Fritz Stern, *The Politics of Cultural Despair* (Berkeley and Los Angeles, 1961); Walter Lacquer, *Young Germany* (London, 1962); Hans Kohn, *The Mind of Germany* (New York, 1960). Buber's recently published correspondence is an excellent source for his

early breathless aestheticism. *Martin Buber, Briefwechsel aus sieben Jahrzehnten,* Herausgegeben und eingeleitet von Grete Schaeder (Heidelberg, 1972) esp. editor's introduction on p. 44 f. For Buber's later reflections on the great aesthetes and poets he so admired in his youth *see* Werner Kraft, *Gesprache mit Martin Buber* (Munchen, 1966). Something of the period's general mood can be sampled in H. Stuart Hughes's excellent *Consciousness and Society* (New York, 1958); Roger Shattuck, *The Banquet Years* (New York, 1968); Holbrook Johnson, *The Eighteen-Nineties: A Review of Art and Ideas* (London, 1913); and Gerhard Masur, *Prophets of Yesterday: Studies in European Culture 1890-1914* (New York, 1961).

7. Paul R. Flohr and Bernard Susser, "Alte und Neue Gemeinschaft: An Unpublished Buber Manuscript," *American Jewish Scholar's Review,* vol. I, 1976, pp. 41-56.

8. For the *Neue Gemeinschaft* circle see Hans Kohn, *Martin Buber, sein Werk und seine Zeit. Ein Versuch über Religion und Politik* (Cologne, 1961), pp. 28-39; Albert von Hanster, *Das Junge Deutchland, Zwei Jahrzehnte unterlebten Litteraturgeschichte* (Leipzig, 1900), pp. 17-20, 59-61, 82, 85. *See also* Buber's introduction to *Gustav Landauer, Sein Lebensgang in Briefe* (Frankfurt, 1929), and Landauer's "Die Neue Welterkentnis," *Die Kultur,* I (1902), 616-17. The major writings of the Hart brothers—leaders of the circle—are *Die Neue Gemeinschaft: Ein Orden vom Wahren Leben* and part two: *Das Reich der Erfullung: Flugschriften zur Begrundung einen Neuen Weltanschauung* (Leipzig, 1901).

9. "Alte und Neue Gemeinschaft," p. 51.

10. Ibid., p. 53.

11. Ibid., p. 55.

12. Landauer's description of one of the circle's meetings is worth citing.

It was a beautiful moment full of religious atmosphere when we set ourselves up on a beautiful spot at the lakeside. There was a wonderful evening light over the lake and the pines, storm clouds in the sky and distant thunder during the recital of the opening poem by Heinrich Hart which was followed by a longer, more serious, profoundly conceived recital of Julius Hart. Life! Life! rang out of these words of both brothers while nature echoed the call.

Gustav Landauer, Sein Lebensgang in Briefe, I, p. 56.

13. *See* "Ein Wort über Nietzsche und die Lebenswerte," *Die Kunst im Leben* (December, 1900), p. 13.

14. *The Philosophy of Martin Buber* volume of *The Library of Living Philosophers,* eds. Maurice S. Friedman and Paul Arthur Schilpp (LaSalle, Ill., 1963), p. 13 fn.

15. Ernst Simon, Introduction to *Teudah Veyeud,* vol. II, *Am Volam* (Hebrew), Zionist Library (Israel, 1961), p. 13. His early descriptions of Herzl have an unmistakable Nietzschean ring. *See* "Er und Wir," *Die Jüdische Bewegung,* vol. I (Berlin, 1920), pp. 198-99.

16. "Ein Wort über Nietzsche," p. 13.

17. "Judaism and Mankind," *Martin Bber: On Judaism,* ed. Nahum N. Glatzer (New York, 1967), p. 29.

18. Buber's early Zionist writings focus on the Jewish 'proletariat'. *See,* e.g., "Herzl und die Historie," *Die Jüdische Bewegung,* I, pp. 164 ff.

19. "Von Jüdischer Kunst," ibid., pp. 61 ff.

20. "Hebrew Humanism," *Israel and the World: Essays in a Time of Crisis* (New York, 1963), p. 240.

21. For an account of the activities and policies of the Democratic Opposition *see* Israel Klausner, *Haopozitzya l'Herzl* (Hebrew) (Jerusalem, 1960).

22. "Er und Wir," *Die Jüdische Bewegung*, I, p. 202.

23. "Die Schaffenden, das Volk und die Bewegung," ibid., p. 73.

24. "Von Jüdischer Kunst," ibid., pp. 64-66.

25. "Die Schaffenden, das Volk und die Bewegung," ibid., pp. 70-73.

26. *Rome and Jerusalem*, trans. Meyer Waxman (New York, 1943), pp. 245-48.

27. Hans Kohn, *Martin Buber sein Werk und seine Zeit*, pp. 14-15, 22.

28. Maurice S. Friedman, ed., *The Tales of Rabbi Nachman* (New York, 1956), p. 10.

29. Maurice Friedman, trans., *The Legend of the Baal-Shem* (New York, 1969), p. 7.

30. *Tales of Hasidim, The Early Masters*, I (New York, 1961), p. 134.

31. Ibid., p. 277.

32. Buber's "conversion" to Hasidism was not quite as sudden as his confessional style would indicate. He had already expressed himself warmly on the subject about a year earlier. He writes flatly: "Der Chassidismus ist die geburt des neuen Judentums." "Kunst und Judentum," *Die Jüdische Bewegung*, I, p. 250. Would Buber's conversion to Hasidism be complete without the following letter from his father? "It would make me happy, were you to forego these Hasidic and Zohar [the major Kabbalistic text] matters that waste the spirit and have such unwholesome effects. It is a pity that you expend your talents on so fruitless a theme and consume so much work and time for something that is useless both to you and the world." *Briefwechsel* I, letter 124. *See also* letter 215.

33. "My Way to Hasidism," *Hasidism and Modern Man*, ed. Maurice S. Friedman (New York, 1958), p. 59.

34. *Tales of Rabbi Nachman*, p. 14. In the same spirit Buber writes:

Just that which you do in the uniformity of recurrence or in the disposition of events, just this answer of the acting person to the manifold demands of the hour, an answer acquired through practice or won through inspiration, just this continuity of the living stream leads—when accomplished in dedication—to redemption. He who prays and sings in holiness, eats and speaks in holiness is mindful of his business, through him the fallen sparks are raised and the fallen words redeemed and renewed.

The Legend of the Baal-Shem, pp. 37-38.

35. "My Way to Hasidism," *Hasidism and Modern Man*, p. 59.

36. *The Legend of the Baal-Shem*, pp. 17-23, esp. p. 19.

37. *Tales of Rabbi Nachman*, p. 10. For critiques of Buber's interpretation of Hasidism *see* Gershom Scholem, "Martin Buber's Hasidism," *Commentary*, vol. 32 (1961), pp. 305-16; Rivkah Schatz-Uffenheimer, "Man's Relationship to God and World," *The Philosophy of Martin Buber*, pp. 403-34, and Mayer Oron, *Chasidut Be'aspaklaria shel Buber* (Hebrew) (Haifa, 1970).

38. "Alte und Neue Gemeinschaft," p. 54. Although Tönnies is not mentioned by name, it is clear that Buber refers to him in his remarks.

39. Tönnies wrote important studies on Hobbes and Marx and was deeply influenced

by their work. *See Thomas Hobbes der Man und der Denker* (Stuttgart, 1896). He also edited Hobbes's *Behemoth* and *The Elements of Law*. For Marx, *see Marx: Leben und Lehre* (Jena, 1921).

40. Talcott Parsons, *The Structure of Social Action* (Glencoe, Ill., 1949), p. 688.

41. Ibid., p. 690.

42. Interestingly, Buber gives the term *Gegenwartsarbeit*, commonly used by the SPD to denote reformist day-to-day activity [*see* Robert C. Tucker, *The Marxian Revolutionary Idea* (London, 1970), pp. 189-90], a distinctly heroic ring. *Die Jüdische Bewegung*, I, pp. 17-22.

43. Despite Tönnies's protestations that the sociologist must "examine" phenomena "with the same attitude of factual objectivity with which the naturalist observes the life of a plant or an animal" [*Gemeinschaft und Gesellschaft* (Leipzig, 1887) preface], there is little doubt as to where his own sympathies lay. *See*, e.g., J. Leif, *La Sociologie de Tönnies* (Paris, 1946), p. 69.

44. Martin Buber, ed., *Die Gesellschaft. Sammlung Sozialpsychologischer Monographien* (Frankfurt am Main, 1906) Introduction to vol. I—Werner Sombart,*Das Proletariat*, p. x.

45. *Philosophy of Martin Buber*, p. 702.

46. For an excellent general discussion see Carlo Antoni, *From History to Sociology* (London, 1962).

47. H. A. Hodges, *Wilhelm Dilthey, an Introduction* (London, 1944), pp. 135-37. *See also* Howard N. Tuttle, *Wilhelm Dilthey's Philosophy of Human Understanding: A Critical Analysis* (Leiden, 1969).

48. Hodges, p. 127.

49. Ibid., p. 125.

50. Ibid., p. 113.

51. Ibid., p. 114.

52. Buber's comments on his relationship to Hasidism express Dilthey's methodological principle excellently. "I had to tell the stories I had taken into myself from out of myself as a true painter takes into himself the line of the models and achieves the genuine images out of the memory formed of them." "My Way to Hasidism," *Hasidism and Modern Man*, p. 61. And again: "I bore in me the blood and spirit of those who created it and out of my blood and spirit it has become new," *Legend of the Baal-Shem*, p. 10. J. Coert-Rylaarsdam writes in regard to Buber's biblical studies: "Only a viewpoint that is biblical in a very profound sense could so consistently illuminate every part of the bible it touches."

53. *Philosophy of Martin Buber*, p. 702.

54. These views are faithfully reflected in Buber's unique 'anarcho-theocratic' interpretation of the development of authority in the biblical narrative. *See Moses: The Revelation and the Covenant* (New York, 1958), *Kingship of God* (New York, 1967), and *The Prophetic Faith* (New York, 1960). Something of this approach may also be found in Buber's drastic account of Jewish history. The direct and intimate relationship to God as found in 'myth', 'saga' and Hasidic popular mysticism is set squarely against the cramping "codification of religious laws" that attempts to "erect an eternal dam against the passion of the people." Myth "is the expression of the fullness of existence, its image, its sign; it drinks incessantly from the gushing fountain of life." "Positive religion," on the other hand, rests on an enormous simplification of the manifold and wildly engulfing

forces that invade us: it is the subduing of the fullness of existence." He concludes that "the history of the Jewish religion is in great part the history of its fight against myth." *Legend of the Baal-Shem*, pp. 11-12.

An interesting (friendly but not uncritical) discussion of Buber's tendency to disparage structure whether as law, ritual or tradition can be found in Ernst Simon, "Martin Buber V'Emunat Yisrael," *Iyyun, A Hebrew Philosophical Quarterly*, vol. 9, no. 1 (January, 1958), esp. pp. 13-24. A more frankly critical view is presented in Gershom Scholem, "Martin Bubers Auffasung des Judentums," *Neue Zuricher Zeitung* (Sonntag 2, April, 1967), p. 6 and continuation (Sonntag 9, April, p. 6). Of great interest and perception is Baruch Kurzweil's "Kavim Le'Dmuto shel Martin Buber," *Haaretz*, June 18, 1965 (Hebrew).

55. *Beitrage zu einer Kritik der Sprache* (Stuttgart, 1906).

56. Ibid., I, p. 2.

57. Ibid. (2nd ed.), I, p. x.

58. Ibid., I, p. 54. Buber is very likely responding to Mauthner's biblical "In the beginning was the word," when he writes in *I and Thou*, "In the beginning was relation."

59. *See* Gershon Weiler, "On Fritz Mauthner's Critique of Language," *Mind*, vol. 67 (1958), pp. 80-87 and Hermann Wein, *Sprachphilosophie der Gegenwart* (The Hague, 1963), ch. 4.

60. There have been a number of recent studies on Landauer. Wolf Kalz, *Gustav Landauer: Kultur Sozialist und Anarchist* (Meisenham am Glau, 1967); Charles B. Maurer, *Call to Revolution: The Mystical Anarchism of Gustav Landauer* (Detroit, 1971). Much the best is Eugene Lunn's *Prophet of Community: The Romantic Socialism of Gustav Landauer*, (Berkeley and Los Angeles, 1973). The most recent work which came to my attention as this book was going to press is Ruth Link-Salinger (Hyman), *Gustav Landauer: Philosopher of Utopia*, (Indianapolis, Ind., 1977).

61. Landauer was then engaged in his Meister Eckhart translation *Meister Eckharts mystische Schriften, in unsere Sprache Ubertragen von Gustav Landauer* (Berlin, 1903) while Buber was preparing his doctoral dissertation on Renaissance mysticism. (*See* fn. 5 this chapter.)

62. Landauer settled accounts with the Hart brothers in *Skepsis und Mystik, Versuch in Anschlus an Mauthners Sprachkritik* (Berlin, 1903), pp. 61-82.

63. Ibid., *passim*. Buber was clearly speaking for himself as well when he discussed Landauer's evaluation of Mauthner in "Gustav Landauer" *Die Zeit*, band 39, no. 506, p. 127. Mauthner remained close to Buber nevertheless, and his "Die Sprach" appeared in Buber's *Die Gesellschaft*, no. 9 (1906). Despite their differences Landauer accepted Mauthner's contention that formal language cannot truly capture the essence of ideas. *See*, e.g., *Der Werdende Mensche*, Herausgegeben von Martin Buber (Potsdam, 1921), p. 21.

64. Hans Kohn, *Martin Buber, sein Werk und seine Zeit*, pp. 28-39 and *passim*.

65. Landauer (and Buber) identified Marxism with its Kautskian, Social Democratic variant. (*See* ch. 4 following.)

66. *Aufruf zum Sozialismus; ein Vortrag* (Berlin, 1919).

67. Ibid., p. 1.

68. Cited by Buber in "Landauer und die Revolution," *Masken*, vol. XIV (1919), pp. 18-19.

69. It appeared from 1906-1912 with a total of forty volumes. Some of the more

important were: no. 1, Werner Sombart, "Die Proletariat"; no. 2, Georg Simmel, "Die Religion"; nos. 4 and 35, Eduard Bernstein, "Die Streik" and "Die Arbeiter Bewegung"; no. 13, Gustav Landauer, "Die Revolution"; nos. 14-15, Franz Oppenheimer, "Der Staat."

70. Ludwig Lewisohn, *Cities and Men* (New York, 1927), p. 200.

71. They are included in *Reden über das Judentum* (Frankfurt am Main, 1923); (English Translation in *Martin Buber: On Judaism*).

72. See *Deutsches Judentum in Krieg und Revolution 1916-1923*, Herausgegeben von Werner E. Mosse (Tubingen, 1971), especially the essays by Mosse, Friedlander, Tramer, and Reichman; Hans-Helmuth Knutler, *Die Juden und die deutsche Linke in der Weimar Republic* (Dusseldorf, 1971), pp. 45-67; Otto Baumgerten, "Die Wirkungen des Weltkrieges auf das Seelenleben des deutschen Volkes," in *Geistige und Sittliche Wirkungen des Krieges in Deutschland*, Herausgegeben von Otto Baumgerten (New Haven, 1927).

73. See "Landauer und die Revolution," *Masken* and *Briefwechsel* I, p. 63, 67-69.

74. See ibid., I, letters 384, 385, 386, 387.

75. "Renewal of Judaism," *On Judaism*, p. 35.

76. Ibid., pp. 34-35.

77. "Judaism and Mankind," ibid., p. 25.

78. Ibid., p. 33.

79. Ibid., p. 28.

80. "Das Gestaltende," *Die Jüdische Bewegung* I, p. 206.

81. Ibid., pp. 206-7.

82. "Renewal of Judaism," *On Judaism*, p. 37.

83. "Das Gestaltende," *Die Jüdische Bewegung* I., p. 209 ff. *See also* ibid. (only the 1916 edition), p. 244. For Buber's later views on the prophet *see The Prophetic Faith*, pp. 111-12, 175-76.

84. "The Spirit of the Orient and Judaism," *On Judaism*, p. 73.

85. Ibid.

86. Ibid., p. 93.

87. Maurice S. Friedman, *Martin Buber, The Life of Dialogue* (New York, 1960), p. 50, fn. 3.

88. "Dialogue," *Between Man and Man* (New York, 1965), pp. 13-14.

89. "With a Monist," *Pointing the Way*, p. 28. First appeared February 1914 in *Die Wiessen Blatter*.

90. *Pointing the Way*, introduction, p. xvi.

91. "On My Philosophy," in *Existentialism from Dostoyevsky to Sartre*, ed. Walter Kaufmann (New York, 1958), p. 133.

92. There is no adequate account of the *Fortokries*. See *Briefwechsel* I, pp. 63-66; Romain Rolland, *Au-Dessus de la Mêlée* (Paris, 1915); Rene Cheval, *Romain Rolland, L'Allemagne et la Guerre* (Paris, 1963).

93. For a discussion of Buber's relation to 'Volkish' ideas *see* the author's "Ideological Multivalence: Martin Buber and the German Volkish Tradition," *Political Theory*, vol. 5, no. 1, February 1977, pp. 75-95.

94. *See* "Bewegung. Aus einem Brief an einen Hollander," *Der Neue Merkur* (München, January-February 1915). *Briefwechsel*, I, letter 250, Martin Buber, *Von Geist des Judentums* (Leipzig, 1916), pp. 46-48; "Die Tempelweihe," *Die Jüdische Bewegung* I, pp. 239-41, "Die Losung," ibid., II, pp. 7-15.

95. See *Briefwechsel* I, letters 264, 306. *See also* "Herut: On Youth and Religion," *On Judaism*, p. 159.

96. *See Deutsches Judentum in Krieg und Revolution 1916-1923*, Herausgegeben von Werner E. Mosse, *passim*.

97. *Prophet of Community*, pp. 317 ff.

98. *Briefwechsel* II, Letter to Ludwig Strauss, 18, dated 22 February 1919.

99. Ibid., I, p. 63, 67-69.

100. "The Holy Way," *On Judaism*, p. 114.

101. Ibid., p. 115.

2 The Narrow Ridge

1. T. M. Knox, trans., *Philosophy of Right* (New York, 1967), p. 103.

2. J. B. Baillie, trans., *Phenomenology of Mind* (London, 1931), pp. 666-67.

3. *I and Thou* was published in 1922, but Buber had started work on it as early as 1917.

4. While certain earlier post-1912 works contain somewhat analogous dichotomies (e.g., "Das Gestaltende," *Die Jüdische Bewegung* 1, pp. 205-16 and esp. *Daniel. Gespräche von der Verwirklichung*, Leipzig, 1913), Buber is there distinguishing between two different types of human actors—"forming" and "formless," "realizing" and "orienting"—with the implicit assumption that the 'heroic' person can choose to reject the type of which he disapproves. It is not that each person is possessed of a dual nature but that there are two types of people. In *I and Thou* it is the world that is inescapably twofold—there is no *I-Thou* as opposed to an *I-It* person. There is a necessary duality in the relationships between man and the world. It "is the sublime melancholy of our lot that every *Thou* must become an *It* in our world." (*I and Thou*, trans. Walter Kaufman, New York, 1970, p. 68.) For the sake of uniformity, I have throughout retained "Thou" in place of Kaufman's "You."

5. Ibid., pp. 143-44. Elsewhere he writes: "According to the logical conception of truth only one of two contraries can be true, but in the reality of life as one lives it they are inseparable." "The Faith of Judaism," *Israel and the World, Essays in Times of Crisis* (New York, 1963), p. 17.

6. "Preface," *On Judaism*, p. 8.

7. *Kampf um Israel. Reden und Schriften* (Berlin, 1933), p. 274.

8. Donald J. Moore, *Martin Buber, Prophet of Religious Secularism* (Philadelphia, 1974).

9. Hans Urs von Balthasar, "Martin Buber and Christianity," *The Philosophy of Martin Buber*, volume of *The Library of Living Philosophers*, eds. Paul Arthur Schilpp and Maurice S. Friedman (La Salle, Ill., 1963), p. 365.

10. Hans Urs von Balthasar, *Martin Buber and Christianity* (London, 1961), p. 46.

11. "Martin Buber and Christianity," p. 351.

12. *Martin Buber and Christianity*, p. 77.

13. "Judaism and Civilization," *On Judaism*, pp. 195-96.

14. "What Is Man?" *Between Man and Man* (New York, 1968), p. 184.

15. Alexander Dru, ed. and trans., *The Journals of Sören Kierkegaard* (London, 1951), p. 46.

16. "The Question to the Single One," *Between Man and Man*, p. 60.

17. Ibid., p. 52.

18. Ibid., p. 64.

19. Ibid., pp. 65-66.

20. Parenthetically, there is considerable intellectual affinity between Buber's existence-utopia 'double-vision' and the 'critical' theory of the Frankfurt School. Very briefly, both oppose 'reification' and stress human possibilities. Buber was in Frankfurt for much of the time that Horkheimer, Adorno Marcuse, Fromm *et al.* were at the Institut for Sozialforschung, and there are some indications of ties between them. See Martin Jay, *The Dialectical Imagination, A History of the Frankfurt School and the Institute of Social Research 1923-1950* (Boston, 1973), pp. 41-85, 21, 33, and 200.

21. "The Question to the Single One," *Between Man and Man*, pp. 73-79.

22. "The Silent Question," *On Judaism*, p. 209. *See also* Franz Von Hammerstein, "Martin Bubers messianische Hoffnung und ihr Verhaltnis zu seine Philosophie," *Judaica* (Zurich), vol. X, no. 2 (June 1, 1954), pp. 65-104.

23. This accounts for the ease of movement between the various disciplines. Buber writes, for example, "The sociological 'utopia' of a voluntary community is nothing else but the immanent side of a direct theocracy." *Kingdom of God* (New York, 1967), p. 139.

24. "What Is Man?" *Between Man and Man*, p. 126ff.

25. Ibid., p. 200

26. Another expression of philosophical individualism which Buber criticizes is that of Sartre. *See* "Religion and Modern Thinking," *Eclipse of God*, pp. 38-40 for comments in this spirit on the Cartesian *cogito*.

27. For Buber on Heidegger *see* "What Is Man?" *Between Man and Man*, pp. 163-81 and "Religion and Modern Thinking," *Eclipse of God*, pp. 70-78.

28. "What Is Man?" *Between Man and Man*, p. 168. For a more complete and balanced account of Heidegger's 'individualism' *see* Magda King, *Heidegger's Philosophy, A Guide to his Basic Thought* (New York, 1964), pp. 104-26 and William Barret, *Irrational Man: A Study in Existentialist Philosophy* (New York, 1962), pp. 206-38, esp. 236-37. An interesting cross perspective between Heidegger and Buber can be found in Paul Christopher Smith, *Das Sein des Du; Bubers Philosophie im Lichte des Heideggerischen Denken an das Sein* (New York, 1966).

29. "What Is Man?" *Between Man and Man*, p. 172.

30. "The Question to the Single One," ibid., p. 41.

31. "What Is Man?" ibid., p. 201.

32. "Dialogue," ibid., p. 31.

33. "What Is Man?" ibid., p. 201.

34. Ibid., p. 175.

35. Ibid., pp. 175-76.

36. Much the most lively and engaging is Malcolm Diamond, *Martin Buber: Jewish Existentialist* (New York, 1960), pp. 15-38. *See also* Robert E. Wood, *Martin Buber's Ontology* (Evanston, 1969).

37. "The Task," *Gleanings* (New York, 1969), p. 99.

38. *Sozialismus aus dem Glauben. Verhandlungen der Sozialistichen Tagung in Heppenheim* (Leipzig, 1928), p. 92.

39. Buber is recorded as having remarked "The narrow ridge is the place where I and Thou meet." Aubrey Hodes, *Martin Buber: An Intimate Portrait* (New York, 1971), p. 58.

40. "What Is Man?" *Between Man and Man*, p. 176.

41. Ibid.

42. *Paths in Utopia*, p. 134.

43. Ibid., p. 133. In this light Eliezer Berkowitz's query: "Community between an individual *I* and individual Thou, yes! But a community of people, a society of men, how?" is seen as entirely misconceived. *A Jewish Critique of the Philosophy of Martin Buber* (New York, 1962), p. 45. *See also* Ernst Simon, "Martin Buber V'emunat Yisrael," *Iyyun: A Hebrew Philosophical Quarterly*, Vol. 9, No. 1 (January 1950), p. 16.

44. "What Is Man?" *Between Man and Man*, p. 176.

45. Ibid., pp. 176-77.

46. Buber regarded Hasidism as "the one great attempt in the history of The Diaspora . . . to found a true and just community based on religious principles." "On National Education," *Israel and the World: Essays in a Time of Crisis* (New York, 1965), p. 159. *See also* "The Silent Question," *On Judaism*, pp. 211-12. "Spirit and Body of the Hasidic Movement," *The Origin and Meaning of Hasidism* (New York, 1960), p. 144ff.

47. *Paths in Utopia*, pp. 139-49.

48. Ibid., pp. 144-45.

49. "Character Change and Social Experiment in Israel," *Israel: Its Role in Civilization*, ed. Moshe Davis (New York, 1956), p. 207.

50. Ibid., p. 210.

51. "Three Theses of a Religious Socialism," *Pointing the Way*, p. 112.

52. *I and Thou*, p. 94. *See also Paths in Utopia*, p. 135.

53. "The Dialogue Between Heaven and Earth," *On Judaism*, p. 216.

3 The Rehabilitation of Utopia

1. Ernst Simon, "Buber or Ben Gurion," *Outlook* (January 1966). Original Hebrew in *Ner*, XI, pp. 3-10.

2. *Paths in Utopia*, p. 8.

3. Ibid., p. 7.

4. "Three Theses of a Religious Socialism," *Pointing the Way*, p. 113.

5. Cf. Eric Voeglin, *Order and History* (Baton Rouge, 1957), vol. III.

6. *Paths in Utopia*, p. 9.

7. Ibid., p. 8.

8. Ibid., p. 7.

9. Buber does very much the same thing for the Zionist idea in *Israel and Palestine. The History of an Idea* (New York, 1952). Although in somewhat different form, one may find a similar approach to Hasidism in Buber's various essays on the subject: Maurice S. Friedman, ed. and trans., *Hasidism and Modern Man* (New

York, 1958); Maurice S. Friedman, ed. and trans., *The Origin and Meaning of Hasidism* (New York, 1960). The same is true of his biblical studies: *Moses* (New York, 1958); *The Prophetic Faith* (New York, 1960); *Kingship of God* (New York, 1967). Buber's method consists of tracing the core idea, the underlying and unifying theme, as it develops and slowly matures into completion. As he says in his foreword to the English translation of his *Paths in Utopia*: "The fundamental question in the making of such a picture is—as in the making of all pictures—the question of what one has to leave out. Only so much of the massive material seemed to me to be relevant as was essential to the idea itself. It is not the false turnings that are important for us, but the single broad highway into which they invariably lead. From the historical process the idea itself rises up before our eyes."

This is a highly subjective methodology that permits the author to set his own organization on an unruly, often chaotic, body of material. If as a theologian he has been accused of "metaphysical impressionism" [Nathan Rothenstreich, "Buber's Dialogical Thought," *The Philosophy of Martin Buber*, p. 132; Hebrew original in *Iyyun*, IX, A (January, 1958), p. 75] judged as a critical scholar he is often close to "intellectual impressionism." But it should be borne in mind that Buber's aim is not 'academic' in the conventional sense. His writings are invariably the product of an 'engaged' reading, and their aim is instruction rather than exposition or explanation.

10. Eduard Zeller, *Outlines of the History of Greek Philosophy* (London, 1955), p. 192.

11. Jowett trans. 1281^a 4-5, book III, chap. 9.

12. The state so evolved is generally termed 'organic'. But it must be kept in mind that for the Greek the notions 'society' and 'state' did not carry the basic duality of meanings that they do for the twentieth-century person. (Both terms are condensed into a single one in the Greek.) The small self-ruling community is both society and state. It is another question entirely whether Aristotle would consider the contemporary state—remote and severed from society—as natural and organic. Thus while Buber is at one with Aristotle in accepting community as organic, he can turn a moment later—without violating the spirit of the Aristotelian dictum— and condemn the state as a "foreign excrescence."

13. *Paths in Utopia*, p. 133.

14. "What Is Man?" *Between Man and Man*, p. 203.

15. "Al Mahuta Shel Hatarbut," *Pney Adam* (Hebrew) (Jerusalem, 1962), pp. 377-93.

16. "Society and the State," *Pointing the Way*, p. 174 ff. Buber is here in full agreement with the well-known Marxist critique: "The bourgeoisie, wherever it has got the upper hand, has put an end to all feudal patriarchial, idyllic relations. It has pitilessly torn asunder the motley feudal ties that bound man to his 'natural superiors' and has left no other nexus between man and man than naked self-interest, than callous 'cash payment'." Karl Marx and Frederick Engels, *Communist Manifesto* in *Selected Works in Two Volumes* (Moscow, 1962), vol. I, p. 36.

17. "The Task," *Gleanings*, p. 99.

18. *Paths in Utopia*, p. 132.

19. Ibid., pp. 7-8.

20. "Warum Muss die Aufbau Palästinas ein sozialisticher sein?" *JSJ*, p. 381.

21. There is, of course, no question of rigor in the picture that Buber draws. It is

admittedly a projection from the anthropological conclusions discussed in the previous chapter. Buber speaks in terms of being a witness to the truth and his writing as personal testimony. "There is and can be no objective criterion which will establish universal standards of judgment regarding the fundamental issues of human existence . . . ." (Diamond, p. 33).

22. "Warum Muss die Aufbau Palästinas ein sozialisticher sein?" *JSJ*, p. 381.

23. *Paths in Utopia*, p. 136.

24. Ibid., p. 133.

25. Ibid., p. 134.

26. Ibid., p. 135.

27. *See* "Hara'yon Hashitufi," *Davar* (January 5, 1945); *see also* chap. 7, "Experiments," in *Paths in Utopia*, pp. 58-79.

28. *Paths in Utopia*, p. 73.

29. Agrarian society, in Buber's eyes, is far more conducive to the realization of community than the mass facelessness of city life. *Towards Union in Palestine* (Jerusalem, 1947), p. 34; "L'Shem Hitbatzrut P'neemit," *Moznaim*, p. 14, 1942, Hebrew Writers' Convention; "The Holy Way," *On Judaism*, p. 144; *JSJ*, pp. 249-71 *passim*. He makes an unconvincing appeal for the growth of community even in large urban centers, but it was clearly a second best. But be that as it may, he is quite emphatic in rejecting any backward-looking romanticism that yearns for a return to old forms and rejects the advances of modern science. Responsibility confronts people in the here and now. What is needed is "finding new means to accomplish old ends." "Character Change and Social Experiment in Israel," *Israel: Its Role in Civilization*, p. 211 f.; *Sozialismus aus dem Glauben*, p. 90f., 121f., 217f.; Kohn, p. 196; *Paths in Utopia*, p. 15.

30. Cited in *Paths in Utopia*, p. 47 (original: *Aufruf Zum Sozialismus*, p. 61).

31. *Israel and Palestine, p. 112.*

32. *See*, e.g., "Binational Approach to Zionism," *Towards Union in Palestine*, pp. 7-13.

33. *See*, e.g., "What Is Man?" *Between Man and Man*, pp. 199-201.

34. The particular influence of Gierke seems to be very strong on this point. Buber quotes him three times in the course of *Paths in Utopia*—each time to the effect that the Middle Ages was a structurally rich era, made up of local associations and communities, while the modern state "devoured" all "intermediate organizations." Gierke was professor at Berlin from 1888 to 1927, and it is quite likely that Buber came to know him, or at least his work, there. This romantic medievalism was strongly present in Landauer as well. *See* Lunn, *Prophet of Community*, pp. 18 f. and 179 f. The romanticizing of the medieval community was, of course, very fashionable in German academia during those years. Not surprisingly, its use by radicals (like Buber and Landauer) was less prevalent than its conservative version, e.g., the work of Scheler and Sombart. For the former *see* John R. Staude, *Max Scheler: An Intellectual Portrait* (New York, 1967), especially pp. 29-61 and Paul R. Flohr, "Werner Sombart's *The Jews and Modern Capitalism*: An Analysis of Its Ideological Underpinnings," *Leo Baeck Yearbook*, 1976, pp. 87-107.

35. "Society and the State," *Pointing the Way*, p. 173.

36. Ibid., p. 173 f.; "What Is Man?" *Between Man and Man*, p. 199 f.; *Paths in Utopia*, p. 130 f.

37. "Society and the State," *Pointing the Way*, p. 174.

38. "To the Clarification of Pacifism," *Gleanings*, p. 212.

39. "Society and the State," *Pointing the Way*, pp. 173-76.

40. *Paths in Utopia*, p. 47. The phrase in Landauer's [*Beginnen: Aufsätze über Sozialismus*, ed. Martin Buber (Cologne, 1924), p. 53].

41. Ibid., p. 46. See Schaeder, p. 216.

42. *Paths in Utopia*, p. 48.

43. In one of his private notebooks (apparently in preparation for *Paths in Utopia*), Buber cites, with obvious agreement, the following quotation from de Tocqueville: "Decentralization, like liberty, is a thing which leaders promise their people but which they never give them. To get it and to keep it the people must count on their own sole efforts: if they do not care to do so the evil is beyond remedy." Alexis de Tocqueville, *Oeuvres*, VIII, p. 32 ff., Buber Archive.

44. "Judaism and Civilization," *On Judaism*, p. 200.

45. "Socialist Experiments in Jewish Palestine," *The New Palestine*, vol. XXXV, no. 1 (October 13, 1944).

46. *See* Ernst Simon, "Darko Hapolitit Ve'tfisato Haleumit shel Martin Buber," introductory essay to the Hebrew edition of his essays, vol. II, *Teudah Ve'Yiud* (Jerusalem, 1961), p. 23.

47. *Paths in Utopia*, p. 48.

48. Ibid., p. 47.

49. Ibid., p. 48.

50. Ibid., p. 50.

51. Ibid., p. 134.

52. Very much the same is true in regard to the ideal vision of 'theocracy' in Buber's various works on the Bible. Ernst Simon, "Nationalismus, Zionismus und der Jüdische-Arabische Konflikt in Martin Bubers Theorie und Wirksamkeit," *Leo Baeck Institut Bulletin* (Tel Aviv, 1966), p. 34 ff.

53. *Paths in Utopia*, p. 134.

54. Ibid., p. 137.

55. Buber expresses the same idea in the realm of personal ethics in a graphic way. "Sometimes striving to be just I go in the dark till my head meets the wall and aches and I know 'Here is the wall and I cannot go further.' But I cannot know it beforehand otherwise." *Interrogations of Contemporary Philosophers*, p. 80.

56. For a statement on the positive value of the state *see JSJ*, p. 295 f. *See also* Buber's criticism of Kropotkin's too-sweeping anarchist position. *Paths in Utopia*, p. 38 f. Buber, in fact, asserts that "in all probability there will never—so long as man is what he is—be freedom, pure and simple, and there will be 'state', i.e., compulsion, for just so long." Ibid., p. 104.

57. S. N. Eisenstadt, "Hagato Hachevratit Shel Martin Buber," *Al Professor Martin Buber: D'vorim Sheneemru L'zichro* (Jerusalem, 1965), p. 14. An inappropriately weak government, Buber would say, may well be the stepping-stone for an authoritarian movement that capitalizes on the confusion and discontent the former produces.

58. *See*, e.g., Niebuhr's statements quoted by Friedman, p. 222; *see also Interrogations of Contemporary Philosophers*, p. 78 f.; Paul Tillich, "Martin Buber

and Christian Thought," *Commentary*, vol. V, no. 6 (1948), p. 521; Balthassar, *Martin Buber and Christianity, passim.*

59. "Warum Muss die Aufbau Palästinas ein sozialisticher sein?" *JSJ*, p. 387.

60. "Bimkom Divrai Vikuach," *Ner* (October 1956). Reprinted in *Teudah Ve'yiud*, II, p. 320 f.

61. "Warum Muss die Aufbau Palästinas ein sozialisticher sein?" *JSJ*, p. 387.

62. *See* note 9, this chapter.

63. In addition, Buber's habit of almost never footnoting sources makes this approach arduously difficult.

64. *Paths in Utopia*, p. 16.

65. Ibid., p. 17.

66. Buber ignores the rather conspicuous element in Saint-Simon's thought that tends to authoritarianism, centralization, and the all encompassing state. The growth of a "new class" of experts who, from their position of pervasive control and management, dispense law administratively, and "objectively," is by no means identical with the basic "restructuring" of society and the withering of authority and compulsion that Buber has in mind. *See* J. L. Talmon, *Political Messianism; the Romantic Phase* (London, 1960), chap. I; Georg G. Iggers, *The Cult of Authority: The Political Philosophy of the Saint-Simonians, A Chapter in the Intellectual History of Totalitarianism* (The Hague, 1958), *passim.*

67. *Paths in Utopia*, p. 18.

68. Although Fourier rejects equality as a strict principle, in effect his scheme, by an intricate distribution formula, does away, in the course of time, with any substantial inequality. *Le Nouveau Monde Industriel et Sociétaire* (Brussels, 1840), vol. II, pp. 109 f. and 123 f.

69. While there is no doubt that Owen's position was influenced by his experience, let it simply be noted that, at least as much as Fourier and Saint-Simon, Owen based his 'philosophic' system on the a priori principle of 'behaviorism' that he seems to have learned from the school of Godwin. His rather naïve formulation of the behaviorist viewpoint is the endlessly repeated justification for all of his programs.

70. *Paths in Utopia*, p. 23.

71. Buber's version of Owen's contribution to utopian socialism is an attempt to read late nineteenth-century German theories of community into early nineteenth-century English socialism. He goes so far as to cite Tönnies's description of community in support. *Paths in Utopia*, p. 21. Owen's notion of community, although it is certainly central to his thought, is not a proto-Buberian formulation. His preoccupation with community stems not from any deep concern with dialogue or fraternity, but with the desire to maximize human happiness, by removing the sources of oppression, giving free outlet to the productive powers of society, developing the potential of each individual, and insuring a smoothly running social unit. Harrison's work on Owen and the Owenites devotes a section to the "Idea of Community," analyzing and tracing the concept to its various roots. The image of community that emerges is quite different from that of Buber. J. F. C. Harrison, *Robert Owen and the Owenites in Britain and American. The Quest for the New Moral World* (London, 1969), pp. 47-63.

72. *Paths in Utopia*, p. 22.

73. Buber devotes his opening pages to demonstrating that Marx and Engels considered Proudhon in the utopian tradition of Saint-Simon, Fourier, and Owen. It is worth remarking that for Marx and Engels, Proudhon was deemed utopian for primarily polemical purposes and not because of any essential bond or intellectual debt to the forerunners. For Buber, by contrast, "Proudhon did not merely continue the evolutionary line of Utopian Socialism, he began it again from the beginning, but in such a way that everything anterior to him appeared completely remodeled." *Paths in Utopia*, p. 27.

74. Ibid.

75. Ibid., p. 34.

76. Landauer presents a similar picture of Proudhon in his *Aufruf zum Sozialismus*, p. 102 f.

77. Marx expresses the same thought in less complimentary fashion: "M. Proudhon, in spite of the great trouble he has taken to scale the height of the *system of contradictions*, has never been able to raise himself above the first two steps of thesis and antithesis." *The Poverty of Philosophy* (London, 1900), p. 87.

78. *Paths in Utopia*, p. 32. Exactly what the nature of this "decisive step" that Proudhon took was, is more difficult to uncover than the above uncritical text would indicate. Buber's formulations in regard to Saint-Simon's and Proudhon's conceptions of societal transformation are nearly identical, e.g., for Saint-Simon: "No longer was one group of rulers to be ousted by another group of rulers, as had happened in all the upheavals known to history. . . . No leadership is required other than that provided by social functions themselves." This will obviate the need for a "political order superimposing itself as an essentially distinct and special class." For Proudhon as was cited in the text above: "It can no longer be a matter of substituting one political regime for another but of the emergence, in place of a political regime grafted upon society, of a regime expressive of society itself." It is certainly true, as Buber writes, that Proudhon "in far greater detail and with far more precision" than Saint-Simon, "brought the problem of structural renewal to the fore"; but it is far less clear what the "decisive step" from "social reconstruction" to "structural renewal" entails. That one started with the state and the other with society is a verbal rather than a substantive distinction, since in practice they seemed to amount to virtually the same thing, in Buber's account. Buber may be referring to Proudhon's accent on "freedom in association," his "mutualism," or his appreciation of the role of labor (as opposed to "all productive forces" of Saint-Simon), but if so, he fails to express this adequately. He does state that the latter factor marks an advance of Proudhon over Saint-Simon, but its connection to "social reconstruction" and "structural renewal" is, again, unclear.

79. Cited by Buber in *Paths in Utopia*, p. 33.

80. Ibid., pp. 28-33. Here, too, Buber assigns to Proudhon views that are very distinctly late nineteenth-century German. For example, Buber attributes the need for decentralization and federation—as if it were implicit in Proudhon—to the breakdown of the rich, communal life of the Middle Ages. This is Gierke (who is cited in support just a few pages later) and not Proudhon. Buber himself asserts that Proudhon was "not an historical thinker" and as such it is strange to hear that Proudhon saw the need for decentralization in terms of an historical analysis.

81. Ibid., p. 37. Buber's discussion of Proudhon's federalism is ambiguous in regard to the nature of the units that are to be the structural cells of the new body politic. At times he seems to realize quite clearly that Proudhon's idea of federal society is concerned "with the larger units to be federated" and that Proudhon does not fill the requirement of dealing with the smaller ones. At other times he speaks of Proudhon as the champion of the local commune. "Proudhon," Buber writes, "turns more and more to 'communalism' and federalism . . ." As previously cited, he saw the new society built upon "the local community or commune—living on the strength of its own interior relationships." It is the latter view that predominates in most of Buber's discussion.

But this does not seem to have been Proudhon's view. His federalism is not based on renewed communal life or on face-to-face socialism but on the attempt to construct society so that the bargaining process between groups does not deteriorate into inequality. Large groups are often necessary for this purpose. In contrasting Proudhon and Buber, we are dealing with the difference between an intensely practical Socialist, whose point of reference is early nineteenth-century laissez-faire capitalism, and a more philosophical Socialist who begins with Tönnies and Gierke. The one goes from federalism to the "peoples' bank"; the other begins with community and ends with dialogue.

Substantially the same criticism is leveled at Buber by Alan Ritter, *The Political Thought of Pierre-Joseph Proudhon* (Princeton, 1969), pp. 127-28 fn. Ritter remarks that Proudhon "besides defending large groups, also denounced the petty surveillance prevalent in the small communities which Buber thinks he favors." As Proudhon writes: "If authority is painful, the jealousy of confreres is no easier thing to put up with . . . In those societies that are best unified, one sees pretention to privilege; that is what makes association odious. There is no need to push association further than need be." *Carnets* (Paris, 1961), VI, vol. 2, No. 87-88. Proudhon writes to the same effect that "Mutuality means to associate men no more than is required by the imperatives of production, the low cost of products, the needs of consumption and the security of the producers themselves." *Oeuvres Complètes* (Paris, 1924), IV, p. 190. For discussions of Proudhon's federalism, *see* Ritter, pp. 118-62; J. J. Chevallier, "Le Fédéralisme de Proudhon et de ses Disciples," *Le Fédéralisme* (Paris, 1956), esp. p. 95 f.; Franz Neumann, *The Democratic and Authoritarian State* (Glencoe, Ill., 1957), p. 218.

82. *Paths in Utopia*, p. 42.

83. Ibid., p. 43.

84. Ibid., p. 45.

85. Ibid., p. 43. Although Buber has framed Kropotkin into his own thought patterns and vocabulary, this does not involve a manifest injustice to the spirit of the latter. He is certainly not so existentially oriented as Buber's last statement would have one believe, but there is very definitely an antidoctrine bias to all his writings. With Kropotkin and certainly with Landauer, Buber is more on home ground in the sense that there is a moral or even spiritual tone to their work that accords with Buber's thought more authentically than the notions of economic balance and equalized bargaining in the thought of Proudhon. This, of course, is not to say that Buber's history has become less schematic or designed. (For example, he omits Bakunin from his utopian odyssey precisely because Bakunin lacks this

moral-spiritual quality. His emphasis is squarely on revolution and what Buber considered doctrinaire, one-sided anarchism.

86. Ibid., p. 44.
87. Ibid, pp.44-45.
88. *Paths in Utopia,* p. 83.
89. *Aufruf zum Sozialismus,* p. 19.
90. "Landauer und die Revolution," *Masken,* XIV, 18/19, 1919, pp. 282-91.
91. Buber's treatment of Moses Hess betrays the same tendencies. *See Israel and Palestine,* pp. 111-22 and Buber's introductions to his edition of Hess's work in Hebrew translation; *Moshe Hess K'tavim Yehudim* (Jerusalem, 1954), and *Moshe Hess K'tavim Klaliyim* (Jerusalem, 1956).

4   The Prophet and the Apocalypse

1. Notably "What Is man?" *Between Man and Man,* pp. 143-45; *Paths in Utopia,* pp. 80-98.
2. Franz Rosenzweig, the intimate friend and colleague, with whom Buber translated the Bible into German, wrote the influential *Hegel und der Staat,* 2 vols. (Munich and Berlin, 1920.)
3. "Die Sowjets und das Judentum," *JSJ,* p. 548. *See also* "The Gods of the Nations and God," *Israel and the World,* pp. 211-12.
4. *See* e.g., "Herzl und die Historie," *Die Jüdische Bewegung,* I, p. 165 f.
5. The Jewish background of Marx's thought has been noted on numerous occasions. But as Shlomo Avineri has stated, this "begs the question" by wholly disregarding the problem of Marx's own awareness of those specific Jewish traditions held responsible for his views. Avineri attributes the Messianic element in Marx's thought to its Hegelian antecedents. *The Social and Political Thought of Karl Marx* (Cambridge, 1968), p. 4. Buber himself notes the rejection, ignorance, and coarseness with which Marx speaks of Jews and Judaism, in light of which it is difficult to maintain that just this was his source of inspiration. "Die Sowjets und das Judentum," *JSJ,* p. 551; Buber's introduction to his edition of *Moshe Hess K'tavin Tzionim V'yehudiim,* p. 18 fn. It is interesting to note the directly antithetical and rather provincial view of Istvan Meszaros in his work on Marx. Spinoza and Marx, he claims, achieved universal greatness by transcending their specific Jewish beginnings, while Hess and Buber, confined by their "Jewish narrowness," produced merely "second-rate" utopias. *Marx's Theory of Alienation* (London, 1970), p. 72.
6. "Believing Humanism," *Gleanings,* p. 120.
7. *The Philosophy of Martin Buber,* p. 35.
8. "Believing Humanism," *Gleanings,* pp. 119-20.
9. *The Philosophy of Martin Buber,* p. 36.
10. Loyd D. Easton and Kurt H. Guddat, eds., *Writings of the Young Marx on Philosophy and Society* (New York, 1967), p. 294.
11. Ibid.
12. *Capital* (New York, The Modern Library, 1936), I, p. 198.
13. *Wrirings of the Young Marx,* p. 292.
14. "What Is Man?" *Between Man and Man,* pp. 198-99.

15. "Distance and Relation," *The Knowledge of Men*, ed. Maurice S. Friedman (New York, 1965), p. 65.

16. Ibid., p. 66.

17. Ibid.

18. *I and Thou*, p. 85.

19. "Distance and Relation," *The Knowledge of Man*, p. 64. For Buber's elucidation of "distance and relation," and their connection with *I-Thou*, see Maurice S. Friedman's introduction to *The Knowledge of Man*, pp. 21-23.

20. *I and Thou*, p. 58. The very onerous problem of what exactly this relation entails in terms of objectivity (Buber denies that it is merely a psychological phenomenon) and mutuality is posed by many of Buber's critics. Buber deals with this point in his afterword to *I and Thou* (written in 1957), pp. 171-82.

21. *Writings of the Young Marx*, p. 409.

22. *I and Thou*, p. 80.

23. "Distance and Relation," *The Knowledge of Man*, p. 69.

24. "What Is Man?" *Between Man and Man*, p. 177.

25. Ibid., "Dialogue," p. 37; "Al Hamashber Hagadol," *Davar* (July 20, 1945). Reprinted in *Teudah Ve'yiud II*, pp. 75-79.

26. "Dialogue," *Between Man and Man*, pp. 36-37.

27. Ibid, p. 37.

28. Ibid.

29. Ibid.

30. Ibid., p. 38. If the Hasidim taught that even a carpenter may hallow this world through his work, it is not the work process itself, its meaningfulness or ability to satisfy human needs, but the holiness of the thoughts that accompanied the activity that mattered. Its value was measured in terms that had nothing at all to do with the real creative effort invested in the table or chair. This point of view accords well with the item just cited since in both cases work is "redeemed" by something besides the work itself.

31. "Education," *Between Man and Man*, p. 83 ff.

32. Ibid., p. 85.

33. Ibid., p. 86.

34. Ibid., p. 87.

35. Ibid.

36. Ibid.

37. *Writings of the Young Marx*, pp. 305-6.

38. Ibid., p. 303.

39. The previously cited phrase (p. 89) "his existence for the other and the other's existence for him," illustrates very much the same stress on complementing one another, reciprocity, and interchange. For example, Avineri, under the heading "Social Man," states: "Since production cannot be carried out single-handedly, Marx deduces man's social, transsubjective nature from his quality as an object-creating being." (p. 86 and f.) *See also Capital I*, pp. 353-68, where Marx discusses the development of the human 'species' capabilities in a chapter significantly titled "Cooperation." Buber, by contrast, sets the condition for genuine relation in transcending just this functionalism. Love "does not cling to an *I* as if the *Thou* were merely its 'content,' or object." *I and Thou*, p. 66. Rather, the lover "turns to

his other human being, the beloved, in his otherness, his independence, his self-reality." *Between Man and Man*, p. 29. They do not exchange fulfillment but include the other in a two-sided act. "Inclusiveness is the complete realization of the submissive person, the desired person, the 'partner,' not by the fancy but by the actuality of the being." *Between Man and Man*, p. 97.

40. "Education," *Between Man and Man*, p. 88.

41. Ibid., p. 87.

42. "What is Man?" Ibid., p. 121f.

43. A pertinent instance of this is Buber's discussion of the shortcomings of human work in the present time and the possibilities for the future. People work with inner drive and enthusiasm in eras of belief when their work, reflecting their belief in "life," takes on meaning. *Arbeitsglaube* reflects *Glaube* in general. *Kampf um Israel*, pp. 281-82.

44. That Buber, practically, if not formally or conceptually, introduces the need for such gradations through the back door is abundantly clear from previous discussions of community as inevitably *I-It* yet highly desirable (*see* chap. 2). Although it is beyond the scope of this work to treat the concept 'dialogue' in Buber's thought fully, it is clear that dialogue is not the I-Thou relationship and takes place at the level of *I-It*.

45. "Dialogue," *Between Man and Man*, p.35.

46. Cited ibid., p. 27.

47. Both Marx and Buber owe a debt to Feuerbach and both advance characteristically "beyond" him. *See* "What Is Man?" *Between Man and Man*, pp. 145-48, 210. Both accept Feuerbach's "anthropological" orientation as a signal advance over Hegel and agree that Feuerbach treats man as too static and opaque a datum. Marx, of course, remedies this by concretion and relativization (which man, what historical circumstances); Buber, by stressing the "real" man and his problematic nature.

48. In a bibliography that he made for himself in preparation for *Paths in Utopia*, Buber included, for the pre-1948 period, only *Die Heilige Familie, Die Deutsche Ideologie*, and *Misère de la Philosophie* (Buber Archive).

49. It is quite true as Beek and Weiland surmise, that Buber wrote—or at least conceived—the bulk of *Paths of Utopia* long before it came to print. (It first appeared in Hebrew as *Netivot B'Utopia* in 1947.) This helps to explain Buber's position on Marx. M. A. Beek and J. Sperna Weiland, *Martin Buber: Personalist and Prophet* (Westminster, Md., 1968) pp. 100-101. Major portions of the work were published as articles in *Hapoel Hatzair* during the early forties.

50. Buber makes the point starkly in his discussion of Marx in *Paths in Utopia*. For the latter, "the organizing activity will begin, i.e., the reconstruction of society, only after the complete overthrow of existing power—whatever organizing activity preceded the revolution was only organization for the struggle." Marx sees the new society growing out of "exclusively political means . . . by ways of sheer suicide, so to speak, on the part of the political principle." pp. 82-83.

51. Avineri, p. 143; Alfred Meyer, *Marxism: The Unity of Theory and Practice* (Cambridge, 1970), pp. 92-100; Georg Lukács, *History and Class Consciousness* (Cambridge, Mass., 1971) pp. 46-255.

52. *Writings of the Young Marx*, p. 431.

Notes

53. "The Spirit and Body of the Hasidic Movement," *The Origin and Meaning of Hasidism*, p. 129.

54. "Judaism and Civilization," *On Judaism*, p. 195.

55. Meyer, p. 96.

56. *Werke*, I, p. 68. Cited by Avineri, p. 137.

57. It should be noted that the unity in Marx is not a static one; he does see room for change. Nevertheless, there is no longer the possibility for real challenge to the new order or the need to struggle for its continued existence. See *The Poverty of Philosophy* (London, 1900), p. 160.

58. *Writings of the Young Marx*, p. 259.

59. "Character Change and Social Experiment in Israel," *Israel: Its Role in Civilization*, p. 207 ff.

60. "Material force must be overthrown by material force. But theory also becomes a material force once it has gripped the masses." *Writings of the Young Marx*, p. 257.

61. *Gleanings*, p. 209.

62. "Character Change and Social Experiment in Israel," *Israel: Its Role in Civilization*, p. 205.

63. "Landauer B'Sha'ah zo," *Hapoel Hatzair* (June 27, 1939), p. 9.

64. "The Question to the Single One," *Between Man and Man*, p. 82.

65. "My Way to Hasidism," *Hasidism and Modern Man*, p. 59.

66. "Religion and Philosophy," *Eclipse of God* (New York, 1957), p. 37.

67. *Sozialismus aus dem Glauben*, p. 90.

68. *Writings of the Young Marx*, p. 401.

69. "Prophecy, Apocalyptic, and the Historical Hour," *Pointing the Way*, pp. 192-207; *Moses* (New York, 1958), pp. 182-90. In the latter work Buber interprets the biblical dispute between Moses and Korah along similar lines.

70. "Prophecy, Apocalyptic, and the Historical Hour," *Pointing the Way*, p. 200.

71. Ibid.

72. Ibid., p. 198.

73. "Plato and Isaiah," *Israel and the World*, p. 111.

74. Ibid.

75. "Prophecy, Apocalyptic, and the Historical Hour," *Pointing the Way*, p. 200.

76. Ibid., p. 201.

77. Ibid., p. 203.

78. "Spirit and Body of the Hasidic Movement," *The Origin and Meaning of Hasidism*, p. 127.

79. "Prophecy, Apocalyptic and the Historical Hour," *Pointing the Way*, pp. 203-204.

80. Ibid.

81. Jacob Taubes, "Buber and the Philosophy of History," *The Philosophy of Martin Buber*, p. 461.

82. *See* Avineri, p. 196 f.

83. The entire plot of *For the Sake of Heaven* (New York, 1961), Buber's epic narrative on early nineteenth-century Hasidism, is centered on the resolute and ultimately self-sacrificing attempt of the Seer of Lublin to bring about the messianic era. The Seer, who roughly represents the apocalyptic viewpoint, says at one point:

"Redemption is no ready-made gift of God, handed down from heaven to earth. The body of this world must travail as in birth and reach the very edge of death before redemption can be born." p. 108. The Yehudi, who represents the prophetic principle, is juxtaposed to the Seer and replies: "Truly it does depend on us; not on our power but on our repentance." p. 114.

84. "What Is Man?" *Between Man and Man*, p. 122.

85. *I and Thou*, p. 100.

86. Ibid.

87. Ibid., p. 101. *See also Good and Evil* (New York, 1953), pp. 63-143.

88. Emmanuel Levinas, "Martin Buber and the Theory of Knowledge," *The Philosophy of Martin Buber*, p. 143.

89. *Paths in Utopia*, p. 96.

90. Ibid., pp. 82-96.

91. Ibid., p. 87.

92. Ibid. *See* Avineri, pp. 174-84, 239-49.

93. *Paths in Utopia*, p. 96.

94. Ibid., pp. 89-94.

95. Ibid., p. 93.

96. D. Riaznov, ed., *Marx-Engels Archiv* (Frankfurt, 1927), pp. 318-41.

97. Quoted by Buber, *Paths in Utopia*, p. 84. Original: *Eighteenth of Brumaire of Louis Bonaparte* in Karl Marx and Frederick Engels, *Selected Works*, vol. 1, pp. 254-55.

98. Most striking are Marx's comments on the Commune. *Civil War in France, Selected Works*, II, pp. 498 f. In light of these comments, Buber's claim that for Marx, the "communes were essentially political units, battle organs of the revolution" is untenable. *Paths in Utopia*, p. 95.

99. *Paths in Utopia*, p. 86; *Marx-Engels Briefwechsel* (Berlin, 1954), vol. III, p. 328, dated 20 June 1866.

100. *Paths in Utopia*, p. 86.

101. In addition, Marx's comments to Engels must be taken against the background of the Austro-Prussian War. The French delegates whom he criticized had entirely discounted nationalism "and even nations as a *préjugé suranné*," and called on the workers not to fight. Marx, who looked to the unification of Germany under a single political leadership as a positive step that could lift Germany out of the semifeudal condition from which it still suffered, opposed the antinationalist and hence, anti-state position of the French delegates. *See* the *Minutes of the Internationale* for June 19th and 26th, 1866, vol. II (Moscow), pp. 200-205.

102. *Selected Works*, I, pp. 383-84.

103. *Paths in Utopia*, p. 103.

104. Ibid, p. 127. Original: J. Stalin, *Works* (Moscow, 1955), vol. XIII, p. 233.

5   Rome, Moscow, and Jerusalem

1. *The Twenty Years Crisis 1913-1939; An Introduction to the Study of International Relations* (London, 1962), pp. 10-12.

2. *I-Thou* and *I-It*, although they do typologically exhibit much that is common

with utopia and existence, are in one important respect quite different. For Buber, *I-Thou* and *I-It* are completely separate and not unifiable. There is no chance to creatively overcome the distance between them. The word realization which is otherwise the key word in Buber's thought, is inapplicable to the philosophy of *I and Thou*. *I-It* must always remain *I-It*; there can be no common ground. It is perhaps the central paradox of Buber's thought structure that its two main pillars— the philosophy of realization and the philosophy of *I and Thou*—are ultimately constituted of very different materials.

3. *The Twenty Years Crisis 1913-1939*, p. 19

4. "Warum Muss der Aufbau Palästinas ein sozialistischer sein," *JSJ*, p. 382. In variations on this theme written after World War II, Buber drops Rome as an alternative. *See Paths in Utopia*, p. 149.

5. "Warum Muss der Aufbau Palästinas ein sozialistischer sein," *JSJ*, p. 382.

6. "Landauer B'sha'ah Zo," *Hapoel Hatzair* (June 26, 1939).

7. *Gleanings*, p. 178. *See also* "Gandhi, Politics, and Us," *Pointing the Way*, p. 137.

8. Ibid.

9. Ibid., p. 128.

10. *See The Prophetic Faith*, esp. pp. 155-235.

11. For a highly interesting discussion of Buber's philosophy of history, *see* Jacob Taubes, "Martin Buber and the Philosophy of History," *The Philosophy of Martin Buber*, pp. 451-68. Buber seems to have been influenced by Landauer in this regard. See *Aufruf zum Sozialismus*, p. 60 f.; *see also* Buber's "Dialogue," *Between Man and Man*, pp. 30-31; "Warum Muss der Aufbau Palästinas ein sozialistischer sein," *JSJ*, p. 383; "The Validity and Limitation of the Political Principle," *Pointing the Way*, p. 215; "Biblical Leadership," *Israel and the World*, p. 124 f.

12. "The Demand of the Spirit and Historical Reality," *Pointing the Way*, pp. 185-86.

13. "Gandhi, Politics, and Us," ibid., p. 129.

14. Ibid.

15. Ibid., p. 127.

16. Ibid., p. 129.

17. But cf. *Two Letters to Gandhi*, p. 19.

18. "Gandhi, Politics, and Us," *Pointing the Way*, p. 130.

19. Interestingly Buber rejects the traditional interpretation of Jesus' famous dictum for one that is characteristically his own. *See* "The Validity and Limitation of the Politcal Principle," *Pointing the Way*, p. 137.

21. Ibid., p. 131.

22. "Warum Muss der Aufbau Palästinas ein sozialistischer sein," *JSJ*, pp. 382-83.

23. "People and Leader," *Pointing the Way*, pp. 148-50.

24. "Achad Haam Gedankrede in Basel," *JSJ*, p. 764.

25. "People and Leader," *Pointing the Way*, p. 151.

26. Ibid., p. 159.

27. Ibid.

28. "Warum Muss der Aufbau Palästinas ein sozialistischer sein," *JSJ*, p. 383.

29. Were force desisted from when it was imperative, for the sake of the prinicple

of purity, one would be approaching the dogmas of Moscow. Were force resorted to when regrets no longer restrained its use, or even used with regret but solely under the dictates of necessity, the principle of Rome would be effective.

In discussing Jesus' statement about the proper renderings to God and to Caesar, Buber concludes, that "What is legitimately done in the sphere of separation [read reality] receives its legitimacy from the sphere of wholeness [read ideals]. Or, more specifically, "giving to the state, giving that which is due it in the sphere of separation, is authorized by the sphere of wholeness . . ." In the above case, however, what is done is validated only by necessity. "The Validity and Limitation of the Political Principle," *Pointing the Way*, pp. 211-12.

30. "Recollection of a Death," *Pointing the Way*, p. 117.

31. *Two Letters to Gandhi*, p. 21; *Pointing the Way*, p. 146. *See also* "Der Weg Israels," *JSJ*, p. 541 and fn., ibid., "Jüdisches Nationalheim und Nationale Politik in Palastina," pp. 333-34, *Two Types of Faith*, p. 15, "Power and Love," *Gleanings*, pp. 44-45.

32. "The Question to the Single One," *Between Man and Man*, p. 69. *See also Gleanings*, p. 209.

33. "The Validity and Limitation of the Political Principle," *Pointing the Way*, p. 217.

34. *The Philosophy of Martin Buber*, p. 722.

35. *Interrogations of Contemporary Philosophers*, p. 80.

36. *The Philosophy of Martin Buber*, p. 724. See note 77, chap. 6 of this work.

37. "Achad Haam Gedankrede in Basel," *JSJ*, p. 763. An interesting but not altogether congruent sidelight to the question of the teacher and political power is Buber's comment that the philosopher-king is not a particularly desirable arrangement. The philosopher-king would either cease being a philosopher or cease being a king. What is desirable, however, is (as Kant contended), that kings set up at their sides teachers who would advise them in critical times. See Itzhak Ivry, *Martin Buber at Eighty*, Jewish Agency for Israel (New York, 1958); Ernst Simon, "Martin Buber and German Jewry," *Leo Baeck Institute Yearbook III* (London, 1958); "People and Leader," *Pointing the Way*, p. 148. This may very well be a counsel of wisdom, but it does not appear to be of a piece with the rest of his thought. The philosopher-king, a hyphenated-unity, would seem to fulfill the highest hopes of "Jerusalem." From a single individual, the voices of both truth and practice would be heard. The revolutionary of Jerusalem is, if not a professional philosopher or a reigning monarch, the amalgam of the two principles represented by them.

38. *See Paths in Utopia*, p. 46 f.; "Validity and Limitation of the Political Principle," *Pointing the Way*, p. 218.

39. Robert Weltsch, "Buber's Political Philosophy," *The Philosophy of Martin Buber*, p. 442.

40. "Validity and Limitation of the Political Principle," *Pointing the Way*, p. 218.

41. "On the Suspension of the Ethical," *Eclipse of God*, pp. 115-20.

42. Weltsch, p. 442.

43. "Religion and Philosophy," *Eclipse of God*, p. 35.

44. "Spirit and Body of the Hasidic Movement," *The Origin and Meaning of Hasidism*, p. 127.

45. "On the Suspension of the Ethical," *Eclipse of God*, p. 120.

46. Ibid., pp. 118-19.

47. "Recollection of a Death," *Pointing the Way*, p. 118.

48. Ibid. See also "The Validity and Limitation of the Political Principle," ibid., p. 218.

49. "Dialogue," *Between Man and Man*, p. 31. *See also Sozialismus Aus den Glauben*, p. 218.

50. "Du Siyach Al 'Biltmore'," *Teudah V'yiud*, p. 339; "Rede Auf dem XVI Zionisten Kongress in Basel," *JSJ*, pp. 522-23; "Jüdisches Nationalheim und Nationale Politik in Palastina," ibid., pp. 334-35.

51. See above, pp. 117-18.

52. See, for example, "Biblical Leadership," *Israel and the World*, p. 124 f.

53. "They live in failure; it is for them to fight and not to conquer." Their lives are enclosed in "failure, in obscurity, even when one stands in the blaze of public life, in the presence of the whole national life . . . The biblical point of view . . . proclaims that the way, the real way from the Creation to the Kingdom is trod not on the surface of success, but in the deep of failure. The real work, from the biblical point of view, is the late-recorded, the unrecorded, the anonymous work." "Biblical Leadership," *Israel and the World*, pp. 127-33.

54. *Pointing the Way*, pp. 220-29.

55. "Genuine Dialogue and the Possibilities of Peace," *Pointing the Way*, p. 236.

56. "Hope for This Hour," ibid., pp. 223-24.

57. Ibid., p. 222.

58. "Validity and Limitation of the Political Principle," *Pointing the Way*, p. 216.

59. Ibid., pp. 212-13. It is odd that Buber should seek to buttress his position from the juxtaposition of the writings of Hobbes and Hegel. Hobbes presents the most thoroughgoing attempt in the history of political theory to base a system on mistrust; nevertheless, he leaves intact a small part of the realm of God. Hegel, whose state is precisely the *Aufhebung* of this universalized mistrust, claims for it, in Buber's view, unlimited authority. Besides, Hegel's thought is based on philosophical considerations that are not related to the issues Buber discusses. Unless, of course, Buber is unmasking.

It should also be noted that Buber's interpretation of Hegel is sharply questioned by modern scholarship. *See*, for example, Herbert Marcuse, *Reason and Revolution: Hegel and the Rise of Social Theory* (Boston, 1960); Eric Weil, *Hegel et l'état* (Paris, 1950); John Findlay, *Hegel: A Re-examination* (London, 1958); and most thoroughly in Shlomo Avineri's *Hegel's Theory of the Modern State* (London, 1972).

60. "Hope for This Hour," *Pointing the Way*, p. 227.

61. "Genuine Dialogue and the Possibilities of Peace," ibid., p. 237. *See also* Itzhak Ivry, *Martin Buber at Eighty*.

62. "Genuine Dialogue and the Possibilities of Peace," *Pointing the Way*, p. 237.

63. Ibid., p. 238.

64. "The Validity and Limitation of the Political Principle," ibid., p. 218.

65. "Abstract and Concrete," ibid., pp. 230-31.

66. Ibid., p. 230.

67. Ibid., p. 231.

68. "Gandhi, Politics, and Us," ibid., p. 136.

6 Jerusalem and Zion

1. See chap. 1, p. 9-11.

2. *Reden über das Judentum* (Frankfurt am Main, 1923).

3. Ernst Simon, "Nationalismus, Zionismus und der Jüdisch-Arabische Konflict in Martin Bubers Theorie und Wirksamkeit," *Bulletin des Leo Baeck Instituts*, 33, 9. Jahrgang (Tel Aviv, 1966), p. 61.

4. *See* Ernst Simon, *Aufbau im Untergang, Jüdische Erwachsenenbildung im nationalsozialistischen Deutschland als geistigen Widerstand*, Leo Baeck Instituts (Tubingen, 1959); Ernst Simon, "Martin Buber and German Jewry," *Yearbook III*, Leo Baeck Institute (London, 1958), pp. 3-39; Ernst M. Wolf, "Martin Buber and German Jewry: Prophet and Teacher to a Generation in Catastrophe," *Judaism*, vol. I, no. 4 (1952), pp. 346-53; Solomon Liptzin, *Germany's Stepchildren* (Philadelphia, 1944), chapter XVII, pp. 255-69; Jacob S. Minkin, "The Amazing Buber," *The Congress Weekly*, vol. XVI (January 17, 1949), p. 10 f.

5. For such a study *see* the authoritative but highly partisan essay of Ernst Simon, "Nationalismus, Zionismus und der Jüdisch-Arabische Konflict in Martin Bubers Theorie und Wirksamkeit," *Bulletin des Leo Baeck Instituts*, pp. 21-84. *See also* Greta Schaeder, *Martin Buber Hebraischer Humanismus* (Gottingen, 1966), pp. 184-236.

6. *See* Hans Kohn, *Martin Buber*, pp. 94 f. and 139 f.

7. *I and Thou*, p. 103.

8. "Nationalism," *Israel and the World*, p. 217.

9. In an unpublished version of the address, Buber interestingly adds the the four-year-old Russian revolution as a contemporary example of this phenomenon.

10. *Rome and Jerusalem*, p. 107.

11. "The Gods of the Nations and God," *Israel and the World*, pp. 200-201.

12. "Hebrew Humanism," ibid., p. 241. See also *Israel and Palestine*, p. 142.

13. "Achad-Haam Gedankrede in Basel," *JSJ*, p. 768.

14. Ibid, p. 763. *See also* Buber's discussion of Mickiewiez and the national idea in "Zur Geschichte der Nationalen Idee," ibid., pp. 320-23.

15. *Rome and Jerusalem*, p. 103.

16. "The Gods of the Nations and God," *Israel and the World*, p. 210.

17. This is parallel to Buber's contention that marriage is the laboratory for social relationships. "The Question to the Single One," *Between Man and Man*, pp. 60-62.

18. "Spirit of Israel and the World of Today," *On Judaism*, p. 183. Note the structural and intellectual similarity to individuals and community. Only individuals who have become "single ones" can constitute a community.

19. *Paths in Utopia*, p. 49.

20. "Der Staat und die Menscheit," *JSJ*, p. 295. Cf. Landauer, *Aufruf zum Sozialismus*, p. 19.

21. "Le'hakarat Ha'rayon Haleumi," *Teudah Ve'yiud*, II, pp. 205-6.

22. "Nationalism," *Israel and the World*, p. 220.

23. Ibid., p. 219.

24. Unpublished version of Buber's address to the Twelfth Zionist Congress in 1921, MS. p. 7 (Buber Archive).

25. "Nationalism," *Israel and the World*, p. 219.

26. Ibid., p. 215.

27. "The Gods of the Nations and God," *Israel and the World*, p. 201.

28. "Nationalism," *Israel and the World*, pp. 222-23; *see also* "Zion und die Jugend," *JSJ*, pp. 700-20.

29. *The Prophetic Faith*, pp. 43-44; *Kingship of God* (New York, 1967), p. 118.

30. "Myth in Judaism," *On Judaism*, pp. 109 f.

31. This is the religious counterpart to Buber's utopian socialist vision. The two works that deal with the socialist and religious aspects are *Paths in Utopia* and *Kingship of God*, respectively; the first makes passing reference to the religious significance of socialism, the latter alludes to the social justice necessary in the Kingdom of God. There is, unfortunately, no thorough attempt at integration. The closest that Buber comes to this is the very short and general "Three Theses for a Religious Socialism," *Pointing the Way*, pp. 112-14.

32. *Israel and Palestine*, pp. 31-35. As opposed to Hermann Cohen, the great defender of nineteenth-century liberal, reform Judaism, Buber grasped Jewish universalism as tied, paradoxically, to real national existence. The reformers, attempting to model their Judaism after the prevailing Western experience, saw national survival merely as the necessary biological vehicle for the perpetuation of the Jewish messianic idea of universalism. They made a virtue of necessity by extolling Jewish universal dispersion as the ideal means of presenting universalism to the world. Zionism appeared to them, not surprisingly, a retrograde step, a failure of nerve that sought national security in place of universal exposure. Buber, as the revolutionary traditionalist, chides his adversaries for not seeing the real source of Jewish uniqueness: the marriage of nationhood and the faith community. Most assuredly, Buber argues, being 'a light unto the nations' is the central Jewish idea, but if we are to set an example worthy of universal emulation, it must be with our lives and our national existence and not merely with our declarations. Zionism is, therefore, particularist in form and universalist in vision. See *JSJ*, pp. 280-308.

33. Samuel 8:5; "Tzionut V'tzionut," *Teudah Ve'yiud*, II, pp. 236-38.

34. *See* "Der Jude in der Welt," *JSJ*, pp. 216-20.

35. *See*, e.g., "The Silent Question," *On Judaism*, pp. 208-9.

36. Ibid., "The Holy Way," pp. 140-42.

37. *Israel and Palestine*, pp. ix-x. The introduction is published separately under the title "Zion und die Nationalen Ideen," *JSJ*, pp. 324-29.

38. *Israel and Palestine*, p. ix.

39. "The Land and Its Possessors" (from an open letter to Gandhi), *Israel and the World*, p. 227. Full version in *Two Letters to Gandhi* (Martin Buber and J. L. Magnes), "The Bond" (Jerusalem, 1939), p. 7. He continues soon after: "That which is an idea and nothing more cannot become holy; but a piece of earth can become holy," see ibid., pp. 227 and 7, respectively.

40. *Israel and Palestine*, p. 8, *see also* p. 142.

41. "On National Education," *Israel and the World*, p. 159. *See also* "The Spirit of Israel and the World of Today," ibid., p. 187 f.

42. "The Silent Question," *On Judaism*, pp. 211-12. *See also* "The Land and Its Possessors," *Israel and the World*, p. 229; *Two Letters to Gandhi*, p. 9.

43. "The Land and Its Possessors," *Israel and the World*, pp. 228-29; *Two Letters*

to Gandhi, pp. 8-10; "Le'ketz Hasimbiosa Hagermanit Yehudit," *Teudah Ve'yiud*, II, pp. 293-95.

44. *Israel and Palestine*, pp. ix-xii, 3-77. *See also* "Das Land der Juden," Die Jüdische Bewegung, I, pp. 191-94; "Die Eroberung Palästinas," *JSJ*, p. 505 f.

45. "Das Land der Juden," *Die Jüdische Bewegung*, I, pp. 191-92.

46. *Israel and Palestine*, p. 142.

47. Ibid., p. xiii.

48. "It must not be forgotten that the genuine messianic idea fulfilled a mighty role in the *Halutzic* movement in spite of its being given a secular dress." "Chinuch Mevugarim," *Teudah Ve'Yiud*, II, p. 204.

49. "Character Change and Social Experiment in Israel," *Israel: Its Role in Civilization*, p. 206. *See also* "The Holy Way," *On Judaism*, p. 130; "Judaism and Mankind," ibid., p. 29; "Judaism and the Jews," ibid., p. 20; "Hitchadshut Chayai Haam," *Teudah Ve'yiud*, II, p. 180 f.

50. "Judaism and Mankind," *On Judaism*, p. 33; "Das Gestaltende," *Die Jüdische Bewegung*, I, pp. 209-13. *See*, e.g., *Writings of the Young Marx*, pp. 209, 430.

51. "Judaism and Mankind," *On Judaism*, p. 23.

52. "Herzl und die Historie," *JSJ*, p. 789.

53. Dated November 4, 1918 (Buber Archive; not included in *Briefwechsel*).

54. "Michtav Le'vaad Hapoel Shel Histadrut Hatzionit," *Davar* (July 27, 1928); "Volker, Staaten und Zion," *JSJ*, p. 287 f.; Israel Klausner, *Haopositzya L'Herzl* (Jerusalem, 1960), p. 241. Weitzmann, in a more sarcastic vein, asked, "I do not understand this term ["cultural home"], what is it, a museum, a hospital?" Cited by Susan Lee Hattis, *The Bi-National Idea in Palestine During Mandatory Times* (Tel Aviv, 1970), p. 87.

55. "Character Change and Social Experiment in Israel," *Israel: Its Role in Civilization*, p. 204.

56. "Rede Auf dem XII Zionistenkongress in Carlsbad," *JSJ*, p. 468 f.; "Kongressnotizen zur zionistischen Politik," ibid., pp. 476-87.

57. *The Jewish State* (London, 1967); *Old-New Land* (New York, 1960).

58. See "Theodor Herzl," "Herzl und die Historie," "Er und Wir," "Sache und Person," "Herzl vor der Palastina-Karte," *JSJ*, pp. 775-808.

59. "Achad Haam Gedankrede in Basel," *JSJ*, p. 768.

60. "Zion und die Jugend," ibid., p. 710.

61. "Our Reply," *Towards Union in Palestine, Essays on Zionism and Jewish-Arab Cooperation*, eds. Martin Buber, Judah L. Magnes, and Ernst Simon (Jerusalem, 1945), pp. 33-36, 47. *See also* "Zion und die Jugend," *JSJ*, p. 706; "The Land and Its Possessors," *Israel and the World*, p. 229.

62. Quoted by Ernst Simon in "Nationalismus, Zionismus und der Jüdisch-Arabische Konflikt in Martin Buber's Theorie und Wirksamkeit," *Bulletin des Leo Baek Instituts*, p. 63.

63. *See* pp. 58 and 78 as well as notes 9 and 91 in chap. 3 of this work.

64. "Zion und due Jugend," *JSJ*, p. 708.

65. Ibid., p. 707.

66. "The Holy Way," *On Judaism*, pp. 142-43.

67. Ibid., p. 143.

68. "Landauer Be'sha'ah Zo," *Hapoel Hatzair* (June 27, 1939).

69. "Hitchadshut Chayai Haam," *Teudah Ve'yiud*, II, p. 185.

70. *Paths in Utopia*, p. 143. Cf. "Character Change and Social Experiment in Israel," *Israel: Its Role in Civilization*, p. 207.

71. *Paths in Utopia*, pp. 142-43. Cf. "Character Change and Social Experiment in Israel," *Israel: Its Role in Civilization*, p. 250 f.; "Social Experiment in Jewish Palestine," *The New Palestine* (October 13, 1944, vol. XXXV, no. 1, p. 24 f.; "Die Halutz und sein Welt," *JSJ*, pp. 353-54; "Hitchadshut Chayai Haam," *Teudah Ve'yiud*, II, p. 187.

72. See *Israel and Palestine*, pp. 154-61.

73. "Hitchadshut Chayai Haam," *Teudah Ve'yiud*, II, p. 181. *See also* "Tzionut Ve'Tzionut," ibid., p. 236.

74. Ibid., pp. 183-84.

75. "Die Halutz und sein Welt," *JSJ*, pp. 354-56; "Achad Haam Gedankrede in Basel," ibid., pp. 764-65; "Chinuch Mevugarim," *Teudah Ve'yiud*, II, p. 407.

76. Ibid., *passim*; "Hitchadshut Chayai Haam," ibid., p. 181 f.; "Volkerziehung als unsere Aufgabe," *JSJ*, pp. 674-84; "Character Change and Social Experiment in Israel," *Israel: Its Role in Civilization*, p. 208.

77. The question of elites in Buber is a characteristically many-sided one. He is without doubt an elitist if the term is intended to mean that a select group is to lead and inspire the rest. But Buber denies any real doctrine of elitism since his elite owes its position to no specialized learning, insight, race, class, party, etc., but only to an essentially human renewal—it begins no higher than humanity begins and is therefore equally open to all. *See The Philosophy of Martin Buber*, p. 724 f.

78. "Character Change and Social Experiment in Israel," *Israel: Its Role in Civilization*, p. 210; "Haim Ve'anachnu," *Teudah Ve'yiud*, II, pp. 298-99; "Hitchadshut Chayai Haam," ibid., pp. 181, 188, 189; "Selbstbesinnung," *JSJ*, pp. 496-97; *Paths in Utopia*, pp. 143-48; "Harayon Hashitufi," *Davar* (January 5, 1945).

79. *Israel and Palestine*, p. 35.

80. "Hitchadshut Chayai Haam," *Teudah Ve'yiud*, II, p. 184.

81. *Israel and Palestine*, p. 35.

82. "Le'shem Hitbatzrut Pneemit," *Moznaim*, no. 14, 5702 (The Hebrew Writers' Conference).

83. "Der Halutz und sein Welt," *JSJ*, p. 356.

84. *Paths in Utopia*, pp. 143-44; "Character Change and Social Experiment in Israel," *Israel: Its Role in Civilization*, pp. 207-10; "Rayonot Al Chinuch Haleumi Ve'hachalutzi," *Teudah Ve'yiud*, II, pp. 387-99.

85. *Paths in Utopia*, pp. 146-48, 58-79; "Character Change and Social Experiment," *Israel: Its Role in Civilization*, p. 210.

86. The earliest explicit published mention of the *Halutzic* and Cooperative movements I have found are in "Selbstbesinnung," *JSJ*, (1926), p. 495 f. and "Achad Haam Gedankrede in Basel," ibid., (1927), pp. 769-70. Buber became interested in Halutzic ideas after the First World War.

87. *Interrogations of Contemporary Philosophers*, p. 74.

88. The two are parallel in substance. The "broad uplands" of the systems that he refers to in regard to the "narrow ridge" may very well be the sweeping and unqualified imperatives of the idea or of reality.

Interestingly, this same finely balanced, narrow ridge philosophy, when seen through unsympathetic eyes, becomes loose thinking and half deliberate ambivalence. "Buber as a Zionist writer is a master of the art of being misunderstood. One type of reader approves of the Zionist Buber and is made to ignore the humanist liberal in him. The other type respects the humanist liberal in Buber and does not recognise the crude nationalism, strongly inherent in Buber's lectures and essays. Thus Buber as a propagandist enjoys the best of two worlds: he is liberal to the liberals and a Jewish nationalist to the Zionists." Ignaz Maybaum, *Trialogue between Jew, Christian, Muslim* (London, 1973), p. 8. *See also* pp. 5-12.

89. These beliefs, he writes, were "utopian," "full of fantasy," "deductive," rather than "empirical," immersed in an "ardent poetic atmosphere," "vague and without solid content." "Gegenwartsarbeit," *Die Jüdische Bewegung*, I, pp. 18-19. This theme of having finally overcome his tendency to the mystical and aesthetic, persists in later years as well. *See*, e.g., a poem he wrote to his wife: "On the Day of Looking Back," *Gleanings*, pp. 48-49. His periodic references to having "overcome," and his rather ubiquitous protestations against being thought of as a quixotic, unrealistic thinker, reflect a continuing concern that he had not, in fact, entirely slain the idealist dragon inside him.

90. "Gegenwartsarbeit," *Die Jüdische Bewegung*, I, pp. 17-22.

91. "Warum Muss der Aufbau Palästinas ein sozialistischer sein?" *JSJ*, pp. 376-87.

92. Ibid., p. 377.

93. Ibid., p. 386.

94. Ibid., p. 378.

95. Ibid.

96. "Rede Auf dem XII Zionistkongress," ibid., pp. 467-75 and "Nationalism," *Israel and the World*, pp. 214-26.

97. "Kongressnotizen zur zionistischen Politik," *JSJ*, pp. 476-87.

98. Buber's draft read:

At this hour at which the representatives of the self-conscious Jewish people meet for the first time after eight years of separation, it shall again be stated before the occidental nations that the strong nucleus of the Jewish people is determined to return to its old homeland and to build there a new life, based on independent work and which shall grow and last as an organic element of a new humanity. No power on earth can shake this determination which generations of our pioneers have confirmed with their life and their death. Any act of violence committed against us for its sake, will put a seal of blood on the deed of our national will.

However, this national will is not directed against another nation. The Jewish people who have been an oppressed minority in all countries for two thousand years, are now, that they are again entering into world history as masters of their destiny, turning away with disgust from the methods of imperialistic nationalism whose victim they have been for so long. It is not in order to displace or to dominate another people that we strive to return into the country to which we are linked through ever-lasting historical and spiritual bonds, and whose soil, so sparsely populated, offers enough space for us and the tribes at present living there, especially if it is intensively and consistently cultivated. Our return to Eretz Israel, which is to take place in the form of an ever-increasing immigration is not intended to encroach upon the rights of others. In a just union with the Arab people we wish to make the common homeland an economically and culturally flourishing community whose structure will guarantee each of its national groups an undisturbed autonomous develop-ment. Our colonization which is exclusively devoted to the saving and renewal of our ethnological existence, does not aim at the capitalistic exploitation of a territory, nor does it serve any imperialistic aim. Its sense is the constructive work of free people on a common soil. In this social character of our national ideal lies the powerful warrant for our confidence that between us and the working Arab people a deep and lasting solidarity of real interests will develop, which must overcome all differences produced by momentary confusions. Out of the consciousness of this union, a spirit of mutual respect and kindness, practised in public and private life, will develop in the members of both peoples. Only then will the reencounter of the two peoples be truly brought about in historical greatness. (Translation by Susan Lee Hattis, *The Bi-National Idea in Palestine During Mandatory Times*, pp. 29-31. Original German in "Rede Auf dem XII Zionistenkongress in Carlsbad," *JSJ*, pp. 474-75, and Ernst Simon, "Zionismus Nationalismus und der Jüdisch-Arabische Konflikt in Martin Buber's Theorie und Wirksamkeit," *Bulletin des Leo Baeck Instituts*, pp. 55-57.)

The resolution which was finally passed by the Twelfth Zionist Congress was worded as follows (quoted from ESCO foundation for Palestine, pp. 276-77):

It was with sorrow and indignation that the Jewish people have lived through the recent events in Palestine [the 1921 Palestine riots]. The hostile attitude of the Arab population in Palestine incited by unscrupulous elements to commit deeds of violence, can neither weaken our resolve for the establishment of the Jewish National Home nor our desire to live with the Arab people on terms of harmony and mutual respect, and together with them to make the common home into a flourishing commonwealth, the upbuilding of which may secure to each of its peoples an undisturbed national development. The two great Semitic peoples united of yore by the bonds of common creative civilization, will not fail in the hour of their national regeneration to comprehend the need of combining their vital interests in a common endeavour. The Congress calls upon the Executive to redouble its efforts to secure an honourable entente with the Arab people on the basis of the Declaration and in strict accordance with the Balfour Declaration. The Congress emphatically declares that the progress of Jewish colonization will not affect the rights and needs of the working Arab nation. (Cited in Hattis, p. 31. German in Ernst Simon, "Zionismus National-ismus und der Jüdisch-Arabische Konflikt in Martin Buber's Theorie und Wirksamkeit," *Bulletin des Leo Baeck Instituts*, pp. 55-57.)

99. "Ha'emet Ve'hateshua," *Teudah Ve'yiud*, II, pp. 341-42. (The essay was written in 1947.)

100. For a carefully argued presentation of the opposite point of view *see* Ernst Simon, "Zionismus Nationalismus und der Jüdisch-Arabische Konflikt in Martin Buber's Theorie und Wirksamkeit," *Bulletin des Leo Baeck Institus*, p. 55 f.

101. *See* above, pp. 164-65.

102. Clearly referring back to this episode, Buber wrote in 1930: "Nor may he [the man of spirit] forget that, if his work is to be done in public life, it must be accomplished not above the fray but in it. He has a task to perform within his party if he knows himself strong and free enough to fight *in it* [emphasis in original] against the lies of party structures. Even if he succumbs, he has done work that will continue to have effect." ("Gandhi, Politics and Us," *Pointing the Way*, p. 137.)

Writing in 1953 he again returns to the same theme:

When men of integrity join a party, they do so out of a conviction that the party strives for a goal of the same character as their own, and that this goal is to be reached solely through the energetic alliance of the like-minded. An actual party, however, consists both of genuinely convinced members and of only ostensibly convinced men who have entered it for all kinds of motives, usually out of an inextricable tangle of motives. It may easily happen, of course, that those of pretended convictions predominate. Be that as it may, it is incumbent on those of genuine conviction to resist within the party, the dominance of the fictitious faction without crippling the party's energy. A thorny business this is; but without it one cannot serve God in the party, one cannot render Him, in the sphere of political organization what is His, God's. ("The Validity and Limitation of the Political Principle," *Pointing the Way*, p. 218. Friedman's translation of the sentence beginning, "Be that as it may . . .," is misleading. It is revised in the above text. Cf. "Geltung und Grenze des Politischen Prinzips," *Werke*, I, 1107.)

If, as Buber himself writes, the revision of political resolutions is the most normal and necessary of occurrences, and nevertheless he was unable to weather its demands, it is difficult to see him "strong enough or free enough" to have any sustained relationship with the real world of day-to-day politics. The confession to Magnes that he could not bring himself to choose once again between "truth" and "realization" is quite close to the position he criticized Gandhi for and in much the same spirit as the group of essays ("Hope for This Hour," "Abstract and Concrete," and "Genuine Dialogue and the Possibilities of Peace," *Pointing the Way,* pp. 220-39) discussed at the close of chap. 5. By contrast the 1953 statement is foresquare back in tradition of the "narrow ridge." Here there are no either-or choices to be made between purity and pragmatism.

103. Hattis, pp. 25-27, 38 f.

104. Ibid., p. 258 f.

105. A good selection of these articles appears in in *Teudah Ve'yiud*, II, pp. 317-44. *Be'ayot*, published by Martin Buber, edited by Ernst Simon (1943-1948), was the major organ for this viewpoint.

106. *Our Reply— Towards Union in Palestine*, Ihud (Jerusalem, 1947), especially pp. 32-36.

107. "Bi-national Approach to Zionism," *Towards Union in Palestine, Essays on Zionism and Jewish Arab Cooperation*, eds. M. Buber, J. L. Magnes, E. Simon, Ichud (Jerusalem, 1947), pp. 7-10.

108. Ibid., p. 11. *See also* Moshe Smilansky's essay, ibid., pp. 57-69. There is another level to the argument that follows a more Marxist vein. If there can grow up a solid and influential network of joint Arab-Jewish economic ventures, he argues, the political superstructure will eventually be forced to reflect it.

109. Letter to the *London Times* (May 5, 1946). Reprinted in the *New York Times* (June 3, 1946).

110. "There are modern Ahad-Haamists founded by Buber, who do not even care about achieving a Jewish majority. For them the freeing of the masses in the diaspora by their millions is not the most important thing. Not the solution of the Jewish problem but the setting up of a center from which the light of the famous 'mission' of Judaism will spread." Meir Yaari, *Iton Bogrim* (Warsaw, June 30, 1930). Cited by Hattis, p. 72.

111. *See* e.g., note 39, this chapter and pp. 149-50.

112. "Bi-national Approach to Zionism," *Towards Union in Palestine*, p. 11.

113. "Tzionut Ve'tzionut," *Teudah Ve'yiud*, II, p. 238.

114. "Compromise as such," Buber told the Anglo-American Committee of Inquiry, "is neither good nor evil, if or when it is fitted by its nature and content to save our cause and if there is no other way of salvation, then it is good." *Our Reply*, p. 34 f.

115. When he died his library was left to the University and National Library in Jerusalem. It contained an estimated 30,000 volumes.

116. Letter to the editor of *Haaretz* (April 28, 1949). Story corroborated and amplified upon by friends and associates of Buber with whom I spoke.

117. "Nasim Ketz Le'fitumai-Hamilim," *Teudah Ve'yiud*, II, pp. 343-44. Also appeared in English in the fairly inaccessible *Freeland* as "Let Us Make an End to Falsities," vol. V, no. 1 (1949).

118. "Haim Ve'anachnu," *Teudah Ve'yiud*, II, p. 300.

119. "Tzionut Ve'tzionut," ibid., p. 237.

120. Ibid., p. 238.

121. *Two Types of Faith*, p. 15.

122. Ernst Simon, "Ben Gurion or Buber," *New Outlook* (January 1966).

123. "Darko Shel Yisrael," *Teudah Ve'yiud*, II, p. 353.

Bibliography

The student of Buber's writings is faced with serious bibliographical difficulties because of the often dizzying variety in which his works appear. Many essays are printed three, four, even five times in different collections, sometimes under different titles, with important stylistic and substantive changes. Some essays show a chronology of editing, reflecting Buber's concerns in various periods. Others show major differences between the text in its original form—as a public address or formalistic piece—and its final form as an essay.

To complicate matters further, Buber wrote (primarily) in two languages, German and Hebrew, and many of his works—particularly after 1938—appear in both languages. Based on a study of the various manuscripts and discussions with his secretary, I strongly suspect that even those works appearing originally in Hebrew were often first drafted in German. (This should not be surprising considering that Buber began to use Hebrew as a spoken and written language only at the age of sixty. Even after he had mastered Hebrew, it betrayed unmistakable signs of German syntax and sentence structure.)

In order to retain a monolingual format, I have used translations when they existed and made my own when they did not. Except for a number of minor stylistic revisions, the translations are unaltered. When translations did not exist, I followed the practice of citing the works from the most complete, authoritative, and accessible collections rather than from the frequently obscure original.

Of great aid to the researcher is the virtually complete (until 1958) bibliography of Buber's works compiled by Moshe Catanne: *Bibliografiyah shel Kitve Mordekhai Martin Buber* (Jerusalem: Mosad Bialik, 1961). A new bibliography of Buber's works prepared by Raphael Buber and Margot Cohn entitled *Martin Buber: A Bibliography of His Writings* which promises to be complete up to 1978 will be published in Jerusalem by the Magnes Press and will likely appear at the end of 1979. A less detailed bibliography that emphasizes English translations and covers the period from 1958 to 1966 is that of Maurice Friedman in *The Library of Living Philosophers* series: *The Philosophy of Martin Buber*, edited by Paul Arthur Schilpp and Maurice Friedman (La Salle, Ill.: Open Court, 1967). Friedman has also compiled a useful bibliography of primary and secondary material in his *Martin Buber: The Life of Dialogue* (New York: Harper & Row, 1960); expanded and updated in later editions. A large and wide-ranging bibliography can also be found in Kees Waaigman, *De Mystiek van Ik en Jij* (Utrecht: Bijleveld, 1976). Bibliographies relating to Buber's early works are included in Hans Kohn, *Martin Buber, sein Werk und sein Zeit* (Cologne: J. Melzer Verlag, 1961) and in Paul Flohr's *From Kultur-Mystik to Dialogue*, unpublished Ph.D. dissertation (Brandeis, 1974).

There is no edition of the complete works of Buber. There is, however, a three-volume edition of his most significant works: *Werke* (Munich: Kosel-Verlag, 1962-1964). The first volume includes *Schriften zur Philosophie*, the second *Schriften zur Bibel*, and the third *Schriften zum Chassidismus*. A fourth volume (by a different publisher) meant to be part of this set is *Der Jude und sein Judentum* (Cologne: J. Melzer, 1963). It includes Buber's Jewish and Zionist writings. Useful bibliographies may be found in volume 1 and in *Der Jude und sein Judentum*. A three-volume edition of Buber's correspondence is worthy of special note: *Martin Buber, Briefwechsel aus sieben Jahrzehnten*, Herausgegeben und eingeleitet von Grete Schaeder (Heidelberg: L. Schneider, 1972-1975).

The Martin Buber Archive at the Hebrew University and National Library in Jerusalem is an indispensable source for everything related to Buber. It contains complete bibliographies of primary and secondary material, a nearly complete collection of all Buber-related material, his voluminous correspondence, his library, and hundreds of manuscripts, documents, memorabilia, and so on.

What follows is a listing of the more significant collections of Buber's work.

German

An der Wende. Reden über das Judentum. Cologne and Olten: Jacob Hegner Verlag, 1952.

Bilder von Gut und Bose. Cologne and Olten: Jakob Hegner, 1952.

Die chassidische Botschaft. Heidelberg: Lamberg Schneider, 1952.

Die chassidischen Bucher, Gesamtausgabe. Hellerau: Jakob Hegner, 1928.

Daniel. Gesprache von der Verwirklichung. Leipzig: Insel Verlag, 1913.

Dialogisches Leben. Gesammelte philosophische und padagogische Schriften (including *Ich und Du, Zwiesprache, Die Frage an den Einzenen, Uber das Erzieherische,* "Uber Charaktererziehung," *Das Problem des Menschen*). Zurich: Gregor Muller Verlag, 1947.

"Drei Satze eines religiosen Sozialismus," *Die Neue Wege,* XXII (1928), 327 ff.

Ekstatische Konfessionen. Jena: Eugen Diedrichs Verlag, 1909.

(editor) *Die Gesellschaft. Sammlung sozialpsychologischer Monographien.* 40 vols. Frankfurt am Main: Rutten & Loening, 1906-1912. Buber's introduction to the series in 1st ed. of 1st vol., Werner Sombart, *Das Proletariat,* 1906.

Der Glaube der Propheten. Zurich: Manesse Verlag, 1950.

Gog und Magog. Eine Chronik. Heidelberg: Verlag Lambert Schneider, 1949.

Gottesfinsternis. Zurich: Manesse Verlag, 1953.

Der grosse Maggid und seine Nachfolge. Frankfurt am Main: Rutten & Leoning, 1922.

Hinweise, Gesammelte Essays (1910-53). Zurich: Manesse Verlag, 1953.

Ich und Du. Nachworterweiterte. Heidelberg: Verlag L. Schneider, 1958.

Israel und Palastina. Zur Geschichte einer Idee. Erasmus Bibliothek, edited by Walter Ruegg. Zurich: Artemis-Verlag, 1950.

Die Jüdische Bewegung. Gesammelte Aufsatze und Ansprachen. vol. II, 1916-1920. Berlin: Judischer Verlag, 1921.

Kampf um Israel. Reden und Schriften (1921-1932). Berlin: Schocken Verlag, 1933.

Konigtum Gottes. vol. I of *Das Kommende. Untersuchungen der Entstehungsgeschichte des messianischen Glaubens.* Berlin: Schocken Verlag, 1932; 2nd enlarged ed., 1936. 3rd rev. ed., Schneider, 1956.

Die Legende des Baalschem. Frankfurt am Main: Rutten & Loening. 1908.

Mein Weg zum Chassidismus. Erinnerungen. Frankfurt am Main: Rutten & Loening, 1918.

Moses. Heidelberg: Verlag Lambert Schneider, 1952.

Nachlese. Heidelberg: L. Schneider, 1965.

Pfade in Utopia. Heidelberg: Verlag Lambert Schneider, 1950.

Reden über das Judentum. Frankfurt am Main: Rutten & Loening, 1923. Reissued by Schocken Verlag, Berlin, 1932.

Die Stunde und die Erkenntnis, Reden und Aufsatze, 1933-1935. Berlin: Schocken Verlag, 1936.

Urdistanz und Beziehung. Heidelberg: Verlag Lambert Schneider, 1951.

Das verborgene Licht. Frankfurt am Main: Rutten & Loening, 1924. (editor) *Die vier Zweige des Mabinogi.* Leipzig: Insel-Verlag, 1914.

Vom Geist des Judentums. Leipzig: Kurt Wolff Verlag, 1916.

Worte an die Jugend. Berlin: Schocken Verlag, 1938.

Zion als Ziel und Aufgabe. Berlin: Schocken Verlag, 1936.

Zwei Glaubensweisen. Zurich: Manesse Verlag, 1950.

Zwiesprache. Berlin: Schocken Verlag, 1932.

Zwischen Gesellschaft und Staat. Heidelberg: Verlag Lambert Schneider, 1952.

Hebrew

The following Hebrew material contains works either written or delivered in Hebrew:

Be'ayat ha'adam. Tel Aviv: Machbarot Le-sifrut, 1943.

Ben am Le'artzo. Jerusalem: Schocken, 1944.

Be'sod siah. Jerusalem: Bialik Institute, 1959.

Gog u-Magog. Tel Aviv: Am Oved, 1967.

Pene adam. Jerusalem: Bialik Institute, 1962.

Te'udah ve-yi'ud. 2 vols. Jerusalem: Zionist Library, 1959.

Major English Translations

Arab-Jewish Unity. Testimony before the Anglo-American Inquiry Commission for the Ihud (Union) Association by Judah Magnes and Martin Buber. London: Victor Gollancz Ltd., 1947.

Between Man and Man. Translated by Ronald Gregor Smith. (Includes "Dialogue," "The Question to the Single One," "Education," "The Education of Character," and "What is Man?") London: Kegan Paul, 1947; Boston: Beacon Paperback, 1955.

Eclipse of God. Studies in the Relation between Religion and Philosophy. Translated by Maurice S. Friedman, et al. New York: Harper & Brothers, 1952; Harper Torchbook, 1957.

For the Sake of Heaven. Translated from the German by Ludwig Lewisohn. Philadelphia: The Jewish Publication Society, 1945.

Gleanings. New York: Simon & Schuster, 1967.

Good and Evil. Two Interpretations. (Includes *Right and Wrong* and *Images of Good and Evil*.) New York: Charles Scribner's Sons, 1953.

Hasidism and Modern Man. New York: The Horizon Press, 1958.

I and Thou. Translated by Walter Kaufman, New York Charles Scribner's Sons, 1970.

Israel and Palestine. The History of an Idea. Translated from the German by Stanley Godman. London: East and West Library; New York: Farrar, Straus & Young, 1952.

Israel and the World, Essays in a Time of Crisis. New York: Schocken Books, 1948.

The Kingship of God. New York: Harper & Row, 1967.

The Knowledge of Man. New York: Harper & Row, 1965.

The Legend of the Baal-Shem. Translated by Maurice S. Friedman. New York: Harper & Brothers; London: East and West Library, 1955.

Moses. Oxford: East West Library, 1946; Harper Torchbook, 1958.

On Judaism. New York: Schocken Books, 1967

On the Bible: Eighteen Studies. New York: Schocken Books, 1968.

The Origin and Meaning of Hasidism. Edited and translated by Maurice Friedman. New York: The Horizon Press, 1960.

"Our Reply," *Towards Union in Palestine, Essays on Zionism and Jewish-Arab Cooperation.* Edited by Martin Buber, Judah L. Magnes, and Ernst Simon. Jerusalem: Ihud Association, 1945, pp. 33-36.

Paths in Utopia. Translated by R. F. C. Hull. London: Routledge & Kegan Paul, 1949; Boston: Beacon Paperback, 1958.

Pointing the Way: Collected Essays. Translated by Maurice S. Friedman. New York: Harper & Brothers; London: Routledge & Kegan Paul, 1957.

The Prophetic Faith. Translated from the Hebrew by Carlyle Witton-Davies. New York: Macmillan Co., 1949.

Tales of the Hasidim, The Early Masters. Translated by Olga Marx. New York: Schocken Books, 1947.

Tales of the Hasidim, The Later Masters. Translated by Olga Marx. New York: Schocken Books, 1948.

Two Letters to Gandhi. With Judah Magnes and including public letters by Buber and Magnes and the original text of Gandhi's statement about the Jews in *Harijan*, November 26, 1938. Pamphlets of *The Bond.* Jerusalem: Rubin Mass, April 1939.

Two Types of Faith. Translated by Norman P. Goldhawk. London:

Routledge & Kegan Paul, 1951; New York: Macmillan Co., 1952.

Works on Buber

This section includes works related to Buber himself. Studies of a more general nature regarding intellectual trends, social background, important figures in Buber's life can be found in the relevant footnotes.

Agus, Jacob B. *Modern Philosophies of Judaism.* New York: Behrman's Jewish Book House, 1941.

Anzenbacher, Arno. *Die Philosophie Martin Bubers.* Vienna: Verlag A. Schendl, 1965.

Balthasar, Hans Urs von. *Martin Buber and Christianity.* New York: Macmillan, 1961.

Beek, M. A. and Weiland, J. S. *Martin Buber: Personalist and Prophet.* Westminster, Md.: Newman Press, 1968.

Ben-Chorin, Schalom. *Zweisprache mit M. Buber.* Munich: List, 1966.

Bergman, S. H. *Faith and Reason: An Introduction to Modern Jewish Thought.* Washington, 1961, pp. 81-97.

Berkovitz, Eliezer. *A Jewish Critique of the Philosophy of Martin Buber.* New York: Yeshiva University, 1962.

Berl, Heinrich. *Martin Buber und die Wiedergeburt des Judentums aus dem Geist der Mystik.* Heidelberg, 1964.

Blau, Joseph L. "Martin Buber's Religious Philosophy," *The Review of Religion,* November 1948.

Bloch, J. *Die Aporie des Du.* Heidelberg: Lambert Schneider, 1977.

Casper, Bernhard. *Das Dialogische Denken. Franz Rosenzweig, Ferdinand Ebner, Martin Buber.* Freiburg, Basel and Vienna: Herder, 1967.

Cohen, Adir. *Martin Buber on Education* (Hebrew). Tel Aviv: Yachdav, 1976.

Dejung, Berta. *Dialogische Erziehung. Martin Bubers Rede über das Erzieherishe. Eine Interpretation.* Zurich: Juris-Verlag, 1971.

Diamond, Malcolm. *Martin Buber. Jewish Existentialist.* New York: Harper Torchbooks, 1968.

Duesberg, Hans. *Person und Gemeinschaft: Philosophishe systematische Untersuchungen des Sinnzusammenhangs von Personaler Selbständigkeit und Interpersonaler Beziehung an Texten von J. G. Fichte und Martin Buber.* Bonn: H. Bovier, 1970.

Eckert, W. P., Wachenger, L., Goldschmidt, H. L. *Martin Buber und des erzieherische Verhaltnis.* Ratingen bei Düsseldorf: A. Henn, 1967.

Flohr, Paul R. *From Kulturmytik to Dialogue.* Unpublished Ph.D. dissertation, Brandeis, 1974.

————. "The Road to 'I and Thou': An Inquiry into Buber's Transition from Mysticism to Dialogue," in Michael A. Fishbane and Paul R. Flohr (eds.) *Texts and Responses, Studies Presented to Nahum Glatzer.* Leiden: E. J. Brill, 1975.

————. "Martin Buber's Concept of the Center and Social Renewal," *Jewish Journal of Sociology*, June 1976.

———— '*Alte und Neue Gemeinschaft,' An Unpublished Buber Manuscript*, edited and introduced by Paul R. Flohr and Bernard Susser, *Association for Jewish Studies Review*, vol. 1, 1976.

Friedman, Maurice S. *Martin Buber: The Life of Dialogue.* New York: Harper & Row, 1960.

Goldschmidt, Herman L. *Hermann Cohen und Martin Buber.* Geneva: Migdal, 1946.

Goldstein, W. *Begegnung mit Martin Buber.* Jerusalem: Edition Dr. Peter Freund, 1943.

————. *Die Botschaft Martin Bubers.* 4 volumes. Jerusalem: Edition Dr. Peter Freund, 1952-56 (Stencil).

————. *Der Glaube Martin Bubers.* Jerusalem: Reuben Mass, 1969.

————. *Jean Paul Sartre und Martin Buber.* Jerusalem: Reuben Mass, 1965.

————. *Martin Buber: Gespräche, Briefe, Worte.* Jerusalem: Reuben Mass, 1967.

Grünfeld, W. *Der Begegnungscharakter der Wirklichkeit in Philosophie und Pedagogik Martin Bubers.* Ratingen: Henn, 1965.

Hammerstein, F. F. von. *Das Messiasproblem bei Martin Buber.* Stutgart: W. Kohlhammer, 1958.

Horowitz, Rivka. *Martin Buber und Franz Rosenzweig: Studien zur Entstehungsgeschichte von 'Ich und Du'.* Heidelberg: Lambert Schneider, 1976.

Bibliography

Kohanski, Alexander. "Martin Buber's Philosophy of Judaism," *Judaism*, vol. 24, no. 1, Winter 1975.

————. *An Analytical Interpretation of Martin Buber's "I and Thou."* New York: Cornell University Press, 1975.

Kohn, Hans, *Martin Buber, sein Werke und sein Zeit.* Cologne: J. Melzer Verlag, 1961.

Kraft, Werner, *Gespräche mit Martin Buber.* Munich: Kosel-Verlag, 1966.

Lang, Bernhard. *Martin Buber und das dialogische Leben.* Bern: H. Lang, 1963.

Michel, Wilhelm. *Martin Buber. Sein Gang in die Wirklichkeit.* Frankfurt am Main: Rutten und Loening, 1926.

Moore, Donald J. *Martin Buber. Prophet of Religious Secularism.* Philadelphia: Jewish Publication Society, 1974.

Mosse, George L. *Germans and Jews: The Right, the Left and the Search for a 'Third Force' in Pre-Nazi Germany.* New York: Howard Fertig, 1970.

Orian, Meyer. *Chasidism According to Buber: A Critical View* (Hebrew). Haifa, 1970.

Pfeutze, Paul E. *The Social Self in the Writings of George Herbert Mead and Martin Buber.* Westport, Conn.: Greenwood Press, 1973.

Poppel, Stephen. "Martin Buber: The Art of the Unpolitical," *Midstream*, Winter 1974.

Reinharz, Yehuda. *Fatherland or Promised Land. The Dilemma of the German Jew 1893-1914.* Ann Arbor: University of Michigan Press, 1975.

Rome, Sidney and Beatrice. *Philosophical Interrogations.* New York: Harper Torchbooks, 1970.

Rosenblüth, Pinchas E. *Martin Buber. Sein Denken und sein Wirken.* Hannover: Niedersächsischen Landeszentrale für Politische Bildung, 1968.

Schaeder, Grete. *Martin Buber: Hebraischer Humanismus.* Göttingen: Vanderhoeck und Ruprecht, 1966. Translated into English by Noah J. Jacobs, *The Hebrew Humanism of Martin Buber.* Detroit: Wayne State University Press, 1973.

Schilpp, Paul Arthur and Freidman, Maurice (eds.). *The Philosophy of Martin Buber* (vol. 12 in *Library of Living Philosophers*). La Salle, Ill.: Open Court, 1967.

Scholem, Gershon. "Martin Buber's Hasidism," *Commentary*, October 1961.

————. "Martin Bubers Auffassung des Judentums," *Neue Zuricher Zeitung*, 1 and 8, April 1967.

Simon, Ernst. "Nationalismus, Zionismus und der jüdische-arabische Konflict in Martin Bubers Theorie und Wirksamkeit," *Bulletin des Leo Baeck Instituts* 33, 9 Jahrgang, 1966.

Singer, Isaac Bashevis. "Rootless Mysticism," review of *Daniel: Dialogues on Realization, Commentary,* January 1965.

Susser, Bernard. "Ideological Multivalence. Martin Buber and the German Volkish Tradition," *Political Theory*, February 1977.

————. 'Alte und Neue Gemeinschaft': An Unpublished Buber Manuscript," edited with an introduction by Paul Flohr and Bernard Susser, *American Jewish Scholars Review*, vol. 1, 1976.

————. "The Anarcho-Federalism of Martin Buber," *Publius*, vol. 9, no. 4, Fall 1979.

Wood, Robert. *Martin Buber's Ontology: An Analysis of "I and Thou."* Evanston, Ill.: Northwestern University Press, 1969.

Waaiman, Kees. *De Mystiek van Ik en Jij.* Utrecht: Bijleveld, 1976.

Index

216